Adventures in Aidland

Studies in Public and Applied Anthropology

General Editor: **Sarah Pink**, University of Loughborough and **Simone Abram**, Town and Regional Planning, University of Sheffield.

The value of anthropology to public policy, business and third sector initiatives is increasingly recognized, not least due to significant innovations in the discipline. The books published in this series offer important insights into these developments by examining the expanding role of anthropologists practicing their discipline outside academia as well as exploring the ethnographic, methodological and theoretical contribution of anthropology, within and outside academia, to issues of public concern.

Adventures in Aidland

The Anthropology of Professionals in International Development

Edited by

David Mosse

berghahn
NEW YORK · OXFORD
www.berghahnbooks.com

First published in 2011 by
Berghahn Books
www.berghahnbooks.com

Library of Congress Cataloging-in-Publication Data

Adventures in Aidland : the anthropology of professionals in
international development / edited by David Mosse.
   p. cm. – (Studies in public and applied anthropology ; v. 6) Includes
bibliographical references and index.
   ISBN 978-0-85745-110-1 (hardback) – ISBN 978-1-78238-063-4
   (paperback) – ISBN 978-1-78238-064-1 (retail ebook)
1. Applied anthropology. 2. Economic development--Social aspects. I.
Mosse, David.
   GN397.5.A38 2011 301–dc22

                                                     2011000953

British Library Cataloguing in Publication Data

A catalogue record for this book is available from the British Library
Printed in the United States on acid-free paper

ISBN: 978-1-78238-063-4 paperback
ISBN: 978-1-78238-064-1 retail ebook

CONTENTS

PREFACE AND ACKNOWLEDGEMENTS

In this volume, anthropologists write about expertise in the realm of international development, and especially the 'thought work' that occurs in organizations such as the World Bank or the World Health Organization, or in donor agencies such as the UK Department for International Development or non-governmental organizations, and within their various networks of professionals. These are the agencies that commonly enough define for us the nature of global poverty or other global conditions – of health and disease, food prices, the water crisis, conflicts and humanitarian crises. Their policy documents and norm-making expert panels provide the vocabulary with which to think about global issues and global governance, and the conditions for improvement, for poverty reduction, service delivery or democratization. Their 'travelling rationalities' (Craig and Porter 2006), produced in international institutions, are transferred to countries around the world. 'Aidland' – 'not a nowhere exactly but inexactly a somewhere with the characteristics of a nowhere' – is a term borrowed from Raymond Apthorpe (see Chapter 10) to capture the aggregate effect of expert thought and planning which is the virtual world of aid professionals. As one anonymous reviewer of this manuscript aptly put it, 'Aidland is the international development parallel to both the finance crises and contemporary US policies, constituted simultaneously as both real and surreal (or virtual), and held together by a puzzling "utopian realism"'.

Such knowledge practices have only recently attracted the attention of social scientists. Anthropologists may be latecomers to this field, but their contribution is distinctive. In particular, most of the authors of this volume have worked for or been a part of one or more of these development organizations. Their insights do not arise from conventional anthropological research projects, but are the result of reflection on the experience of living and working as part of the interconnected expert world of international development. This is 'insider ethnography' or 'auto-ethnography', offering the fruits of an anthropological reflexive capability from those who might describe themselves as observant participants as much as participant observers.

Debates about 'applying' anthropology in development (or previously colonial) interventions and the relationship between anthropology and professional work are as old as the discipline itself. This series of 'Studies in Public and Applied Anthropology' makes an important contribution to the debate on consultancy, building social knowledge into policy prescription or business management and other ways in which anthropology seeks to become an expert field (e.g., Stewart and Strathern's 2005 collection on *Anthropology and Consultancy*, and Sarah Pink's 2005 collection on *Applications of Anthropology*). This volume, however, shifts concern from the usual 'applied' question of how to make planning knowledge out of ethnography to the question of how to make ethnography out of planning knowledge; equivalently it is less a matter of putting theory into practice than of putting practice into theory (as a recently proposed conference puts it: Amy Pollard, pers. comm.).

Each of the authors of this volume has tried to find an ethnographic voice from within professional practice. Maia Green provides an ethnographic view of her own work on framing policy categories at the 'conceptual interface of mind and text' in a UK government department for international development in London and as consultant to a multilateral agency. Tania Li provides an analysis of the World Bank's turn to ethnography as an instrument for its large-scale interventions in Indonesia, while David Mosse offers an ethnography of anthropologists at work in the World Bank's headquarters in Washington D.C. Desmond McNeill and Asun Lera St Clair provide an account of the social processes of expert knowledge formulation as participants in the globally influential World Development Report 2006 on Equity and Development. Ian Harper writes from intimate professional knowledge of the world of international health experts in Nepal. Rosalind Eyben describes the everyday sociality of aid professionals in Bolivia from the position of her own role as Head of Mission of the UK DFID in the country. Dinah Rajak and Jock Stirrat reflect on a world of expatriate experts in Colombo, Bangkok and Ho Chi Minh City from their own movements in and out of this world. David Lewis analyses life histories of agency personnel in the UK voluntary sector and international NGOs, and finally, reflecting on a long career as an anthropologist and development consultant, Raymond Apthorpe enters expert domains as the allegorical reality of 'Alice in Aidland'.

In each case the world of international development and the professional and public engagement involved become a site for 'fieldwork', where 'the field' is no longer a place but a shift in location that is the pretext for anthropological writing. And, as in any anthropological practice, insight comes from combining the experience of insider participation with the detachment of an outsider; the ability to stand outside the taken-for-granted frameworks and to see the arena of international development as a foreign country – the social life and cultural practice of Apthorpe's Aidland – asking as one would of any unfamiliar culture not whether but how it works. Some find that negotiating an ethnographic exit from insider professional roles can be as difficult as gaining research access to relatively closed institutions. Indeed, the authors here reveal both the insights and also the difficulties that arise from the essential tension between identification and distanciation that characterizes anthropology as a discipline.

Several of the chapters of this volume began as contributions to an invited panel on 'Cosmopolitanism and Development' at the 'Cosmpolitanism and Anthropology ASA (Association of Social Anthropologists) Diamond Jubilee Conference 2006', convened by Pnina Werbner at Keele University. However, the book did not remain tied to cosmopolitanism as an organizing framework. Indeed, the contributors share a critical awareness that claims to 'cosmopolitanism' implied in international development policy or global governance are inherently problematic, and that international experts are always embedded in local social networks and institutions that influence and 'localize' policy worlds. Many of us have intimate knowledge of the way that global policy is shaped by interests, strategies, professional rivalries or insecurities within relatively small communities of border and agency crossing experts – communities of which, for a time, we may also have been members.

So, this book is a contribution to the anthropology of contemporary knowledge practices, the construction and transmission of knowledge about global poverty and its reduction, community development or disease control, among other themes. The book is equally interested in the social life of development professionals, in the capacity of ideas to mediate relationships, in networks of experts and communities of aid workers, and in the dilemmas of maintaining professional identities. Going well beyond obsolete debates about 'pure' and 'applied' anthropology, the book examines the transformations that occur as social scientific concepts and practices cross and re-cross the boundary between anthropological and policy-making knowledge. As will become clear, such an ethnographic approach to international knowledge and development expertise implies serious reflection on the claims of anthropology's own expert knowledge practices and a new awareness that ethnographic knowledge has to be negotiated alongside other forms of knowledge.

I would like to thank Pnina Werbner for the initial invitation to organize the original ASA 2006 panel, as well as the other contributors to that panel whose papers are not published in this collection – Janine Wedel, Gerhard Anders, Philip Quarles van Ufford and Oscar Salemink – but whose influence on the thinking in the book will be clear. I would also like to thank panel discussants James Fairhead, Deborah James and Alpa Shah for their input, as well as our two anonymous manuscript reviewers for highly pertinent suggestions. Above all, I would like to thank the authors for their stimulating contributions. Finally, I would like to thank those at Berghahn Books who have seen this book through production, especially Marion Berghahn and Mark Stanton.

David Mosse
London, November 2009

References

Craig, D. and D. Porter. 2006. *Development Beyond Neoliberalism: Governance, Poverty Reduction and Political Economy.* London and New York: Routledge.

Pink, S. 2005. *Applications of Anthropology: Professional Anthropology in the Twenty-first Century.* Oxford and New York: Berghahn Books.

Stewart, P. and A. Strathern. 2005. *Anthropology and Consultancy: Issues and Debates.* Oxford and New York: Berghahn Books.

Chapter 1

INTRODUCTION
The Anthropology of Expertise and Professionals
in International Development

David Mosse

This is a book about experts and professionals in the world of international development. It brings together ethnographic work on the knowledge practices of communities of development advisors, consultants, policy makers, aid administrators and managers – those involved in the construction and transmission of knowledge about global poverty and its reduction. Recently, anthropological interest in contemporary knowledge practices has turned ethnographic attention to professional fields as diverse as global science research (Fairhead and Leach 2003), international law (Riles 2001), finance (Riles 2004, Miyazaki and Riles 2005, Holmes and Marcus 2005, Maurer 2005), accounting and audit (Power 1997, Strathern 2000), academic research and its funding (Brenneis 1994) and journalism (Hannerz 2004, Boyer and Hannerz 2006). Anthropology's encounter with international development has perhaps been longer and more intimate than any of the others (Ferguson 1997). This invites reflection on the relationship between policy making and anthropological knowledge. After all, as Maia Green notes in Chapter 2, both share a concern with categorization and social ordering, but '[w]hereas anthropology interrogates categorical constructions with a view to disassembling and hence render meaning explicit, policy makers are concerned with reassembling and reconstruction' (this volume); they aim to alter social ordering, not just to interpret it, and to effect such transformations through the channelling of resources.

The anthropological critique of development initially began by dichotomizing the programmer's 'world-ordering' knowledge and the indigenous knowledge that it dismissed while pointing to the ignorance and incompatibility involved in development encounters (Hobart 1993). However, the closer ethnography got to development practices, the harder it was to sustain the distinction. Attention shifted to dynamic knowledge interfaces and battlefields (Long and Long 1992), and to frontline workers in development who participated in apparently incommensurate rationalities, skilfully translating between them, but only ever being partly enrolled onto the outside planners' projects (Long 1992, Lewis and Mosse 2006). But little attention was given to the knowledge practices at the top, which were commonly dismissed as ahistorical and depoliticizing managerial prescriptions that were inherently repressive or governmentalizing, being oriented towards the reproduction of power and knowledge hierarchies and stabilising boundaries around development professionals and those subject to development (Long 2001: 340).

This not only disabled anthropologists' own engagement with visions of the future, social reconstruction or the connection to people's capacities to aspire (Green, this volume, Appadurai 2004, cf. Quarles van Ufford et al. 2003), it also diverted attention from the knowledge producers themselves, anthropologists among them. One problem is that in anthropological hands, policy discourse is disembedded from the expert communities that generate, organize (or are organized by) its ideas. The products of the policy process, visible as documents, are privileged over the processes that create them (e.g., Escobar 1995); whereas documents can better be seen *as* sets of relations (Smith 2006). Consequently, the rich literature on the intended and unintended effects of development interventions on populations, regions and communities is hardly matched by accounts of the internal dynamics of development's 'regimes of truth' or of the production of professional identities, disciplines and the interrelation of policy ideas, institutions and networks of knowledge workers who serve the development industry.

This book is about life within what Raymond Apthorpe (Chapter 10) refers to as Aidland. Its chapters constitute 'aidnography' that 'explores the "representations collectives" by which Aidmen and Aidwomen say they order and understand their world and work'. The book closes with Apthorpe's lighthearted allegorical pondering on the adventures of Alice in Aidland, a mysterious world in which she finds places-that-are-not-places, non-geographical geography, undemographical demography, un-economics and history made from policy design. In Aidland's political mathematics 'doubling' aid will 'halve' poverty, but its morality is that of the return gift, accruing larger benefits at home, protected by Aidland's 'firewalls against accountability'. Why, Apthorpe asks, 'does the bubble that is Aidland not burst?' Other chapters in this volume offer versions of an answer which remind us that Aidland may look like another planet, but its reality is not virtual. 'The perpetuating institutions and "mechanisms" involved lie in the distinctly unvirtual *Realpolitik* of states, inter-state organizations, and international non-governmental organizations' (Apthorpe, Chapter 10 this volume).

The broad questions implied in Apthorpe's hyperbolic satirical sketch are how does international development produce 'expertise' and how does such knowledge work within the global aid system? This opening chapter provides the context for a discussion of such questions about expertise and professionalism, first by identifying recent policy trends within the aid industry; second, by setting out some different approaches to the study of expert knowledge; and third, by turning to the identity and social world of border-crossing professionals themselves. The chapter sets out an overall argument presented by the book as a whole. This concerns, first, the way in which extraordinary power is invested in 'global' policy ideas, models or frameworks that will travel and effect economic, social and (within a 'governance agenda') political transformation across the globe and, second, the way in which, in reality, policy ideas are never free from social contexts. They begin in social relations in institutions and expert communities, travel with undisclosed baggage and get unravelled as they are translated into the different interests of social/institutional worlds and local politics in ways that generate complex and unintended effects. And yet, in addition, the work of professionals of all kinds is precisely to establish (against experience) the notion that social and technical change can be and is brought about by generalizable policy ideas, and that 'global knowledge' produced by international organizations occupies a transcendent realm 'standing above' particular contexts (cf. Mitchell 2002), and a globalized 'present' that compresses historical time.[1] Such notions of scale and temporality are also constitutive of professional identities in development.

Finally, this introduction raises some important problems of method for anthropology. These arise from the authors' concern with process rather than product, their interest in understanding international knowledge making, rather than debating policy ideas, and by the ethnographic engagement with expert informants that this involves.

'Travelling Rationalities'

Perhaps never before has so much been made of the power of ideas, right theory or good policy in solving the problems of global poverty. There is today unprecedented expert consensus on how global poverty is to be eliminated and the poor governed, brought about by new processes of aid 'harmonization' or 'alignment'.[2] Meanwhile, an emphasis on partnership, consultation and local ownership set the ideological conditions for aid such that aid agencies claim they no longer make interventions at all, but rather support the conditions within which development can happen (Wrangham 2006). At the same time, a growing demand for domestic and transnational accountability and transparency of aid signals a distrust of expert knowledge, even though the 'accountability tools' and arrangements put in place in fact further entrench expertise (Boström and Garsten 2008a).[3]

Between global expert consensus and citizen participation, much disappears from view: the institutional conditions of global policy thinking at the point of origin; the enclave agencies and expert communities involved in the unseen processes of international transmission; and the political processes and institutional interests which interpret and transform global policy at its points of reception. I will return to this ethnographic agenda but, first, what are the characteristics of the new expert consensus?

At the centre of the consensus is a marrying of orthodox neoliberalism and a new institutionalism, the latter being the notion that poverty and violence are the result of bad governance and what is needed are stronger institutions, or example, institutions for the delivery of services accountable to the poor (Craig and Porter 2006: 4–5). This is not a return to state provision but a matter of giving resources to governments to make markets work so as to reduce poverty (Fine 2006) or, as Craig and Porter put it, disaggregating and marketizing the state, that is, breaking up existing forms of state rule (dismissed as corrupt or patrimonial) and then 'using markets to replace and reconstruct the institutions of governance' (2006: 9, 100), while at the same time re-embedding markets in regulatory and constitutional frameworks such as the rule of law or freedom of information.

It is the characteristics of policymaking relating to 'neoliberal institutionalism', not the details, that are relevant here. First, the process involves what Craig and Porter (2006) refer to as 'vertical disaggregation': the delegation upwards of rule making and policy framing from poor country governments to the international stage, international agencies, private organizations, non-governmental organizations (NGOs) or companies; and the delegation downwards of risk to 'responsibilized' regions, localities, communities and ultimately individuals. Second, the policy models involved are formalistic, that is, framed by the universal logic of new institutional economics (rules/incentives) and law (rights/accountability/transparency). These are 'travelling rationalities' with general applicability in which 'the universal [is asserted] over the particular, the travelled over the placed, the technical over the political, and the formal over the substantive' (Craig and Porter 2006: 120), in which (as both Eyben's and Rajak and Stirrat's chapters – Chapters 7 and 8 in this volume – will point out) processes take over from places and categories from relations.

This is relevant for our understanding of expertise. The combination of formalism and internationalization ('delegation upwards') allows a technicalization of policy and the centralization of expertise. This enhances the status of a certain transnational class of experts entrenched at the national level in ways that involve unprecedented convergence (Woods 2006: 66, 67, 68). Development policy trends of the 1980s in particular demanded high levels of expertise and produced economic models that were rapidly internationalized, often in the context of crisis or uncertainty (2006: 66–67). Economics retained its pre-eminence as the diagnostic and rulemaking discipline of Aidland (ibid.).[4]

Then, the linking of formalism and 'delegation downwards' extends (quasi-) formal modelling from national economies to the intimate spaces of communities, bringing new interest in re-engineering institutions and state-citizen relations by changing incentive structures, modifying rules, introducing new forums for accountability or conflict resolution, or local competitive bidding for resources (e.g., Barron et al. 2006); in short, an interest in 'get[ing] social relations right' (as Woolcock, cited by Li, Chapter 3 in this volume, puts it). In Chapter 3, Tania Li shows how this, in turn, requires new forms of expertise and the deployment of social science (including ethnography) 'to render society technical', that is, conceived in terms of calculative rationality, neoliberal ideas of self-organization or the deficits/surpluses of social capital, so as to allow expert-designed interventions (see also Li 2007). Taking the case of a very large World Bank 'community-driven development' programme in Indonesia, Li shows how ethnographic description is used to identify norms, social practices and incentives for such 'remedial interventions'. Here she understands 'social development' as a neoliberal governmental assemblage in which communities come to govern themselves in line with designs shaped by expert conceptions of society that allow economic and political structures to remain unaltered.

The point is that with such moves of decentralization and participation, expert knowledge does not work to impose universal modernist designs from the centre (the usual critique of technocratic knowledge, e.g., Scott 1998), but rather to disembed and recombine local institutions, processes or technologies. Through participation in expert designs for farming, microplanning or resocialization, citizens themselves become 'expert' at rationalizing – disembedding and recombining – elements of their own institutions or socio-ecologies, and acquire a new technical (disembedded) view of themselves and of processes of social or ecological change. Compliant citizens become 'empowered' by expert knowledge or, as Arun Agrawal (2005) recently argued in the case of Indian forest protection, their subjectivities are shaped by participation in formal institutions.[5]

Expert Models Unravelled

Ultimately, however, institutions or technologies (national or local) fashioned by expert techniques come to be re-embedded in relations of power that alter their functionality, as is plain from recent ethnographies of neoliberal reform. Gerhard Anders' (2005) study of the life of civil servants in Malawi under the shadow of 'good governance' reform is a good recent example, showing how expert models of public sector reform did not enhance efficiency and transparency, but rather revealed faults and fissures, fragmenting the civil service and intensifying internal divisions within a professional hierarchy (e.g., between winners and losers, young economists and 'old school' officials). Anders' work is part of a literature describing the many and unpredictable ways in which development's 'travelling rationalities' (and technologies) get translated (back) into local social and political arrangements – perhaps through the interests of local collaborators, official counterparts or brokers – with unanticipated, maybe even perverse effects sometimes exacerbating the crises they claim to address. A retired Malawian Principal Secretary told Anders of his experience in government negotiating teams of feeling 'outmatched and overwhelmed by the "expert knowledge" of World Bank delegates', but equally of being bewildered by their 'lack of insight into local conditions and their arrogant belief in the market'. However, rather than challenge unrealistic models, government representatives adopted a 'sign first, decide later' approach (Anders 2005: 83–84). The reform agenda is subsequently ignored and is subjected to delaying tactics and reversals, for example, when bureaucratic patrons rehire client employees following public sector reform retrenchment exercises.

In their recent book, Craig and Porter (2006) show more broadly how local power easily colonizes the spaces created by national poverty reduction strategy (PRS) programmes, turning new rules to different ends. Their careful case studies from Vietnam, Uganda, Pakistan and New Zealand show that donor-established liberal frameworks of governance (under PRS) are incapable of disciplining existing power. Instead they have the effect of pulling 'a thin institutionalist veil over fundamental (often territorial) aspects of poverty, and making frail compromises with territorial governance around community, local partnership and some kinds of decentralization' (2006: 27). They disabuse the formalist 'delusion that agency can be incentivized to operate independently of political economy' (2006: 11, 120) or that political orders can be reorganized by international policy or aid flows (cf. Booth 2005). In these cases, the effects of policy and expertise are real enough, but the point is that they do not arise from pre-formed designs imposed from outside, or from their own logic, but are brought through the rupture and contradictions they effect in existing social, political and ecological systems and their logics (Mitchell 2002: 77; cf. Mosse 2006d).

Development professionals are not ignorant of these facts. Many understand all too well that formal models are slippery in application, finding 'fraught accommodation with the political economy of place, history, production and territorial government' that liberal doctrines can produce markedly illiberal consequences (Craig and Porter 2006: 120) and that the largely technocratic buy-in to the poverty reduction policy consensus does not erase national or local politics (Booth 2005). Technocratically excluded politics have even become the object of new technical instruments, such as the U.K. Department for International Development (DFID)'s 'Drivers for Change', which is intended to analyse the agents, institutions and structures of power driving change; however, because of the strong institutional push towards universal policy models and the 'etiquette of the aid business', these remain peripheral to mainstream aid negotiations (Booth 2005: 1).

The fact is that development policy remains resolutely optimistic about the power of its favoured approaches and institutional solutions, overplaying the impact and blurring the distinction between normative representations and actual outcomes (Craig and Porter 2006: 11; see also Green, Chapter 2 this volume). Expert ideas at the centre seem remarkably resilient in the face of contrary evidence – not only the high-profile blindness of orthodox neoliberals to the warning signs, for example, of economic freefall in Mexico in 1994, the East Asian crisis in the late 1990s or the social effects of market liberalization in Russia starkly portrayed by Joseph Stiglitz (2002), but also the many technical 'fads' and fashions such as the 'Training and Visit' approach to agricultural extension that continued to be upscaled, internationalized and packaged into multimillion dollar loans long after it had lost credibility externally (Anderson, Feder and Ganguly 2005).

Economists such as Easterly (2002, 2006a) argue that it is the selective examination of incentives in aid implementation that leaves (false) hope for the grand new scheme and the one big push, whether it be Jeffrey Sachs's *The End of Poverty* (2005) or Gordon Brown's big financial allocations for meeting the Millennium Development Goals (Easterly 2006b). Such optimism is premised on denied history as well as concealed politics and hidden incentives. The problem, as Pritchett and Woolcock put it, is of 'skipping straight to Weber', that is, transferring from place to place principles of bureaucratic rationality, which carry with them institutional mythologies that conceal the fact that in reality institutional solutions 'emerge from an internal historical process of trial and error and a political struggle' and that part of 'the solution' is to hide this fact (Pritchett and Woolcock 2004: 201).

Over-ambition about the manageability of institutions for global poverty reduction is, of course, politically necessary in order to mobilize support for international aid. Here is the conundrum: the more technical (or managerial) the policy model is, the more it can mobilize political support, but the less that is actually managed; and the less that is managed, the more necessary is a managerial (or technical) model in order to retain support and legitimacy. The world of policy may be a 'chaos of purposes and accidents' (Clay and Schaffer 1984: 192), but its knowledge workers are engaged in a constant refutation of this fact.

Development's 'travelling orthodoxies' ought to be fragile in the face of historical reality, local politics and perverse incentives, but they are not. In fact, they are remarkably resilient. In asking how expert optimism is sustained, we turn from the characteristics of policy thought and its weak purchase on local reality to the institutional processes that produce it. How have development knowledge processes been studied ethnographically?

Paradigm Maintenance: Ethnographies of Expert Knowledge

There are already a number of different approaches to the study of expert knowledge or policy making in international development. First, there are those concerned with the political economy of knowledge, its relation to institutional power and the maintenance of organizational legitimacy. Several such studies focus on the World Bank as the most prominent knowledge making development institution. For example, commenting on World Bank economic expertise, St Clair points to 'a circular dynamic between expertise, audiences, and the legitimacy of that expertise': 'many of the audience bureaucracies that legitimise the Bank's knowledge claims have eventually become dependent on the money delivered by the Bank to carry out work that has been defined and promoted by the Bank's experts' (St Clair 2006a: 88). In a similar manner, Goldman (2005) shows how World Bank expertise in the environment and sustainable development defines problems in ways that legitimize (and require) the role of the Bank and its interventions. As a 'regime of truth' and a framework for intervention, the Bank's new 'green neoliberal' policy gives birth to 'new experts, new subjects, new natures, and a new disciplinary science of sustainable development, without which power could not be so fruitfully exercised' (Goldman 2005: 156).

These critical accounts focus both on the quality and the accountability of expert knowledge. Several suggest that World Bank research uses data that are privileged, confidential or otherwise unavailable for public scrutiny, which may derive from unreliable national surveys or from research funded by Bank operations with restricted 'terms of reference' linked to the interests of loan management, and which contribute to Bank research which is policy-supporting or overly self-referential (Goldman 2005: passim, Bretton Woods Project 2007, Broad 2007). However, for Goldman, St Clair and others, the issue is not so much that World Bank data and reports are open to criticism – the poverty of the science of poverty – but the way in which they acquire discursive dominance among their prime audience of policy makers who have discretionary power (within the Bank or in recipient countries), without any expectation of democratic accountability (Goldman 2000, St Clair 2006a: 82, 84–86; 2006b: 59). Although the science of global poverty is as much in need of public debate as other science-policy contexts such as climate change, pollution effects or public health, there is no balancing citizen participation in the definition of knowledge about global poverty, no hybrid panels with non-expert participation that acknowledge that 'these problems are not only about science, but also about social relations and value choices' (St Clair 2006a: 82).[6] In Chapter 5 of this volume Desmond McNeill and Asun Lera St Clair illustrate precisely this subordination of value choices to economic expertise in the processes of the Bank's World Development Report 2006 on 'Equity and Development'. To do this they first examine what kind of evidence is considered relevant for asserting that equity matters and, second, whether the argument that it does should be made on intrinsic or instrumental grounds. This leads to a reflection on the wider question of the 'management' of the issue of human rights within an institution whose professional language is economics. Here the Bank's thought work has to be understood in terms of its wider relationships with audience and clients.

A second ethnographic approach focuses on the transmission mechanisms of expert knowledge. Some of these operate externally, through the participation of a wide range of professionals in transnational agencies, firms and NGOs, or through 'national capacity building', funded 'research institutes, training centres, and national science and policy agendas' (Goldman 2005: 175). Janine Wedel (2000, 2004) offers a striking account of policy shaping through extra-institutional networks in her work on the U.S. economic aid programme to Russia, and the description of crony relationships between expert players from Harvard and their Russian partners in the so-called Chubais Clan. Other transmission mechanisms operate internally within institutions, as part of the everyday practices of professionalization, ideological control, internal career building, the self-disciplining of aid bureaucrats and the various 'paradigm maintaining' incentives which may be intensified and globalized by electronic communications both between the head office and regional staff, and across institutions (Goldman 2005: 175; Broad 2007). In Chapter 2 Maia Green opens up this professional world within one major donor, while Rosalind Eyben (Chapter 7) shows how the spread of prior reputation between institutions ensures conformity and compliance of thought and action within global expert communities.

Commenting on overplayed expert models, Ngaire Woods suggests that the International Monetary Fund (IMF) and the World Bank experts are required to be positive so as to avoid self-fulfilling economic downturns or critical reports that would exclude them from sensitive national statistics or would lead to the loss of important clients – or, worse still, 'signal a failure of the Fund and Bank's more general project of persuading countries to liberalize and deregulate their economies' (Woods 2006: 58). As Robert Wade put it, '[l]ike the Vatican, and for similar reasons, [the World Bank] cannot afford to admit fallibility' (quoted in Goldman 2000). The interlinking of the orthodoxies of different international aid organizations now lends further stability to established models (Eyben, Chapter 7 this volume). And approaches to programme evaluation that distribute events either side of a divide between the intended and the unintended allow failure itself to sustain rather than challenge dominant paradigms.[7]

However, beyond this, the tendencies towards 'group think', censorship and reliance on templates arise from the self-disciplining of professionals who, Ngaire Woods argues, strategize to minimize individual risk by dispersing accountability and blame (in case of failure) to the institution as a whole (Woods 2006: 62–63; cf. Goldman 2005: 126–46). Development experts here mirror the intellectual self-disciplining of professionals of all kinds, as described by Jeff Schmidt (2000), through processes of professional training and systems of qualification, among others. Schmidt's argument is that the 'ideological discipline' and 'assignable curiosity' of professional subjectivity are governmental effects. These involve unstatedly ideological and system-maintaining political work in which both professional careers and academic research are implicated. Yashushi Uchiyamada, in an intriguing analysis of his Kafkaesque experience of working in a strongly hierarchical Japanese aid 'bureaucratic machine', argues further that self-discipline occurs not autonomously, but through the pairing of junior 'clerks' under supervision in a manner that renders them uncritical, silent 'motifs' (living motifs) arranged spatially and relationally so that they themselves work, unintentionally, to (re)produce the wider form (Uchiyamada 2004: 13). This pattern replicates itself through immanent power which is both architectural (spatial) and brings together present-day and archaic Japanese political forms, while resting on compliance born of mundane incentives such as attractive remuneration, travel, high lifestyles and 'self-sacrifice for the sake of the family' (2004: 18).

Another ethnographic approach shifts attention away from the rationality of power – disciplining or governmentalizing – towards the more ambiguous processes of actual knowledge production, to actor worlds and the social life of ideas revealed through the still rare fine-grained anthropology of policy (Shore and Wright 1997, Wedel et al. 2005). This has two reciprocally connected aspects. One is the importance of actor relationships in the shaping and salience of policy ideas; the other is the importance of policy ideas in mediating professional relationships. These will be considered in turn.

Experience suggests that decision-making knowledge, including apparently hard economic facts and statistics, are the outcome of complex relationships including negotiations over status, access, disciplinary points of view, team leadership struggles, conflict management or compliance with client frameworks defining what counts as knowledge (Wood 1998; Harper 1998). In his engaging story of a World Bank-funded consultancy on economic analysis of food policy in Sierra Leone in the mid 1980s, Peter Griffiths (2004) poignantly reveals expert knowledge as the product of semi-clandestine detective work, negotiating gossip, absent data and misinformation, wishful thinking or deliberate lying, not to mention dangerous driving, loneliness, alcohol and sex – a panoply of experiences, quick impressions and hunches stabilized as statistics and rational processes (tables of figures and logical frameworks). Then, in his ethnography of the work of IMF missions, Richard Harper (1998, 2005) illustrates the way in which financial figures are made authoritative not by being challenged or changed, but through a social process in which IMF economists shape a national authority's perspective, and a ritual process that achieves a kind of 'moral transformation' of figures into agreed economic facts; that is, properly interpreted usable numbers.[8] The point is that expertise is relational and expert knowledge is social: 'numbers and persons go hand in hand' (Harper 2005: 326; Porter 1996). Clearly, to be 'expert' requires skilful negotiation, enrolling supporters and maintaining coalitions within a development system (Mosse 2005a). Moreover, expertise can fail. Relations may not produce agreement; it may not be possible to determine the facts for social rather than technical reasons.

Furthermore, Ikenberry showed how in the foundation of the IMF and World Bank themselves, actual policies were not driven by pre-existing expert consensus: 'Rather, what became a consensus was forged in response to policymakers' exigencies and questions. Politics drove the technocrats not vice versa' (Woods 2006: 68–69, citing Ikenberry 1992). However, Janine Wedel's research on the expert networks involved in the process of Russian privatization shows that transnational experts, through their multiple roles and tight networks, also constitute themselves as powerful political actors with their own independent interests that militate against the coherence of policy and the interests of states or international agencies (2000, 2004). Wedel's remarkable ethnographic work describes the extraordinary influence and power of transnational U.S.-Russian 'transactors' or 'flex groups' (as she calls them) having limited accountability, being able to operate across national and public/private boundaries to pursue their own ideological and material interests.

The other aspect of an actor-focused approach to expertise is the one that focuses on the importance of policy ideas themselves (and their artefacts: papers, reports, diagrams, etc.) in mediating social and professional relationships. Policy ideas gain currency because they are socially appropriate; perhaps because, as I have argued for the idea of 'participation' in a DFID-funded agricultural project (Mosse 2005a), they can submerge ideological differences, allowing compromise, room for manoeuvre or multiple criteria of success, thus winning supporters by mediating different understandings of development (such as those of plant geneticists, soil engineers, economists, marketing managers, social anthropologists, donor advisers, government officials, NGOs and activists). The idea of 'participation' here is a necessary concept, a good 'translator' in actor-network theory terms (e.g., Latour 1996). So, ideas are 'cutting edge' or able to legitimize financial aid flows because they have social efficacy as well as intellectual merit or because they function as 'boundary objects', allowing dialogue but preserving a certain structure of institutional power (St Clair n.d.).

In Chapter 4 of this volume I provide another example of the social efficacy of expert ideas showing how in 2003–4 non-economist social scientists in the World Bank HQ were defining social development concepts and packaging them as corporate knowledge 'products' so as to manage their relationship with the dominant disciplines and power holders in the Bank (economists, task managers, vice-presidents and regional budget holders), in order to deal with their structural vulnerability in an 'economics fortress' (Cernea 1995: 4) and thus to attend to their own 'system goal' of protecting professional space. Such ethnography examines the 'social work' that expert ideas do at their point of formulation, showing how professional relationships are mediated by the strategic use of concepts formulated (in part) with that function in mind. It shows how global policy is the product of village politics – in this case, those of 1818 H. Street in Washington D.C.[9]

As Maia Green (Chapter 2 this volume) points out, through the medium of key concepts or categories, professional relationships are routinely 'transformed *into* documentation', perhaps as meeting minutes, reports, policy statements or technical documents that are the vehicle for the travelling ideas of development. Documents contain hidden relational baggage: statements that are best understood as bargaining positions in ongoing disputes over policy within or between professional teams, or as negotiating positions for future disagreements. Documents themselves are then also the means for agency, through tactical readings, soliciting comments and the inclusions/exclusion of email circulation lists, as well as public airings of policy choices. Documents are not to be analysed as dead artefacts; they are alive with the social processes that produced them and they have a 'performative quality' and social effects, even though the salience of policy ideas that they convey summarize and hide this 'politics of interaction' (see Green, Chapter 2 this volume; cf. Riles 2006, Smith 2006).

However, one thing that anthropologists immersed in the world of 'global policymaking' are good at demonstrating is the thinness of this concealment; that is, the lack of coherence behind apparent documented consensus. In her recent study of expert negotiations on pension reform in Mexico, for example, Tara Schwegler (2009) was struck by the underlying incoherence and instability of a World Bank-led neoliberal policy framework. The policy narrative did not gain unity and coherence as one ascended the hierarchy from local interests to international players. No one could give a definitive account of the framing of reform. The top people had authority, but did not know about critical decisions below. There were different accounts of the policy process which were themselves statements about the power relations through which Schwegler's informants defined each other. Expert knowledge was always 'anticipatory', that is, shaped in ways that anticipated the reaction of others. In this political field of policy, each player preserved a sense that they had succeeded. Examples could be multiplied to show how fragile and responsive to politics expert consensuses actually are.

Given how prevailing expert models are both shaped and unravelled locally in political relations, it is not the failure of harmonized development policy to execute planned social transformation that is remarkable, but rather its success. What is striking is the capacity of professionals (who are by no means ignorant of these processes) to sustain neoliberal institutionalist models as a structure of representation, an accepted interpretation of what is going on and what can be accomplished. There is a striking expert capacity to represent complex events in formalistic terms that allow social change to be understood as subject to policy levers acting directly on the behaviour of economic agents through manipulable structures of incentives so as to produce accountability, efficiency and equity (Craig and Porter 2006: 20; Mitchell 2002: 266–67). And, of course, this is a collaborative capacity since, through the 'politics of the mirror', in-country experts work with their international counterparts to preserve the fiction that the processes of neoliberal reform are locally owned (Anders 2005: 113).

Timothy Mitchell's insight in *Rule of Experts* (2002) is precisely this – that the pervasive 'gaps' between policy and practice, ideal and actual, and representation and reality are not a disappointment but are actively maintained by the operations of expertise in order to preserve policy as a structure of representation. This allows actual practice to be seen as the outcome of the policy ideal and to reproduce a sphere of rational intention that can appear external to and generative of events, so as 'to rearrange power over people as power over ideas' (Mitchell 2002: 90). As ethnographers of expertise in development, we then have to examine the professional processes that make and stabilize the efficacy of 'global' policy regimes.[10]

There is an additional and final approach to expert and institutional knowledge that begins not with the political economy of global institutions, internal processes of transmission or self-discipline, nor even the strategic deployment of ideas, but with the analytical forms of expert ideas themselves. In her important departure from conventional concerns in the sociology of knowledge, Annelise Riles (2001) takes the case of the production of legal knowledge by human rights NGOs in the lead up to the Beijing Conference on Women in 1995 to direct our attention to the effects of knowledge forms, their precedence over content, style over substance (a counterpart to Uchiyamada's [above] replication of institutional form that vacates policy ideas of their content – Uchiyamada 2004: 9). By studying forms such as the network, the bracket, the system or the matrix as documents and diagrams, she reveals professional knowledge as 'an *effect* of a certain aesthetic of information' (Riles 2001: 2, original emphasis). In fact, she does more – she repositions our investigation of development professionals so that it takes place inside the knowledge forms themselves. Studying experts through their own knowledge forms, which are also their modes of sociality (as in the network), is an approach increasingly relevant for communities formed around formalist knowledge where 'the global' is not a spatial scale but, as Riles argues, something generated internally through mundane tools like the network or matrix; 'an aspect of late modern informational aesthetics' (2001: 20).

The World of Professionals

Strangely late and reluctantly, anthropologists have turned to the study of the social and cultural lives of global professionals themselves, their class position, biographies, commitments and anxieties. The chapters in this volume show how international experts are, like their policy models, mobile and separated from contextual attachments yet, paradoxically, are a highly visible group in the capital cities of the developing world where, far from instantiating a cosmopolitan outlook that 'encompass[es] the world's [cultural] variety and its subsequent mixtures', they occupy cultural enclaves of shared consumption, lifestyle and values (Friedman 1997: 74). As Freidman puts it, 'while representing [themselves] as open and including the entire world [international experts are] socially at least as restricted as any other strong ethnic identity' (Ibid, 2004: 165; cf. Argenti-Pillen 2003). Friedman's further argument is that claims to cosmopolitanism are expressions of the class position of a global elite whose power is effected through 'clubs' and that actually displays a 'retreat from the social' that takes the form of a global 'top lifting' and an exit from representative democracy 'upwards into the stratosphere of governance' (Freidman 1997; 2004: 167). The ethnographic accounts offered here make a different point by showing how homogenized development policy knowledge has its social basis in the locally transient but internationally permanent and close-knit communities of experts whose reach, intensity and centralization is increased by electronic information and communication technologies (Eyben, Chapter 7 this volume).

In Chapter 6, Ian Harper reveals the parochialism of internationals as against the cosmopolitanism of 'locals' by contrasting two groups of international health workers: on the one hand, global experts (development consultants and advisers) and, on the other hand, Nepali health worker migrants to countries like the U.K. and the U.S.A. First, he shows how the universalizing knowledge of global experts is 'closed off from other epistemologies' (and other health systems) through the 'spatial dynamics around where knowledge is produced and stabilised': the 'walling off' of 'fortress' hospitals bounded from 'the cacophony of the street'. In contrast, the migrant health workers cross boundaries between health systems and languages. They cannot isolate themselves from the demands of those who are poorly paid, have low status or are socially insecure in the countries to which they migrate. It is these migrant health workers who are cosmopolitan in Hannerz's sense of displaying a 'reflexive distance from one's own culture'; they are 'open to new ways of knowing and being' (Hannerz 1996).

Rosalind Eyben (Chapter 7) reflects on her own role as 'head of mission' of the U.K. DFID in Bolivia and focuses on the everyday sociality of aid professionals in the country – the social round, the party and picnic circles, the strategic inclusions, exclusions and reciprocities, the rituals of entry and exit into expatriate communities, and the circulation of 'prior reputation' between them. In offering important insights into how expert communities are forged nationally and globally, Eyben takes up the point that 'the efforts at constructing and sustaining such a community are an essential component of a harmonized approach to aid'. Correspondingly, policy disagreements rupture social relationships. As in Harper's chapter, it is clear that sustaining expert communities involves a retreat from the street outside, from awkward complexity and dangerous contradictions, and the need for intermediating brokers, simplifying templates and inherited stereotypes.[11] In a postscript, Eyben reflects on the impact of major political change on the maintenance of aid community relations in Bolivia.

In Chapter 8, Dinah Rajak and Jock Stirrat offer a parallel analysis of the way in which development professionals fail to be cosmopolitan. They see this failure as a feature of isolated expatriate social worlds, as well as an effect of standardized neoliberal policy thought, which denies both difference – so that to the expert all countries appear the same – and its own historical specificity. However, they argue that the 'parochialism' of rootless professionals takes a specific form: nostalgia. International experts not only create self-enclosed social worlds that are a nostalgic parody of 'home', but they also bring an 'imperial nostalgia' (Rosaldo 1989) to their imaginings of the countries in which they work. They 'mourn the passing of what they themselves have transformed' (ibid: 69), that is, an anterior traditional order eroded by the 'discontinuities, disjunctures and displacements' of development itself. Through collecting the past as artefact, inhabiting old colonial hotels and rest houses or visiting 'the field', the necessary oppositional framework of the 'under-developed' and the 'developed' is stabilized. Youthful ideas of unmediated cross-cultural contact that drew many into development are contradicted by professional lives in parochial development enclaves – a 'small tragedy' from which nostalgia rather than cosmopolitan sensibilities is born.

David Lewis (Chapter 9) uses life histories to further explore the complexities of professional identities and their relationship to dominant paradigms in development, this time among U.K. voluntary sector and NGO workers. These personal narratives reveal career histories shaped by values, political and religious commitments, experiences or family background (diplomatic, colonial or missionary; cf. Stirrat, n.d.). Lewis also makes a further point, noting how professionals' life stories of ambition, adventure or self-realization also work to instantiate and reproduce sectoral divisions and dominant policy models. In particular, two prominent rationalities of aid or governance become compacted in the stories they tell. The first is a colonially-rooted discourse that separates poverty at home from poverty in the developing world (denying the 'interconnectedness of global social inequality' or the poverty-related domestic issues of immigration and racism). The second is a tripartite model of the state, the market and the 'third sector' (including NGOs), which allows neoliberals to conceptualize a 'good governance' agenda that finds synergies between these three sectors or to speak of 'comparative advantage' and other reassuring policy simplifications. Lewis' informants may have become prisoners of the policy categories they reproduce, but the 'three sectors' and the 'home/away' models present an interesting contrast. While the boundaries of the 'three sector model' are maintained conceptually (in policy) even as they are crossed/complicated in practice, the home/away away model is actually dismantled conceptually – as policy, the distinction disappears in the common ideas on poverty, the same micro-finance models or Participatory Learning and Action (PLA) methods – but the division is reproduced/reinstated in practice in professional networks.

In different ways these ethnographers reveal an awkward tension between the maintenance of professional modes of thought and identities, and the world with which these have to engage. On the one hand, professionals – and here I am thinking of international agency staff, consultants, fieldworkers, NGO staff, even missionaries and anthropologists – have to secure their place within particular institutional and social contexts, which (as I have suggested) are hugely complex. They work hard to maintain relationships, negotiate their position within agencies or on consultancy teams, build networks so as to negotiate their presence within foreign bureaucracies or NGOs for access and influence, and manage interfaces within and between agencies. Theirs is the messy, practical, emotion-laden work of dealing with contingency, compromise, improvisation, rule-bending, adjustment, producing viable data, making things work, and meeting delivery targets and spending budgets. In doing so, they have to negotiate national identity, race, age or gender. They have to manage personal security, family relations, loneliness, stress and anxiety – issues which have hardly been touched upon in the literature – while also shoring up their motivation within moral-ethical or religious frameworks which remain private.

On the other hand, as experts and professionals, they have to make themselves bearers of travelling rationalities, transferable knowledge and skills, context-free ideas with universal applicability or purified moral action – whether in the realms of plant science, water management, environmental protection, economic analysis, institutional capacity building, health sector reform or people's empowerment, whence come the cosmopolitan and technocratic claims. Status and professionalism are produced by recovering the universal from the particular, technocratic knowledge from the illicit relationships on which it is actually based (Riles 2004), conceding what is known from experience to the simple instrumentality of the models of employers, bosses or supporters (Verma 2008), or wider paradigms of the 'industry'. For different reasons, both the World Bank's investors and borrowers and the charitable donors to Oxfam or Care require the 'illusion of certainty' from their experts (Woods 2006).

Of course, the 'instruments' of professional practice facilitate as well as require the disembedding of models from the politics of programme relations and the separation of expert diagnosis from the multiplicity of points of view. Among these instruments are deductive 'terms of reference', the time-pressured information gathering, reporting templates (prescribed sections on strategy, progress and recommendations), charts, matrices, 'accountability tools', 'logframes' or classifications that have effects of their own. While these interpret situations for higher policy, they also produce standards for judgement and stabilize a given framework of interpretation (Mosse 2005a, Riles 2001, Goldman 2005: 168).[12] As Mitchell (2002) argues, expertise is made and has effects not through the imposition of designs that pre-exist events but by relocating the site of the production of significant knowledge from the periphery to the centre. The participatory turn in international development has made the constitution of expert development identities yet more complex. Professionals of participatory programmes have to deny or conceal their own expertise and agency (and their practical role in programme delivery) in order to preserve an authorized view of themselves as facilitators of community action or local knowledge, as 'catalysts', hastening but not partaking in the reaction (White 1999). 'No, my contribution is nothing' proclaims one Indian community worker, 'because I am only [a] facilitator and mobilise the community who have the main power' (Mosse 2005a: 154). Where 'expert' action is inaction, or expertise requires self-effacement, it is harder to constitute professional identities.[13] Such development workers (often in NGOs) have to simultaneously find ways of engaging deeply with communities while making themselves professionally absent. The dilemma is well captured in Celayne Heaton Shrestha's (2006) study of identity formation among Nepali NGO workers who, to be progressive and professional and to 'embody' the universal value of *bikas* ('development'), have to transcend social difference by 'bracketing' those aspects of themselves related to personal history, gender, ethnicity or class, and yet to be moral and thus capable of acting in local social arenas they have to respect social difference. 'Bracketing' is their way of saying that 'difference makes no difference'.

Therefore, to the professionals who face the problem of stabilizing universals of expert knowledge, we must add those NGO employees, charity workers, missionaries or other 'professional altruists' (Arvidson 2008) whose commitment is to moral rather than purely technical universals; whose professional subjectivity is framed by stories of facilitation, altruism, heroic commitment and sacrifice, which involve processes of 'moral selving', that is, making the self virtuous through action and reflection (Arvidson 2008, drawing on Allahyari 2000). These processes also involve a denial of agency, context and identity in ways that are experienced as difficult. For example, equipped with an ideal image of their work, Allahyari's charity workers experienced moral and emotional anxiety when confronted with reality, which led to the avoidance of situations, distancing themselves from clients, the transfer of blame onto ungrateful recipients or becoming closed to communities – a 'failure of sympathetic identification' (Graeber 2006) that is equivalent to the 'retreat from the local' that Harper and Eyben identify among aid professionals.

Development expertise involves, as Quarles von Ufford and Salemink (2006) put it, a curious but inevitable 'hiding of the self in our relations with others'. To be on the receiving end of professional concealment is to be subject to the peculiar diagnosis or unexpected remedy, the unanticipated change in expert judgement or shift in policy, or the mystifying withdrawal of support, all of which can have the dramatic effect of rupturing relationships, precipitating crises or producing failure (see Mosse 2005a: Chapter 8). From this suspicion of experts and what they do not reveal comes the demand for public visibility, openness and transparency. However, efforts to embrace transparency bring their own dilemmas, even eroding professional trust. As Garsten and Lindh de Montoya (2008b: 7) point out, the more professionals attempt to reveal through evidence, facts and figures or 'access points' for public-expert mediation, the greater the public awareness of its ignorance of expert knowledge systems and the greater the suspicion of concealment. At the same time, transparency produces new regimes of professional self-regulation ('regulation by revelation') of workers with public diaries, in open-plan offices in glass buildings who exercise even greater control over their professional conduct and selves (2008a: 5, 12).

The constant demand to turn the political into the technical, to represent the mess of practice in ordered expert or moral categories, the management of demands for transparency and the fragility of professional identities that depend upon these processes is not easily handled. Development professionals are often intensely aware of their dilemma and the contradictions they face: the complexities of relationship and meaning, and the 'instrumentalism which is [also] the condition of their daily work' (Riles 2006: 60). Backstage scepticism and the escape into irony, self-criticism, spoof or humour are common responses (cf. Riles 2004). Indeed, there is little external criticism of development practice that is not prefigured within expert communities. Sometimes, like Riles' human rights lawyers, experts attempt to marginalize themselves from the zealous naivety of 'true believers' and from their own power (ibid.). This may be a mark of the 'true expert' (Riles 2006: 58); but so too is resignation to the immovable dominance of official knowledge which ensures that for many scepticism is closeted and concealed.

Only occasionally do aid professionals offer fuller first person accounts of the real micropolitics of their own expert practice, revealing for the general reader the chaotic, arbitrary underbelly of 'objective' economic data, or the rough politics of loan negotiation in developing counties. Peter Griffith's *The Economist's Tale* (2003) and John Perkins' *Confessions of an Economic Hit Man* (2003) are striking accounts of the moral ambiguity of expert roles: the first is a tale of heroic struggle, while the second is a regretful confession of harm done (see also Vaux 2001). As development experts, anthropologists too have chosen positions of reflective marginality in order to study themselves as well as those for (or with) whom they work, aiming at insights that cannot be gained from within expert frames or management cycles (Eyben 2003, Mosse 2005a, Riles 2006: 53).[14] For professional altruists (charity workers or missionaries), the escape into irony or sceptical expressions of doubt may be more difficult and the experience of contradiction more personally devastating, which may have some part to play in the high levels of stress and their emotional consequences reported in psychological studies of aid workers and missionaries (e.g., Lovell-Hawker 2004, Foyle 2001).

The vulnerabilities of being expert only increase with the growing intensity of targets and uncomprehending demands of audit and accountability across the board (Strathern 2000). With the rising scale of ambition in international development come spectacular possibilities for failure, in which enterprises do not simply fail, they fail in detail. But my point here is that failure is not simply a plan unrealized, it is also the unravelling of professional identities. Failure may be regarded as the irruption of precisely those things that professionalism necessarily suppresses – events, contingencies and relationships. While success buries the individual action or event and makes a project a unified source of intention and power directing attention to the transcendent agency of policy and expert design (and hence replicability), failure fragments into the dynamics of blame (Latour 1996: 76). While success emphasizes the professional, the policy and the collective, moments of failure search out the individual person. Failure points to the contingent, the arbitrary, the accidental, the exceptional and the unintended. By releasing the anecdotal, failure can unravel the work of expertise or professional identity formation; it may license the expression of suppressed and scattered doubts, drawing attention to the informal processes underlying official actions. Narratives of failure individualize downwards to the actions/events of junior people, or upwards, for example, to the singular actions of a corrupt senior official. While stories of success emphasize the system and expert ideas (they are theory-rich), those of failure are inherently event-rich.[15]

From the Ethnography of Failure to the Failure of Ethnography

Researching professional lives, 'studying up' (Nader 2002 [1969]) or 'through' (Wedel 2004) and writing ethnographic accounts of those expert communities open up important methodological and ethical issues quite separate from the matter of techniques for describing networks or 'following the policy' (Shore and Wright 1997). There are aspects of professional identity discussed above that perhaps make ethnographic description difficult, contested or impossible.

First, it may simply be impossible to subject expert communities to ethnographic description. For those close to (or members of) professional communities, it becomes impossible to provide accounts of their own social relations and politics because ethnographic subjects refuse to be objectified in these terms (Riles 2006: 63; 2001: 18). Miyazaki and Riles (2005) regard the 'ethnographic failure' that is associated with attempts at research on/with expert subjects whose parallel theorizing already incorporates sociological analysis as an 'end point' of anthropological knowledge. For an anthropological process premised upon difference, this 'epistemological sameness' indicates the 'failure to know the ethnographic subject' or rather the failure of ethnographic knowledge to be accepted as such (2005: 327). This descriptive failure results from the inability to 'objectify' or to 'localize' expert subjects and to maintain a 'defining distance' between the ethnographer and the subject.

Holmes and Marcus (2005) suggest that this can be averted and ethnography can be 're-functioned', in part, by recourse to experts' own sceptical or self-critical moves. Writing of professionals in the financial world, these authors refer to the existence among experts of a 'self-conscious critical faculty that operates … as a way of dealing with contradictions, exceptions, facts that are fugitive, and that suggest a social realm not in alignment with the representations generated by the application of the reigning statistical mode of analysis' (2005: 237). Making use of this 'para-ethnographic' dimension of expert domains, Holmes and Marcus invite anthropologists to find a 'collaborative' mode of research with those expert subjects who are neither natives nor colleagues, but who stand as counterparts (2005: 248). As outsiders or insiders, ethnographers may then draw on the 'kind of illicit, marginal social thought' that exists among managers, international experts and field staff, scientists or consultants (my colleagues and myself) whose practices are dominated by official technical discourse. Holmes and Marcus suggest that such anecdotal or intuitive thought, deployed 'counterculturally and critically' both by privileged and subordinate actors within development systems, provides a bridge 'to further the production of fundamentally *anthropological* knowledge' (ibid.).

This, indeed, was my own strategy in producing an ethnography of an international development intervention (Mosse 2005a). However, 'collaborative ethnography', even 'self-ethnography',[16] founded on the para-ethnographic may not be so easy to pull off in practice. Holmes and Marcus themselves identify the key aspect of the problem when they refer to the 'implication for these [technocratic/managerial] regimes of the return of ethnography derived from the subversive para-ethnography by some strategy of overture, writing, and representation back to the project's originating milieu' (2005: 241). When presented with my own ethnographic (or para-ethnographic) account of the social production of success and failure, my expert and professional subjects (and colleagues) raised objections. They sought to interrupt the publication and advanced official complaints to my university, to the publisher and to my professional association, insisting that the ethnography was inaccurate, disrespectful and – most significantly – damaging to professional reputations (see Mosse 2006a).

Indeed, the question of professionalism was at the very centre of this particular controversy. My point above was that in deferring to the instrumentality of expert models, professionals are required to deny context, contingency, compromise, even their own agency, and to suppress the relational – all those things from which ethnography is necessarily composed. Little surprise, then, that the parts of the ethnography that my colleagues regarded as 'defamatory and potentially damaging to professional reputations'[17] were precisely those that mentioned unscripted roles, relationships, events or interests; those parts that concerned the real-life connections of consultant work, that alluded to competing rationalities (of donors, clients, staff and beneficiaries) or provided unofficial interpretations.

One colleague, for example, wrote that he took 'exception to the idea that we [international consultants] were motivated by seeking to secure an enduring relationship with the donor or project/area as a site for research and future consultancy income', insisting that, 'we were a professional team'. A description of the wider social context of consultancy work also questioned professionalism, as did comments on informal processes such as the many ways in which lethargic bureaucratic processes of approval and budget release had to be 'facilitated' – 'the many courtesy calls, foreigner visits, cards, gifts, overseas training opportunities' (Mosse 2005a: 123). The same is true of references to informal brokerage, the chameleon-like manipulation of insider/outsider roles or the out-of-sight economy of favours and obligations existing on the margins of legitimacy (ibid.: 125). My colleagues could of course themselves describe such roles and relationships, and did so in the course of the interviews, but they were professionally committed to their denial. Similarly, in her interviews with development professionals in the U.K., Kaufmann notes the desire to rewrite the script of the 'informal and chatty discourse [into] a formal and jargon-ridden one', as well as an anxiety about anonymity (1997: 111).

Any notion of self-interest, not least the observation that, proportionately, we expatriate experts were far greater beneficiaries than tribal villagers of the aid gifts we were honoured for bringing (or that some thirty-seven percent of project costs went to technical cooperation, mostly to U.K. institutions and consultants), or that it is the expectation of trainers, consultants and U.K. universities, as well as project workers and managers, to profit from the flow of aid into projects (Mosse 2005a: 126–30, 249), also undermined professionalism. In an ethical register, such comments in my text were 'unnecessary' because professionals' work in development is charitable. '"Profit"', my colleague wrote to me, 'is the wrong word … we all could have earned more doing something else. We chose not to because we believed in what we were doing'. In other places, the description of the contradiction between actions/events and authorized models was itself regarded as damaging to professionalism. This included accounts of the realities of implementation pressures (budgets and targets) and the actions of workers who were meant to facilitate a community-driven process, or the suggestion that the scientifically demonstrated benefits of new farmer-first technologies could disappear when re-embedded in complex micro-environments, networks of obligation, debt and migration of tribal farmers. Such accounts 'questioned our professionalism' and threatened to damage professional reputations.

My 'para-ethnographic' work encountered a professional habitus that automatically transferred the actuality of events into the preconceived categories of legitimate meaning and ideal process: 'decisions taken democratically by the committees', relationships denuded of power/interest, the power-free flow of information, or the absence of pressure on staff to meet targets, the threat of transfers, etc. It brushed up against self-representations that required the erasure of discrepancies of practice, disjunctures, the effacing of individual action or denial of relationships. Quite inevitably, such ethnographic description is experienced as disempowering or threatening to a professional (or epistemic) community formed around shared representations (Mosse 2006a). Even so, the attendant upset and anger that revealed a fundamental antipathy between professional identity and the ethnographic project was a shock to me. Perhaps it should not have been. After all, such ethnography examines the instability of meaning rather than defining successful outcomes of expert design, and draws attention to the irrelevant, the routine and the ordinary. It intercepts the interlinked chains of theory, events and professional reputations in development. The ethnographic concern with individual actions and events (rather than policy theory) connects it to narratives of failure such that ethnographic description is read as negative evaluation (ibid.), and when it turns its attention to the unnoticed effects of analytical forms (documentary artefacts, networks, matrices, annual reports, etc.: Riles 2001) it detracts from the substance of official narratives.

From another point of view, however, we anthropologists of professionals are making arrogant claims to understand and represent others. In various ways we make ourselves cosmopolitan by rendering other experts 'local', whether World Bank officials (Mosse), aid consultants (Rajak and Stirrat) or international health experts (Harper). Ethnography denies to others their cosmopolitan claims by contextualizing, localizing and placing them in relationships. It may reduce 'the global' claimed of international networks to an effect of the aesthetic of trivial knowledge practices (Riles 2001), and it is clear that when anthropologists point to the relational or the arbitrary – the compromises and discrepancies – in development, or when they prioritize form over content, they can demean and provoke rage. Claims of damage to professional reputations may follow; defamation cases may be threatened. Our ethnographic 'localizing strategies' cause damage to cosmopolitan claims that are always fragile.

However, matters do not end here; that is, with objections raised against illicit accounts that subvert official technocratic/managerial views or intercept the rule of experts. First, anthropological knowledge may itself be delegitimized as 'unethical' when professional groups use the rubric of research ethics codes either to claim harm as human subjects of research, suffering damage to professional reputations, or to assert control over the research process by extending the demand for 'consent' from data gathering to analysis, research outputs and especially publications (see Mosse 2006a, b, c). Second, professional groups may challenge not the factuality of an ethnographic account but its social base. Those who objected to my ethnography of the DFID project in western India challenged an account that departed from consensual, participative truth making, but more significantly they sought to reincorporate the ethnographer into a set of project relations of power and authority (see Mosse 2006a). Indeed, while my expert colleagues took exception to my ethnographic interpretation of relationships as prior to knowledge (and to my description of the investments directed to maintaining these relations as part of the execution of a programme), their own means of contending with ethnographic objectification was precisely to set the demands of professional relationships against anthropological knowledge production. In other words, my informants sought to unravel my ethnographic data back into the relations of our professional team. So, anthropologists' professional interlocutors may themselves work to localize our own cosmopolitan claims and to unravel our professional anthropological knowledge. The way in which expert informants raise objections may challenge the basis of ethnographic description through the erasure of the boundary between ethnographic writing and the relations of fieldwork, and by the refusal to engage with a textual representation and the insistence on re-incorporating its author into the moral relations of a project. Given the essentially relational nature of ethnographic knowledge – in the sense that knowledge is collaborative and dialogical, gained by way of relations, and that (in consequence) the relationships between researcher and object of enquiry become a property of the object itself (Hastrup 2004: 457) – ethnographic representations always have the potential to unravel when our informants (as did mine) attempt to unpack our 'evidence' back into relationships with them.

Expert informants offer an epistemological threat by localizing/parochializing ethnographic cosmopolitanism, re-embedding academic knowledge, denying the worth of 'evidence' or social research, resisting the boundary making between field relationships and research that is the pretext for description (Mosse 2006a).[18] This traces another route to Miyazaki and Riles' ethnographic 'end point' when expert subjects make a 'radical disjuncture between the moment of ethnography [the ethnographic encounter] and the moment of writing [the description and analysis] untenable' – when there is a failure 'to assert analytical control over the material' (2005: 326–28). Sometimes, anthropologists will find it impossible to mark a boundary and 'objectify' cosmopolitan colleagues as social actors; they may fail to exit from professional communities so as to allow the production of ethnographic description (or the analysis may have to sidestep into mimicry or parallel modes, as in Riles 2001, 2006). At other times such boundary making may be contested through objections, as I have described.

It is now widely recognized that the right to academic knowledge can no longer be taken for granted and has to be negotiated alongside other forms of knowledge. Particular dilemmas (ethical and epistemological) arise where the users of research are also the subjects of research (and vice versa), and where research generates information on 'non-public' aspects of systems of public knowledge within which, when published, it also circulates. Anthropologists now have to find modes of post-fieldwork interaction with professionals and public knowledge regimes that solicit responses/objections to ethnographic representations without requiring resolution or consensus, while still acknowledging the genuine underlying tensions of epistemology and purpose.

Notes

1. Call for papers for seminar series 'Conflicts in Time: Rethinking 'Contemporary' Globalization', Laura Bear, London School of Economics (January 2007).
2. The new drive to expert consensus and 'harmonization' is evident, for example, in a series of donor-sponsored and UN agency-coordinated High Level Forums on Aid Effectiveness, in Rome (2003), Marrakech (2004), Paris (2005) and Accra (2008), and on health Millenium Development Goals (MDGs) in Tunis (2006). A recent visit to China (July 2008) reminded me that this common approach to aid and state-society relations also has an important exception (or variant).
3. Boström and Garsten (2008b) throw light on the contradictory implications of transnational accountability for expert knowledge regimes in international development. On the one hand, the rising demand for accountability (including the demand for a negotiation of the meaning of 'accountability' itself) implies a loss of trust in experts. On the other hand, the reorganization of agencies for accountability – the demand for new 'accountability tools', for 'inspection regimes', for numbers, 'robust' output data, and credible accounts of institutional performance – all involve greater dependence on expertise.
4. Of course, the dominance of economic reasoning and quantitative modelling in international development is just part of a widely-explored historical trajectory. At its broadest, Charles Taylor recalls that the pre-eminence of economics is rooted in a rise of 'the economy' in the Western social imaginary from the eighteenth century, 'as an interlocking set of activities of production, exchange, and consumption which form a system with its own laws and its own dynamics' (2007: 171). As a social order caused by human needs and mutual benefits, it replaced the older notion of polity as a normative order ('form at work in reality'), opening social order up to explanation and planned intervention. The particular importance of quantification and number in the bureaucratic and administrative techniques of government and planning is taken up by Porter (1996,

2003). His specific point, that quantification was a political project (to manage populations) before it was a scientific or economic project, is relevant to the present argument. Quantification was part of the centralization of control and decentralization of responsibility (2003: 98) established as a relationship of governance that required central expertise as well as local self-monitoring, for instance through systems of financial accounting (complicated by tax law). The quantification of public policy – the use of instruments such as cost-benefit analysis in project appraisal, policy argument and political justification – increased demand for expertise and technocratic rule. Meanwhile, the presumed neutrality and communicability of numbers (linked to presumed uniform categories: Bowker and Star 2000) make them the quintessential form of translocal knowledge in development.

5. The processes by which a participatory project makes experts out of locals by disembedding their knowledge from its social context has been explored in the case of participatory agricultural development in tribal India (Mosse 2005a, 208). In this case, expert engagement, whether of plant breeders, soil scientists, microfinance specialists or (like myself) anthropologists, had the effect of disembedding technology from agrarian relations, and money (microfinance) from social obligation. In the participatory plant breeding (PPB) programme, it was precisely the separation of farmers' knowledge from social and political relationships that legitimized it as 'expert' or 'scientific', in contrast to research station scientists, who were too embedded in the political matrix of professional career building (Chambers et al. 1989). People participate in expert designs through PPB techniques, participatory rural appraisal (PRA), even ethnography, which allow communication to 'learning elites' who direct the process (Wilson 2006).

6. For an economist's view on the risks that might be involved in the democratization of expertise in international development, see Collier 2007.

7. This does not negate Ferguson's point that failure may also disguise other political effects which transcend developers' intentions (1994: 255).

8. Uchiyamada offers an interesting case of a reverse ritual process aimed at effecting the transformation of information into non-information. A senior officer in a Japanese aid bureaucracy 'morally erases' the minutes of an internal seminar emailed in error by a junior clerk to external participants (which was embarrassing because the email contained a record of internal process). The erring junior is sent a large number of empty envelopes, asked to 'recall' the email from each recipient, print it and return it to the Secretary General for destruction (2004: 8).

9. In a paper prepared at the conference at which this book project began, Philip Quarles van Ufford and Oscar Salemink (2006) extended this interest in the work that development ideas accomplish not by transforming the Third World, but by redefining the identities of those in power in 'the West', with a critical engagement with the moral philosophy of Martha Nussbaum. Through ethnographic cases set in Vietnam and Indonesia, they showed how development's moral and expert 'care of the other' is shaped by an unrecognized 'domestic' self-interest and a necessary 'care of the self'.

10. Bowker and Star's (2000) work on the social life of professional standards and classifications, specifically the International Classification of Diseases (ICD), has an important bearing on this discussion. They follow Latour (1987) in viewing the fact, the datum or the category as a consequence, not a starting point, and then retrieve the stripped-out political and ethical work of individual and organizational agents that make up a classification infrastructure (Bowker and Star 2000: 266). Moreover, they show how classifications and standards regulate information flows, organize institutional memory and provide a means to professionalize (or to become subject to professional surveillance). Classifications mediate communication between groups and the formation of cross-cultural professional communities, but at the same time lose definition under local interpretation as they are contextualized into 'informal' counterparts.

11. Other ethnographic accounts reveal just how complex the processes of expert isolation can be and how mediated the relationship between global expertise and local experience is.

Argenti-Pillen (2003) shows how Western mental health professionals working in the field of humanitarian aid in Sri Lanka are disabled by their exclusion from a complex politicized translation process in which Sinhala intellectuals-collaborators promote Buddhist nationalist language (subjugating villager expressions of trauma) through the translation of a locally unintelligible international humanitarian discourse on war trauma.

12. Riles (2004) describes a technical intervention in Japanese banking specifically designed to resolve the dilemma, that is, to erase relations (with clients) that are a necessary part of technical knowledge through a mechanism to inbuild 'realtime' processes (2004: 398).

13. The dilemma has not escaped those outside experts responsible for community-driven development, who, as Li (Chapter 3 this volume) shows, resolve the paradox by emphasizing the expert design of 'meta-rules','mediating institutions' and 'minimum standards' for the *local* crafting of rules and solutions.

14. Riles (2006) is especially interested in how anthropological ideas of culture are appropriated as a mode of critique or irony by critical human rights lawyers. But since these ironical commentaries remain within the 'iron cage' of legal instrumentalism, anthroplology (or culture) itself becomes instrumentalized in very unanthropological ways. The closest parallel in the world of international development (but also a more extreme case) is the 'critical' introduction of the idea of social relations and culture within economics discourse in the World Bank and their instrumentalization, notably in the concept of 'social capital' (see Mosse, Chapter 4 this volume).

15. The distinction between 'success' and 'failure' as contexts of narration may be relevant to variation in the patterns of remembering and forgetting that Bloch analyses in relation to the differences between official histories (prototypical representations) and event-driven accounts (1998).

16. Something Riles (2006) describes as 'circling back', referring to her return as an ethnographer to the community of human rights lawyers of which she was a member.

17. Unattributed quotations are from correspondence with my critics who I refrain from identifying.

18. In my own case, this boundary was reasserted procedurally and institutionally in a way that reminds us that in the end anthropological knowledge is a 'social achievement' (Crick 1982: 20, cited in Hastrup 2004: 456) (Mosse 2006a).

References

Agrawal, Arun. 2005. *Environmentality: Technologies of Government and the Making of Subjects*. Durham, N.C.: Duke University Press.

Allahyari, R. 2000. *Visions of Charity: Volunteer Workers and Moral Community*. Berkeley, C.A.: University of California Press.

Anders, Gerhard. 2005. 'Civil Servants in Malawi: Cultural Dualism, Moonlighting and Corruption in the Shadow of Good Governance', Ph.D thesis. Rotterdam: Erasmus University.

Anderson, Jock R., Gershon Feder and Sushma Ganguly. 2006. 'The Rise and Fall of Training and Visit Extension: An Asian Mini-drama with an African Epilogue', *World Bank Policy Research Working Paper* 3928, May 2006.

Appadurai, Arjun. 2004. 'The Capacity to Aspire: Culture and the Terms of Recognition', in V. Rao and M. Walton (eds), *Culture and Public Action*. Stanford, C.A.: Stanford University Press.

Argenti-Pillen, A. 2003. 'The Global Flow of Knowledge on War Trauma: The Role of the "Cinnamon Garden Culture" in Sri Lanka', in J. Pottier, A. Bicker and P. Sillitoe (eds), *Negotiating Local Knowledge: Power and Identity in Development*. London: Pluto Press.

Arvidson, Malin. 2008 'Contradictions and Confusions in Development Work: Exploring the Realities of Bangladeshi NGOs', *Journal of South Asian Development* 3(1): 109–34.

Barron, Patrick, Rachael Diprose and Michael Woolcock. 2006. 'Local Conflict and Community Development in Indonesia: Assessing the Impact of the Kecamatan Development Program'. *Indonesian Social Development Paper No. 10*. Jakarta: World Bank.

Bebbington, A., S. Guggenheim, E. Olson and M. Woolcock. 2004. 'Exploring Social Capital Debates at the World Bank', *Journal of Development Studies* 40(5): 33–42.

Bergman, Carol (ed.). 2003. *Another Day in Paradise: Front Line Stories from International Aid Workers*. London: Earthscan.

Bloch, M. 1998. *How We Think They Think. Anthropological Approaches to Cognition, Memory and Literacy*. Boulder, C.O.: Westview Press.

Booth, David. 2005. 'Missing Links in the Politics of Development: Learning from the PRSP Experiment', *ODI Working Paper* 256. London: Overseas Development Institute.

Boström, Magnus and Christina Garsten. (eds). 2008a. *Organising Transnational Accountability*. Cheltenham: Edward Elgar.

Boström, Magnus and Christina Garsten. (eds). 2008b. 'Organising for Accountability', in M. Bostrom and C. Garsten (eds), *Organising Transnational Accountability*. Cheltenham: Edward Elgar, pp. 1–26.

Bowker, C. Geoffrey and Susan Leigh Star. 2000. *Sorting Things Out: Classification and its Consequences*. Cambridge, M.A.: MIT Press.

Boyer, D. and U. Hannerz. 2006. 'Introduction to Special Issue on "Worlds of Journalism"', *Ethnography* 7(1): 5–17.

Brenneis, Don. 1994. 'Discourse and Discipline at the National Research Council: a Bureaucratic Bildungsroman', *Cultural Anthropology* 9: 23–36.

Bretton Woods Project. 2007. 'Knowledge Bank-rupted: Evaluation Says Key World Bank Research "Not Remotely Reliable"', Bretton Woods project update 54, January 2007, retrieved from http://www.brettonwoodsproject.org/art-549070.

Broad, Robin. 2007. '"Knowledge Management": A Case Study of the World Bank's Research Department', *Development in Practice* 17(4): 700–8.

Cernea, Michael M. 1995. Social Organisation and Development Anthropology. Environmentally Sustainable Development Studies and Monograph Series No. 6. Washington: The World Bank.

Chambers, R., A. Pacey and L.-A. Thrupp. 1989. *Farmer First: Farmer Innovation and Agricultural Research*. London: Intermediate Technology Publications.

Clay, E. and B. Schaffer (eds). 1984. *Room for Manoeuvre: An Exploration of Public Policy in Agriculture and Rural Development*. London: Heinemann.

Collier, Paul. 2007. *The Bottom Billion: Why the Poorest Countries are Failing and What Can Be Done About It*. Oxford: Oxford University Press.

Craig, David and Doug Porter. 2006. *Development Beyond Neoliberalism: Governance, Poverty Reduction and Political Economy*. London and New York: Routledge.

Crick, M. 1982. 'Anthropological Field Research, Meaning Creation and Knowledge Construction', in D. Parkin (ed.), *Semantic Anthropology*. London: Academic Press, pp. 15–37.

Easterly, William. 2002. *The Elusive Quest for Growth: Economists' Adventures and Misadventures in the Tropics*. Cambridge, M.A.: MIT Press.

———. 2006a. *The White Man's Burden: Why the West's Efforts to Aid the Rest Have Done So Much Ill and So Little Good*. New York: Penguin.

———. 2006b. 'The Big Push Déjà Vu: A Review of Jeffrey Sachs's *The End of Poverty: Economic Possibilities for Our Time*', *Journal of Economic Literature* XLIV: 96–105.

Escobar, Arturo. 1995. *Encountering Development: The Making and Unmaking of the Third World*. Princeton, C.T.: Princeton University Press.

Eyben, Rosalind. 2003. Donors as Political Actors: Fighting the Thirty Years War in Bolivia. *IDS Working Paper* no. 183, April. Brighton: Institute of Development Studies.

Eyben Rosalind with Rosario León. 2005. 'Whose Aid? The Case of the Bolivian Elections Project', in D. Mosse and D. Lewis (eds), *The Aid Effect: Giving and Governing in International Development*. London: Pluto Press.

Fairhead, J. and M. Leach. 2003. *Science, Society and Power: Environmental Knowledge and Policy in West Africa and the Caribbean*. Cambridge: Cambridge University Press.

Ferguson, J. 1994. *The Anti-politics Machine: Development, De-politicisation and Bureaucratic Power in Lesotho*. Minneapolis: University of Minnesota Press.

———. 1997. 'Anthropology and its Evil Twin: Development in the Constitution of a Discipline', in F. Cooper and R. Packard (eds), *International Development and the Social Sciences: Essays in the History and Politics of Knowledge*. Berkeley, C.A.: University of California Press.

Fine, Ben. 2006. 'What Future for the World Bank?', Meeting 2 of 'Mapping the Future of the Bretton Woods Institutions: Challenges for the Mandate and Governance of the IMF and World Bank' series, 12 September. Retrieved 21 September 2006 from http://www.odi.org.uk/speeches/bretton_woods_sept_06/12%20Sept/index.html.

Foyle, Marjory F. 2001. *Honourably Wounded – Stress among Christian Workers*. London and Michigan: Monarch Books.

Friedman, J. 1997 'Global Crisis, the Struggle for Cultural Identify and Intellectual Pork-barrelling: Cosmopolitans, Nationals and Locals in an Era of Dehegemonization', in P.Werbner (ed.), *The Dialectics of Hybridity*. London: Zed Press, pp. 70–89.

———. 2004. 'The Relocation of the Social and the Retrenchment of the Elites', in B. Kapferer (ed.), Forum on the Retreat of the Social: The Rise and Rise of Reductionism', *Social Analysis* 48(3): 162–68.

Garsten, Christina and Monica Lindh de Montoya (eds). 2008a. *Transparency in a New Global Order: Unveiling Organizational Visions*. Cheltenham: Edward Elgar.

——— and ———. 2008b. 'Introduction: Examining the Politics of Transparency', in C. Garsten and M. Lindh de Montoya (eds), *Transparency in a New Global Order: Unveiling Organizational Visions*. Cheltenham: Edward Elgar, pp. 1–24.

Goldman, Michael. 2000. 'The Power of World Bank Knowledge'. Briefing, Bretton Woods Project, 25 May 2000. Retrieved 18 March 2008 from http://brettonwoods project.org/article.shtml?cmd[126]=x-126-15931.

———. 2005. *Imperial Nature: The World Bank and Struggles for Social Justice in the Age of Globalisation*. New Haven and London: Yale University Press.

Graeber, David. 2006. 'Beyond Power/Knowledge: An Exploration of the Relation of Power, Ignorance and Stupidity', LSE lecture. 25 May 2006. Retrieved from http://www.lse.ac.uk/collections/LSEPublicLecturesAndEvents/pdf/20060525-Graeber.pdf.

Griffiths, Peter. 2004. *The Economist's Tale: A Consultant Encounters Hunger and the World Bank*. London: Zed Press.

Hannerz, U. 1996. *Transnational Connections: Culture, People, Places*. London: Routledge.

———. 2004. *Foreign News: Exploring the World of Foreign Correspondents*. Chicago: University of Chicago Press.

Harper, Richard. 1998. *Inside the IMF: An Ethnography of Documents, Technology, and Organizational Action*. Orlando, F.L.: Academic Press.

———. 2005. 'The Social Organisation of the IMF's Mission Work', in Marc Edelman and Angelique Haugerud (eds), *The Anthropology of Development and Globalisation: From Classical Political Economy to Contemporary Neoliberalism*. Oxford: Blackwell, pp 323–34.

Hastrup, K. 2004. 'Getting It Right: Knowledge and Evidence in Anthropology', *Anthropological Theory* 4(4): 455–72.

Heaton Shrestha, Celayne. 2006. '"They Can't Mix Like We Can": Bracketing Differences and the Professionalization of NGOs in Nepal', in D. Lewis and D. Mosse (eds), *Development Brokers and Translators: the Ethnography of Aid and Agencies*. Bloomfield, C.T.: Kumarian Press.

Hobart, Mark 1993. 'Introduction: The Growth of Ignorance?', in M. Hobart (ed.), *An Anthropological Critique of Development: The Growth of Ignorance*. London: Routledge.

Holmes, Douglas, R. and George E. Marcus. 2005. 'Cultures of Expertise and the Management of Globalisation: Towards a Re-functioning of Ethnography', in Aihwa Ong and Stephen

Collier (eds), *Global Assemblages: Technology, Politics and Ethics as Anthropological Problems.* Oxford: Blackwell. pp 235–52.

Ikenberry, John. 1992. 'A World Economy Recovered: Expert Consensus and the Anglo-American Post-war Settlement', *International Organisation* 46(1): 289–321.

Kaufmann, Georgia. 1997. 'Watching the Developers: A Partial Ethnography', in R.D. Grillo and R.L. Stirrat (eds), *Discourses of Development: Anthropological Perspectives.* Oxford and New York: Berg.

Latour, Bruno. 1987. *Science in Action: How to Follow Scientists and Engineers Through Society.* Cambridge, M.A.: Harvard University Press.

———. 1996. *Aramis, or the Love of Technology*, trans. Catherine Porter. Cambridge, M.A.: Harvard University Press.

Lewis, David and David Mosse (eds.). 2006. *Development Brokers and Translators: The Ethnography of Aid and Agencies.* Bloomfield, CT: Kumarian Press.

Li, Tania Murray. 2007. *The Will to Improve: Governmentality, Development, and the Practice of Politics.* Durham, N.C.: Duke University Press.

Long, N. 1992. 'From Paradigm Lost to Paradigm Regained? The Case for an Actor-oriented Sociology of Development', in N. Long and A. Long (eds), *Battlefields of Knowledge: The Interlocking of Theory and Practice in Social Research and Development.* London: Routledge.

Long, N. and A. Long (eds). 1992. *Battlefields of Knowledge: The Interlocking of Theory and Practice in Social Research and Development.* London: Routledge.

Long, Norman. 2001. *Sociology of Development: Actor Perspectives.* London and New York: Routledge.

Lovell-Hawker, Debbie. 2004 *Debriefing Aid Workers: A Comprehensive Manual.* London: People in Aid.

Maurer, Bill. 2005. *Mutual Life, Limited: Islamic Banking, Alternative Currencies, Lateral Reason.* Princeton, C.T.: Princeton University Press.

Mitchell, Timothy. 2002. *Rule of Experts: Egypt, Techno-Politics, Modernity.* Berkeley, C.A.: University of California Press.

Miyazaki, Hirokazu and Annelise Riles. 2005. 'Failure as an Endpoint', in Aihwa Ong and Stephen Collier (eds), *Global Assemblages: Technology, Politics and Ethics as Anthropological Problems.* Oxford: Blackwell, pp. 320–31.

Mosse, D. 2005a. *Cultivating Development: Ethnography of Aid Policy and Practice.* London: Pluto Press.

———. 2005b. 'Global Governance and the Ethnography of International Aid', in D. Mosse and D. Lewis (eds), *The Aid Effect: Giving and Governing in International Development.* London: Pluto Press.

———. 2006a. 'Anti-social Anthropology? Objectivity, Objection and the Ethnography of Public Policy and Professional Communities', *Journal of the Royal Anthropological Institute* 12(4): 935–56.

———. 2006b. 'Ethics and Development Ethnography', *Anthropology Today* 22(3): 23–24.

———. 2006c. 'A Disquieting Clash of Culture', *Times Higher Education Supplement* 1(739) (21 April): 18–19.

———. 2006d. 'Rule and Representation: Transformations in the Governance of the Water Commons in British South India', *Journal of Asian Studies* 65(1): 61–90.

Nader, Laura. 2002 [1969]. 'Up the Anthropologist. Perspectives Gained from Studying Up', in D. Hymes (ed.), *Reinventing Anthropology.* Ann Arbor, M.I.: University of Michigan Press, pp. 284–311.

Perkins, John. 2003. *Confessions of an Economic Hitman.* London: Plume.

Porter, Theodore M. 1996: *Trust in Numbers: The Pursuit of Objectivity in Science and Public Life.* Princeton, CT: Princeton University Press.

———. 2003. 'The Management of Society by Numbers', in John Krige and Dominique Pestre (eds), *Companion to Science in the Twentieth Century.* London: Routledge, pp. 97–110.

Power, Michael. 1997. *The Audit Society: Rituals of Verification.* Oxford: Oxford University Press.

Pritchett, Lant and Michael Woolcock. 2004. 'Solutions When the Solution is the Problem: Arraying the Disarray in Development', *World Development* 32(2): 191–212.

Quarles van Ufford, P., A. Kumar and D. Mosse. 2003. 'Interventions in Development: Towards a New Moral Understanding of our Experiences and an Agenda for the Future', in P. Quarles van Ufford and Ananta Giri (eds), *A Moral Critique of Development: In Search of Global Responsibilities*. London and New York: Routledge.

Quarles van Ufford and Oscar Salemink. 2006. 'After the Fall: Cosmopolitanism and the Paradoxical Politics of Global Inclusion and Authenticity', Paper prepared for the *Panel on Cosmopolitanism and Development, Association of Social Anthropologists Diamond Jubilee Conference, Keele, U.K., April 2006*.

Riles, Annelise 2001. *The network Inside Out*. Ann Arbor, M.I.: Michigan University Press.

———. 2004. 'Real Time: Unwinding Technocratic and Anthropological Knowledge', *American Ethnologist* 31(3): 392–405.

———. 2006. 'Anthropology, Human Rights, and Legal Knowledge; Culture in the Iron Cage', *American Anthropologist* 108(1): 52–65.

Rosaldo, R. 1989. 'Imperialist Nostalgia'. *Representations* 26: 107–22.

Sachs, Jeffrey. 2005. *The End of Poverty: Economic Possibilities for Our Time*. New York: Penguin.

St Clair, Asunción Lera. 2006a. 'The World Bank as a Transnational Expertised Institution', *Global Governance* 12: 77–95.

———. 2006b. 'Global Poverty: The Co-production of Knowledge and Politics', *Global Social Policy* 6(1): 57–77.

———. n.d. 'Ideas in Action: Human Development and Capability as Boundary Objects', Paper for the *Human Development and Capability Association (HDCA) 'Ideas Changing History' Conference*. Panel on Theorizing Ideas in the Multilateral System, The New School, New York, September 2007.

Scott J. C. 1998. *Seeing Like a State: How Certain Schemes to Improve the Human Condition Have Failed*. New Haven, C.T.: Yale University Press.

Schmidt, Jeff. 2000. *Disciplined Minds: A Critical Look at Salaried Professionals*. Lanham, MD): Rowman & Littlefield.

Schwegler, Tara. 2009. 'Take It from the Top (Down)? Rethinking Neoliberalism and Political Hierarchy in Mexico', *American Ethnologist* 35(4): 682–700.

Shore, C. and S. Wright (eds). 1997. *Anthropology of Policy: Critical Perspectives on Governance and Power*. London and New York: Routledge.

Smith, Dorothy. 2006. 'Incorporating Texts into Ethnographic Practice' in D.Smith (ed.), *Institutional Ethnography as Practice*. Lanham, M.D.: Rowman & Littlefield.

Stiglitz, Joseph. 2002. *Globalization and its Discontents*. New York: W.W. Norton & Co.

Stirrat, R.L. 2000. 'Cultures of Consultancy', *Critique of Anthropology* 20(1): 31–46.

———. n.d. 'Mercenaries, Missionaries and Misfits: Representations of Development Personnel', Paper presented at SOAS, London, March 2005.

Strathern, Marilyn (ed.). 2000. *Audit Cultures: Anthropological Studies in Accountability, Ethics and the Academy*. London: Routledge

Taylor, Charles. 2007. *A Secular Age*. New Haven, C.T.: Harvard University Press.

Uchiyamada Yashushi. 2004. 'Architecture of Immanent Power. Truth and Nothingness in a Japanese Bureaucratic Machine', *Social Anthropology* 12(1): 3–23.

Vaux, Tony 2001. *The Selfish Altruist: Relief Work in Famine and War*. London: Earthscan.

Verma, Ritu 2008. 'At Work and at Play in the "Fishbowl": Gender Relations and Social Reproduction among Development Expatriates in Madagascar', in Anne Meike-Fechter and Anne Coles (eds), *Gender and Family among Transnational Professionals*. London: Routledge.

Wedel, J. 2000. *Collision and Collusion: The Strange Case of Western Aid to Eastern Europe*. New York: Palgrave.

———. 2004. 'Studying Through a Globalizing World: Building Method through Aidnographies', in J. Gould and H. Secher Marcussen (eds), *Ethnographies of Aid – Exploring Development Texts and Encounters*. International Development Studies, Occasional Papers No. 24. Roskilde: Roskilde University, pp. 149–73.

Wedel, J., C. Shore, G. Feldman and S. Lathrop. 2005. 'Toward an Anthropology of Public Policy', *The Annals of the American Academy of Political and Social Science* 600: 30–51.

White, Shirley A. (ed.). 1999. *The Art of Facilitating Participation: Releasing the Power of Grassroots Communication*. London: Sage.

Wilson, Gordon. 2006. 'Beyond the Technocrat? The Professional Expert in Development Practice', *Development and Change* 37(3): 501–23.

Wood, G.D. 1998. 'Consultant Behaviour: Projects as Communities: Consultants, Knowledge and Power', *Project Appraisal* 16(1): 54–64.

Woods, Ngaire 2006. *The Globalizers: The IMF, the World Bank and their Borrowers*. Ithaca, C.A.: Cornell University Press.

Wrangham, Rachel 2006. 'Development People: Professional Identities and Social Lives', Unpublished paper for the 'Beyond Result: Failure as a Moral, Economic, and Socio-political Discourse' Workshop. Cambridge, 20 March.

Chapter 2

CALCULATING COMPASSION

Accounting for Some Categorical Practices in International Development[1]

Maia Green

Introduction

This chapter explores the practice of policy making in international development though an examination of the work that goes into the establishment and dissemination of core categories of the development imaginary – the targets of legitimate intervention. Following some key moments in the social life of a development category, that of children affected by HIV and AIDS, I show how policy coalitions and the relations which sustain them comprise 'communities of practice' (Wenger 1998) which come into being around particular objects of development. It is through these personal and professional networks, and the practices and institutions which sustain them, that the categories of international development practice become salient.[2]

As communities of practice organized around categorical positions, policy communities seek to affect development practice in order to enhance the significance of the categories they promote. This is achieved through fostering relationships, the production of documentation and the positioning of persons, documents and the categories they support at points of influence within the international development system. Just as development documents are claimed by those who spend their lives working on them to be 'living documents', multiply authored and endlessly reworked, development categories are living categories. Not only are they (like the documents in which they appear) perpetually recreated but in having the potential to influence outcomes, they have, in John Law's sense of the term, attributes of agency (1994: 34).[3]

Arguing against perspectives which have focused on policy as documentary style (Shore and Wright 1997; Apthorpe 1997), I show how the social process of policy making depends on special forms of social organization and categorical thinking constituted through the iteration of development's organizational form, within and outside documents (Riles 2001). Based on my experience of policy making in a bilateral donor organization and of working as a consultant for the leading international agency supporting a dispersed policy community around the child affected by HIV and AIDS, I show how policy communities establish themselves around significant categories and how these processes of relationship building are essential to the constitution of development orders. These transient coalitions of individuals representing the positions of diverse agencies and activist perspectives aligned around particular categories and the interventions which support them are important players in the international development scene, not only as influences on development agendas, but as the relations which make and remake the international development order.

Although the concern of policy communities with categorization makes them a potentially privileged site for anthropological attention, anthropologists are largely absent from policy communities. Anthropology (like other social sciences) has paid little attention to the practices and social processes of policy making (Bebbington et al. 2004: 34; Cooper and Packard 1997), tending instead to privilege documents as policy artefacts and their analysis as 'discourse' (Green 2007). Furthermore, anthropology as a discipline has absented itself from the production of development categories. Professional anthropologists tend not to engage in the craft of policy making (Okongwu and Mencher 2000: 109). Although many people with anthropological training work (as I did) in international development, most are employed as generic specialists in the social, that is, as providers of 'technical assistance' in the fields of social development and social policy (Green 2006). If employed specifically as anthropologists undertaking the work of cultural brokerage in the 'field', they are far removed from the policy process and from the centres of agency power (Horowitz 1996; Ferguson 1997).

This disciplinary absence from the production of development categories is paradoxical, given anthropological claims to special knowledge about the social processes of categorization on the one hand and, on the other, to knowledge about the societies which are often the subjects of development. Absence does not imply that the kinds of representations produced by anthropology have little impact on development categories. Indeed, the reluctance of anthropologists to engage in policy processes may actually encourage the perpetuation of policy categories which have little traction on the slippery slopes of social relations and the messiness of everyday life (cf. Mitchell 2002: 145–46). It is my contention that this situation arises not so much because international development policy makers fail to acknowledge the utility of anthropology, as some anthropologists would doubtless claim, but because of the problematic relationship between the epistemic practices of anthropology and the wider project of modernity (see below). Reflecting on development practice from the perspective of anthropology permits a double reflexivity which acknowledges the nature of knowledge practices in anthropology and international development. These practices and modes of representation, as well as the kinds of interventions they support, are very different and have different political implications (Green 2009). If anthropology privileges deconstruction as the basis of its critical engagement with development, the constructivist orientation of development knowledge making has greater potential for realizing positive social transformation. Doing this effectively demands the kinds of insights offered by anthropology.

Children and AIDS: An Unstable Category

Between twelve and fifteen percent of all children in Sub-Saharan Africa are currently described as 'orphans' in the documentation produced by international development agencies.[4] A large proportion of these, around 12.3 million, are thought to have lost one or both parents as a consequence of HIV/AIDS. Millions of other children who have not lost parents are nevertheless rendered vulnerable by the poverty and social devastation associated with the pandemic.[5] The category of children affected by HIV and AIDS is the subject of ongoing debate and renegotiation among agencies and activist lobby groups with different programming agendas. During this process the category has shifted from narrowly defined 'AIDS orphans' to the more encompassing category of 'orphans and vulnerable children' (OVC). Some seek to widen the category, to loosen the association with HIV and AIDS and to facilitate the inclusion of other categories of children. Others, in particular those agencies whose funding depends on narrow programming resourced within AIDS budgets, strive to maintain the boundaries of the category to legitimate a series of programmatic responses targeted specifically at what in policy terms are delimited as the social consequences of AIDS on children. Over the next few years a substantial increase in funding to support children affected by HIV and AIDS is anticipated as a result of the combined spending of initiatives such as the former U.S. President's Emergency Plan for HIV and AIDS Relief (PEPFAR) and innovative public and philanthropic endeavours such as the Gates Foundation and the Global Fund. Important questions had to be resolved before this money could be spent. Which children? How could they be supported? Are all children in affected communities made vulnerable by HIV and AIDS? Moreover, if AIDS impacts on children not so much because of the disease itself but because of structural failings in the economy, public services and the like, would money not be better spent rehabilitating state systems to reduce the negative social and economic impacts of the epidemic (see also Farmer 1999)?

These questions remain the focus of urgent debate and policy framing across a range of multilateral, governmental and non-governmental organizations (NGOs) involved in programming around children and HIV and AIDS. The stakes are high. For some agencies and programmes, funding increases represents the welcome possibility of expansion. For others, changes in policy direction, and hence what is supportable, may call into question the sustainability of long established approaches. Moreover, there is now enough money available to support significant institutional change, at least in some countries. Community and NGO responses are no longer the only possible avenue of support for children in communities affected by AIDS. Investing in the capacity of states to institute national programmes and to assume responsibility for the welfare of children is a real possibility, albeit one dependent on the willingness of donors to reinvest in the state, which recent policies have so assiduously dismantled (Stavrakis 2002). Finally, the stakes are high for the large numbers of children and families in situations where HIV and AIDS are contributing to hardship and poverty, particularly in Southern and Eastern Africa.

There are no 'right' answers. Responses to the question of priorities for AIDS and children articulate divergent moral and political standpoints incorporated into policy positions that are justified technically on the basis of evidence of best practice. The kinds of answers sought through evidence and research are determined by the ways in which the questions are framed. These in turn are framed partly in terms of the availability of funding directed at specific development categories (the framing of what is possible) and partly in terms of the politics of what should be done and for whom (the framing of what is desirable) – what Nancy Fraser has referred to as 'the politics of needs interpretation' (1989: 145). These two axes of possibility and desirability are often, but not necessarily, related. Resource availability is a function of the politics of choice which prioritizes certain categories of spending. However, the generality necessary to deal in practice and on paper with budgeting very large amounts of money means that there is considerable scope within funding streams for contestation over which categories count and how they should be counted. Some answers become, for a time, more acceptable than others, as the basis of a policy consensus on the kinds of activities which merit spending. Much work in international development is concerned with making certain answers seem acceptable and certain policy categories self-evident. This is achieved through specialized practices of knowledge making and the promotion of relationships and networks within the new institutional structures of international development assistance premised on harmonization. Within this emergent architecture of country ownership, national strategies and partnerships between recipients and donors, knowledge within an evidence based paradigm is claimed to drive development programming. Knowledge coalitions and shared targets are now more central to the operation of international development than at any time previously (Watts 2003; Mosse 2005a).

Globalizing Development

The right kind of knowledge as the basis for interventions is not necessarily that concerned with a problem or issue, but that which is counted as relevant and useful enough to achieve the social status of evidence. Evidence-based policy making depends on the negotiated positioning of social actors who can make claims for relevance on the relations between the problem and the intervention which predetermine what kinds of knowledge will be accorded useful status (Strathern 2006; Lambert 2006). In international development, as in aligned fields of government, notions of legitimate knowledge encompass understandings of the proper way to go about designing an approach, a perspective which is simultaneously moral and technical (cf. Harper 2000). Toolkits, frameworks and the standardized approaches they promote enable this knowledge to be locally operationalized across different contexts (Goldman 2005). The globalization of policy categories and implementation frameworks occurs across a marketplace of ideas in which the brokering of knowledge is a central pillar of the development economy. Think tanks, universities, development studies institutes and the research divisions of development agencies and civil society organizations produce a seemingly endless flow of ideas, concepts and solutions for policy makers to work with.

Despite the potential autonomy of countries to make policy choices, categories for development thinking are restricted in practice by what is available and the need for what seems to be transferable, in that donors and recipients whose approaches are harmonized can, in 'reading from the same page', share a common understanding. Common understandings are temporally bounded by the requirements of implementation. As international development is essentially concerned with resource transfers in support of policy objectives, and hence with practices of contracting and calculation, agreements are not merely conceptual. Categories of intervention are situated within management relations which permit development spending to be targeted and outcomes to be claimed. Making categories count, in terms of the spend they command and the range of quantitative evidence to support the extent of their needs, is central to the project of development. Development categories become powerful and significant when they can legitimate a larger spend.

The social relations which constitute international development as a global project are situated within transnational networks, materialized through conventions and practices of networking, regional and international meetings, and organizational hierarchies which scale up from the sub-national, via the national and the regional, to the global apex. This template is replicated across and within the international development system. It applies to the transnational organization of multilateral agencies, such as the UN system, with global, regional and national offices. It is reiterated within the offices of international agencies whose hierarchy of activities is replicated and organized through desks representing regions and countries cross-cut by sectors as ways of conceptually and practically organizing the range and target of interventions. The application of this template is not limited to the organization of institutions on the ground and in the documentation of relationships between the various hierarchical tiers that comprise subsections of a single agency. It is replicated in the conceptual ordering of development imagined as a set of causative transformations which scale up or down along a pyramid of levels of social and political organization, and across time and space (Ferguson and Gupta 2002; Craig and Porter 1997). This ordering is materialized through specialized practises around development planning which constitute projects as manageable 'slices' of social reality (Groves 2002; Green 2003). While it is possible to perceive these practices in essentially representational terms, as self-referential ends in themselves which in being performed create the relationships which the network sets out to effect (Riles 2001: 130–42), this perspective is partial. The ultimate end of development relationships is to control or influence resource flows in support of specific objectives.

Producing Policy

This chapter is written from a different perspective than is usual in the anthropology of development. I write not as a participant observer, but as (to adopt David Mosse's term) an 'observant participant' (2001). Unlike those who have written about their observation of the practice of others, my description and the analysis which follows is based on a reflexive consideration of my own practice, first as a policy maker within the U.K. government department dealing with international development and later as an external consultant to a multilateral organization charged with promoting policy shifts around children and AIDS. Working as a policy analyst or adviser entails not so much defining what development policy should be as ensuring that agency activities support the achievement of the particular policy visions. At the present time, such visions support the Millennium Declaration and numerous other UN declarations as well as, bilaterally, the objectives and commitments of national governments including the government of which our agency was part and the numerous national governments with whom we had 'development partnerships'. My role as an adviser in a policy section was to contribute to the representation and selection of activities which supported policy objectives, to analyse them for potential social impact and use claims about likely impacts to achieve support for policy positions.

Working with other specialists responsible for different kinds of analytical input, depending on the way in which the agency organized its work and the way it approached what it represented as a problem, the bulk of my work over a period of fifteen months involved dealing with documentation of various sorts and organizing and attending meetings.[6] The daily practice of working in the agency entailed the purposive manipulation of text; the specialized reading and writing practices around documents and emails, with view to making documents work, that is, to contribute to achieving particular objectives. This capacity of certain documents and the categories which they evoked was not in fact a quality of the documents themselves, or their style or content (Apthorpe 1997), but depended on the social context of the relationships in which they were embedded (Harper 1998: 43) and which could accord documents a certain performative quality – that is, certain documents and certain categories had particular social effects.[7] Consequently, the other main component of daily practice centred on the nurturance and maintenance of social relationships within and outside the agency. Some of this was achieved through the everyday strategies of writing and documentation, through copying in key people who could influence others to adopt certain perspectives, soliciting comments and opinions, and sharing reports and evaluations. Public events and face-to-face meetings were also valued as a means of furthering particular relationships, nurturing supportive coalitions around particular policy choices and contributing to the global circulation of policy categories.[8]

Meetings were usually structured around particular texts and were aimed at achieving 'buy-in' among constituencies within the agency in support of particular positions.[9] 'Buy-in' was not only metaphorical. Support from across sectors and regions could affect funding decisions and was expressed in budgetary commitments. The social process of commenting on documents via email was similar in effect to meetings, in that a wider group of individuals was copied in, enabling a simulation of virtual consensus and giving included individuals the right to respond to particular documents. The right to inclusion was positional, depending on person's office or position. Other individuals would be copied in according to their personal influence and potential for furthering the agendas of emerging coalitions. These same processes of reading, writing, commenting and coalition building were reiterated across the agency through its network of region and country offices and in the interdisciplinary teams constituted around specific projects within and across country programmes. They were echoed across the other agencies with which it dealt, either as co-funding partners in supporting the new national strategies of poverty reduction via budgetary support and basket funding or as recipients of development assistance.

Substantial effort went into the promotion of social networks and coalition building through the organization of large meetings and events at which international and cross-agency constituencies could be brought together. These events were also structured around documents promoting key categories, but made use of selected invitees from other sectors to support the reality and objectivity of categorical representations. This was particularly the case with researchers whose evidence could be brought to bear publicly to support certain policy positions, and also with representatives from governments in countries where equivalent policy options were being implemented. What mattered at such meetings was the right kind of 'buy-in'. In this context this referred to the level of seniority of attendees, and hence their capacity to determine spending decisions with their own agencies and governments. The presence of senior and powerful attendees also added credibility to the arguments made implicitly and explicitly through the structure of the event. Networking and coalition continuity were perpetuated outside one-off meetings through a range of international working groups, formally timetabled meetings within the global calendar of the international development system and the various official and informal networks in which stakeholders were multiply engaged.

Such meetings provided an interface between what was represented as the formal knowledge sector of development research institutions and development organizations. In actuality, because of funding relationships in which most research was explicitly commissioned by development agencies and because of shared agendas about what constituted relevant knowledge, legitimating knowledge generally originated within the ambit of the international system (Goldman 2005; Moore 2001). It could be strengthened on occasion from external sources, where synergies existed and similar ideas were promoted in cognate fields of policy and inquiry. Intellectual buy-in here was important in promoting the dissemination of concepts through further meetings, conferences, publications and working papers, and ultimately into the kinds of apex documents like the annual World Development Report which, because of its predetermined policy significance, can modify contemporary policy agendas. Meetings, like staff, were organized hierarchically, in relation to the scale of representation and influence. Those which provided the impetus for policy shifts were those which were global in scope and aspiration. Smaller meetings and events within policy worlds were structured to feed into more important meetings, influencing, disseminating approaches and ultimately amending or setting agendas. This process operated across sectors and issues, and constituted a map of action for policy workers across government and civil society organizations. As meetings and coalitions were organized around documentation of various sorts, getting documents right was enormously important. New documents were the main outcome of international meetings. These set out new commitments (financial or moral) on particular issues, which themselves became staging posts in successive sequences of meetings (Riles 2001). Important documents included formal agreements, meeting reports, programmatic statements in the form of frameworks and handbooks, situation reports with programmatic intention and documents that combined these dimensions, particularly at a global level, which provided a set of agreed parameters for approaching an issue and a range of advocated interventions.

Situating Children

Despite the frequency of meetings and the work involved in organizing them, the bulk of my everyday work took place at the computer, at the conceptual interface between mind and text. Most creative work entailed thinking about policy and articulating this in a structured way according to accepted documentary conventions to make it work within the articulated tiers of the policy implementation process. Moreover, most of my thinking and writing was premised on the explicit utilization of categories, of core concepts and notions which were multivalent and multireferential, in that each condensed a sequence of policy associations, and through which once could think, envision and convey the conceptual reordering of states, societies and sectors, which is the purpose of international development spending.[10] Some of this work entailed changing categories, trying to introduce new categories or modify the ways in which current categories were situated in relation to their contexts and associations. This process has been described somewhat differently by Shore and Wright (1997: 19–21) and Apthorpe (1997: 45), who show how policy makers struggle to create new associations for politically salient terms. Something of its essence is also conveyed in Nancy Fraser's use of the notion of 'keyword' (1994: 310) with its multiple politically laden evocations, and in the work of Stacy Pigg on development categories (1992; 1997).[11]

Our concern with categorical statements was more than a concern with moral weightings and associations, or with the moral force of categorical assertions, although this had its place. It was concerned with reordering, with working out and delineating the categorical representations through which certain policy reorderings could become first thinkable, malleable and ultimately real. Development categories, the representations through which spending is justified, are more than an 'Esperanto of global social categories' (Pigg 1992: 512), although they can operate as such. They are significant insofar as they facilitate or legitimate the direction of resource transfers in support of policy objectives. Much effort in international development practice is directed towards consolidating the credibility of categories or presenting new ones, to making some categories more significant. This is effected through a range of inscriptional practices, the presentation of evidence and findings to define the parameters of a category and the construction of documentation which effects the category by ensuring its strategic position within a policy stream to justify a spend. This explains the preoccupation with documentary processes in development agencies, the sheer amount of time and effort spent in writing and reading, in discussing documents and in contributing to new ones (Harper 1998: 248).

Documentary practices in development are social practices. Development documents are not only socially produced, often by teams, or at least commented on and reworked by others in a hierarchy. They also operate within the social contexts of projects and programmes of managed spending to mark stages in the project lifecycle, and hence transitions in the social networks around which a project is created. Social networks and the forums through which projects are discussed are transformed into documentation as stakeholder perspectives, participatory inputs or the minutes of a design team meeting. Policy documentation and framework documents operate at apex levels, providing the rationale for incorporation into lower tier documentary processes. Policy documents and significant categories have wider communities of reception and impact . As policy spirals downwards through regions and countries and through the different tiers of management, significant categories come to be applied globally in policy documents and the programmes they support. They assume status as part of the conceptual toolkit which determines the parameters of the thinkable in the international development community. Significant categories supported by resources are more than representational. In initiating programmes and appearing as effected outcomes in the further rounds of documentation and evidence gathering that feeds the development process, they assume agency within agencies, driving policy development (Goldman 2005).

Just as meetings are nested within a hierarchy of meetings, of which some have substantial impact, some documents assume status as drivers of policy thinking – either as the basis of agreements about what is accepted, as statements on knowledge about what are defined as important development issues, such as the World Development report for example, or as de facto manuals of accepted approaches. Effecting influence meant getting concepts to the right meetings and into the right documents. Which documents these were varied of course, depending on the issue and sector involved. During the period when I was doing this work, the key document for approaching the problem of children and AIDS was a joint UNICEF/ UNAIDS document, *A Framework for the Care and Support of Orphans and Vulnerable Children Living in a World With HIV and AIDS* (UNICEF 2004 a). Published in 2004, the *Framework* outlined a consensus among lead agencies, including not only UNICEF, UNAIDS and the World Bank but also the international NGO community, about what were considered to be the most effective strategies for supporting children affected by the pandemic. As a document supporting a significant category and seeking to enhance its significance, the *Framework* was in turn supported by another document setting out the quantitative case as evidence for the urgency of intervention (UNICEF 2004b). In the case of children and AIDS, key meetings hinged on those events specific to the AIDS sector, such as the annual AIDS conferences, and because of child welfare dimensions, a series of biannual inter-agency meetings called the Global Partners' Forum (GPF) which brought together a cross-section of interests with a view to influencing other agency agendas. As a key meeting on a road map of planned international policy meetings, the GPF was influential. It was preceded by other meetings, some of which were scheduled into the event calendar of policy influence and some of which were organized specifically in order to influence the GPF agenda.

The lead player in the children and AIDS policy field was UNICEF, as the agency with overall responsibility for children. My role, initially within an agency which supported UNICEF, was to contribute to new thinking about vulnerability and children for the framing of the OVC category in alignment with the social protection thinking our policy team was promoting. Later I was contracted by UNICEF to organize an additional meeting which would gather international knowledge and policy professionals together in a discussion that would put state-supported social welfare in contrast to community support on the table as a possible means of intervention for children affected by HIV and AIDS. This meeting brought together a policy community around social welfare and children, which included representatives from agencies and policy communities outside the AIDS sector, such as those promoting universal benefits, old age pensions, food security and so on. Because the aim of the meeting was to bring in outside knowledge and to establish the credibility of a perspective which was more associated with social policy perspectives outside the normal frames of development thinking, the meeting itself was situated partly outside the formal development order of workshops and events, and associated institutions, at Wilton Park, a venue partly funded by the U.K. government, which specializes in debating issues in international relations.

The Wilton Park meeting was structured around a background paper I had been contracted to prepare as an independent consultant. This paper, with the title 'Strengthening National Responses for Children Affected by HIV and AIDS: What is the Role of the State and Social Welfare in Africa?', marshalled knowledge from various sources both inside and outside development to support arguments about a range of other interventions for securing the welfare of children (Green 2005). The tabling of social welfare was formalized at the GPF the following year (UNICEF/UNAIDS/ DFID 2006), where, contracted once again by UNICEF and informed by the consensus established at the previous meeting, I produced the background paper which formed the basis of the Forum's recommendation on social welfare which would eventually feed into a new apex document, as a companion piece to the *Framework* (UNICEF 2007).

Moral Accounting

The category of 'orphans and vulnerable children' (OVC) as a significant category is delineated in detail in the apex document, the joint UNAIDS/UNICEF *Framework for the Care and Support of Orphans and Vulnerable Children Living in a World with HIV and AIDS*. OVC as a development category encompasses children made vulnerable by other causes, but the acronym has particular salience within the AIDS sector, recurring within national and agency plans around HIV and AIDS. The OVC category is utilized in the policy documentation of national governments, key bilaterals, some NGOs and the World Bank, which helpfully publishes an OVC Toolkit (2005) so that development managers and World Bank staff can determine whether and on what basis to 'invest' in this important group. UNICEF, an initial proponent of the OVC category, has since recognized that the category is too restricted, limiting the kinds of normative advocated responses to children made vulnerable by HIV and AIDS to those developed within the AIDS sector, and has shifted to an emergent category of children affected, in the broadest sense, by HIV and AIDS (CABA).[12]

AIDS sector responses to children have taken as their starting point the exceptionality of AIDS and the special requirements of children whose parents are sick or who have been bereaved due to the disease. Interventions, influenced by thinking around home-based care, have prioritized community support for those orphaned by the disease, along with psychosocial services to help children deal with traumatic loss and access to education, which is viewed not merely as a good in itself but instrumentally as a means in the longer term to equip children with the means to reduce their future risk of infection. Finally, attention is given to securing the inheritance and legal rights of individual children.[13] This palette of appropriate interventions presents the problems of children who have lost parents due to AIDS in ways which justify a limited portfolio of responses. In the context of high prevalence countries in Sub-Saharan Africa, which have minimal social welfare provisions and where many people live in extreme poverty, the agent of vulnerability is represented biologically rather than structurally.

In the documentation and thinking of many agencies, children who have lost parents to AIDS are differentiated from children who have lost parents to other causes. This is partly due to the consignment of funding within AIDS budgets and associated ideas about the exceptionality of the disease. It is also due to the representation of the OVC as a category highly deserving of assistance. OVC in such representations appear as overburdened, perhaps heading a household comprised of younger siblings, excluded from school, denied access to education, deprived of their inheritance, marginalized within their communities and traumatized by the experience (Bray 2003). OVC are not only at risk themselves, but represent a risk to society as a whole. Orphans in general, and the products of child-headed households in particular, are represented as being likely to resort to criminality, to be at high risk of becoming street children or sex workers and, by missing out on education, to put themselves at higher risk of contracting AIDS themselves in later life (Subbarao and Coury 2005). Spending to support OVC, because it reduces these risks, is consequently to be perceived as an investment. OVC as a category are especially deserving of support for other reasons relating to the representation of children as the ultimate targets of development and humanitarian assistance (Briggs 2003). The child in such representations is frequently isolated from the network of social relations in which he/she is embedded and which in actuality contribute to poor outcomes for children. Children orphaned by AIDS occupy a privileged place in the representation of need because they can be inserted into the long standing discourse about the deserving poor and the parameters of legitimate – that is, acceptable – dependency (Fraser and Gordon 1994; Block and Somers 2003).[14] In the policy discourse around HIV and AIDS which has situated responses to the disease within the health sector, focusing almost exclusively on modes of transmission and infectivity (Packard and Epstein 1991), the OVC embodies the innocence of childhood made victim by the moral failure of parental sexuality (Seidel 2000; Packard and Epstein 1991).

The OVC as currently constituted is not merely an emotionally compelling category. It has become part of the 'built moral environment' (Bowker and Star 1999: 326) of the international development order in which it is materially embedded. Situated within documents, frameworks, policy instruments and departments, the OVC is a key word and a budget line. OVC Action Plans drive programming in affected countries where teams within ministries and AIDS Commissions are responsible for achieving OVC outcomes. As a significant category, the OVC category drives the formation of communities of practice (Wenger 1998) around its implementation and evolution. Two institutional processes drive the export of the OVC category and its institutionalization within the documentation, practices and thinking of a numerous agencies and governments internationally. These are, firstly, the enormous increases in funding to support children in the category and, secondly, the institutional and programmatic practices initiated through multilateral agreements which have resulted in the institutionalization of OVC capacity within national planning processes, often within the national institutions and committees which have been established to manage national responses to HIV and AIDS. OVC are now embedded in the ministries and NGOs of many countries, and in the conceptual tools of the transnational cadre of planners, social analysts and agency staff tasked with ensuring their assistance.[15] OVC as a category exists in its current form because of the nature and institutional requirements of international development as a project of spending. It is a category of management accounting, enabling a directed spend which can be subject to audit. The need for accountability explains the concern across agencies to develop and refine 'tools' for monitoring spending and impact around OVC programming, rather than a reflection on the quality and relevance of what is being programmed and for whom.[16] Finally, OVC is a category of moral accounting, embodying the attributes of children as the acceptable face of dependency strictly limited to the household and community, and structures of traditional support which must assume responsibility for supporting additional children.

Reframing Responsibility for Children

The situation of OVC within community responses works well in the context of the current emphasis on civil society and non-state action as prime modalities for addressing the social and economic consequences of the pandemic. This kind of policy argument is of course not restricted to thinking about HIV and AIDS. It characterizes both the neoliberal reformist polices which have dominated development policy towards Africa over the past fifteen years and colonial and postcolonial commitments to community development models which were also premised on notions of community responsibility (e.g., Lewis 2000). State dismantling combined with programming for the civil society sector has further hollowed out public services and the potential capacity for a state-directed response in many countries (Eriksen 2001; Gryzmala-Busse and Jones Long 2003). It has also restricted the conceptual space to think coherently about what the social impacts of HIV and AIDS really are – and for whom – and the kinds of interventions which would be most effective (Baylies 2000). A focus on the individually affected 'orphan', deprived of property rights and education and hence at higher adult risk of HIV, may fit the current policy frameworks and needs interpretations.[17] It does not accurately capture the extent to which such children remain enmeshed within social relations and households, and the extent to which risk is dispersed amongst these wider groups who bear the social and economic costs of the disease (Rugalema 2000; Bujra 2004; Baylies 2000b).

More fundamentally, the category of OVC does not map consistently on diverse social realities in different parts of affected countries in Africa. Demographic data demonstrate that the majority of orphans are in fact what are termed in the policy vocabulary single orphans who have lost only one parent. The majority of such orphans live with their surviving parent, usually their mother. Moreover, orphan status in itself is not an indicator of vulnerability. The majority of orphans are older children, aged between seven and fourteen years. Among children who have lost parents, those who have lost mothers or who are fostered with distant kin or strangers fare worse than those who have lost fathers or remain with close relatives (Madhavan 2004: 1445; Nyambedha et al. 2003). Children from poor households, including those which have taken in orphans, experience worse outcomes than children from richer households (Bicego et al. 2003; Nyangara 2004: 22; Ainsworth and Filmer 2002). Finally, child-headed households account for less than one percent of all households, even in highly impacted communities (Nyangara 2004: 21).

This gap between representation and reality has implications for what I have referred to as the normative advocated response, the interventions around inheritance rights, access to education and traditional community support. However, it also presents an opportunity or entry point for those seeking to move forward other policy agendas, to provoke debate about the scope of responses to OVC and to align OVC with a broader social policy agenda. This aims to resituate OVC outside the AIDS sector and, in so doing, to reframe the problems as social, economic and structural. These problems cannot be addressed by civil society or the market, but demand a new normative advocated response in the form of state action and the establishment of systems of entitlement which can help families and households. If the construction of significant categories in international development provides a focal point around which communities of practice temporarily coalesce, it follows that the process of contesting categories involves equivalent social processes of reconstruction and the formation of new alliances and coalitions. This is achieved through the working up of documentation to support categorical reordering, the presentation of evidence, the search for authority and the opportunities presented by wider policy shifts and trends which change the parameters of the spendable, opening up the potentiality of new normative advocated responses.

The process I am describing leading up the 2006 GPF was structured around hierarchies of meetings and documentation, the alignment of positions of support from knowledge providers and lead agencies, and the constitution of a dispersed policy community which coalesced temporarily around this particular agenda. Recommendations from the GPF informed a new apex document which sought to move the *Framework* forward. The paper on 'The Enhanced Protection for Children Affected by AIDS' published by UNICEF and UNAIDS in 2007 serves as a 'companion paper' to the *Framework*, shifting the normative advocated response to include social welfare interventions, building state capacity and the consideration of direct instruments for social outcomes, such as cash transfers to poor families and households (UNICEF/UNAIDS 2007). Social welfare as a response to children affected by HIV and AIDS represented a radical shift in policy thinking not only because it reframes the issue as social and political, but because it changes the parameters of responsibility for welfare outcomes as potentially an obligation of states. Getting social welfare on policy agendas as a discussion point and incorporated into documents subtly moves the boundaries of the thinkable around normative advocated responses not only to HIV and AIDS, but to poverty and inequality. Achieving this involves the efforts and construction work of many people and institutions, widening the perspective, enabling the stresses on a wider range of social relations to be brought into view and to make the case for considering direct support for individuals with responsibility for children. This is achieved through the kinds of policy processes to which I have already referred; documents, meetings, networking, each with their own place in the transitional structure of international development ordering across time and space.

Construction and Deconstruction: Anthropological Engagement Beyond Criticism

Attempting to shift the situation of the child affected by AIDS and hence the chain of inferred causality associated with it away from community systems towards state systems is an ongoing process, just as the category itself has a history of evolution in relation to the intersection of various policy agendas. The end of the Washington Consensus, the expansion of welfare states in Southern Africa, the obvious failure of post-adjustment and market reforms to impact on child poverty, projected increases in aid spending and the new voice of the African Union contribute to a climate in which new ideas are thinkable, if not yet accepted. Agency staff aligned around new policy frameworks, many of whom had previously worked in the social sciences and were familiar with the critical analysis of aid, speak openly of 'changing the discourse' (after Ferguson 1990). This process is not simply about increasing the fit between category and reality, making the categorical target of spending as sociologically evident as possible, although there is evident concern to render categories and interventions more effective. The long term project of policy communities and the actors which comprise them is supporting the kinds of intervention which will positively change the reality in which the category sits, a purposive reordering.

This kind of approach to categories and to social order more generally presents an interesting contrast with knowledge practices in anthropology. Whereas anthropology interrogates categorical constructions with a view to dissembling and thus render meaning explicit, policy makers are concerned with reassembling and reconstruction. The aim of policy makers is not merely to describe and interpret social ordering, but to alter it; to contribute to the process of social ordering in terms of concepts, categories, institutions and relations through which the assemblage both social scientists and policy makers recognize as 'society' is constituted. Engagement in this process of social ordering is not confined to the manipulation of symbolic abstractions. It is not a kind of reverse engineered actor-network theory or reassembling. Its intention is to effect transformations in the relations, institutions and categories through which societies are ordered. This can be both negative and positive. The balance or reordering and the political consequences of who gets what under which conditions are the political choices made by policy makers and governments when they create polices which aim to achieve specific ends.

Like policy making and, arguably, government more generally (Foucault 2002), anthropology is fundamentally concerned with categorization as the enactment of social imaginaries and social ordering (Taylor 2004; Durkheim and Mauss 1963; Douglas 1996). However, unlike policy making, with its emphasis on construction and reconstruction, anthropology's concern has been with deconstruction, with the critical analysis of social categories and their relationship to systems of order. Despite emergent critiques of assumptions inherent in the Durkheimian position and a theoretical shift towards social constructivism, the emphasis within anthropology remains on previously established categories as constructs rather than on the social processes through which categorical orders are perpetually made (cf. Law 1994; Latour 2005). Where categories are demonstrated to be the result of political process and active human agency, anthropology is keen to demonstrate knowingly that such processes are concerned with facilitating or enabling the capillarity of power. This kind of understanding has implications for the ways in which anthropology as a discipline apprehends categorical orders as the objects of criticism rather than reconstruction. The genealogy of knowledge in the context of modernity becomes essentially a concern with the social imposition of order through a discipline to which the subjected subject willingly subjects. Such perspectives are reiterated in anthropology's approach to the related problematics of social organization, economy and government. While this perspective provides a basis from which critical engagement with powerful concepts becomes possible, it simultaneously risks restricting this relation to criticism (Anderson 2003; Green 2009). In representing order as repressive and power as pervasive, particularly in the context of neoliberal governance, anthropology seems to preclude the possibility for the emancipatory potential of categorical reorganization. If the neoliberal political imaginary had to be established conceptually in order to work effectively, that is, representationally, it is surely possible for it to be reimagined and re-presented. To claim otherwise is not only to deny the capacity of human agents to change their perception of the world, but to alter the ways in which that world is organized (Habermas 1987; Fraser 1989). It amounts to a denial of the possibility for the self-conscious reflection on the meaning of categories and their place in the order of structuring.

Policy making is explicitly political. Just as political ends articulate vastly different visions of equity and order, so the content of different policies and the associations each invokes provide the basis for political contestation, within local communities, within national governments and internationally. This contestation is often sought by those working on policies as a means to further political objectives. In the example of the OVC, the policy community with which I was working were aiming to shift the meaning of the causes of the orphans' vulnerability away from a disease only and into structural relations which demanded a response from government. This would entail thinking about the social relations in which these children were embedded in new ways, and ultimately in transforming the quality of their relations with state systems. In this commitment to aspects of enlightenment values of social improvement, policy makers within international development were self-consciously engaged in what those following Habermas would recognize as an offshoot of the project of modernity.

Modernity is a deeply troubling concept for anthropology and for social science more generally (Taylor 2004; Kahn 2001; Cooper 2005). It can connote either the high modernism and tendencies to state control described by James Scott, or its intellectual equivalent, assumptions of progress, rationality and Western scientific achievement justly critiqued by the postcolonial studies movement and postmodernism. It can also convey a tendency towards an increasing purity of organizational forms (Law 1994: 7–9) or, related to this, towards the categorical basis of modernist thinking in the West which through its attitude to nature as separate from society seeks to establish a rigid boundary or 'great divide' between the moderns and others, twentieth-century Euro-American (scientific) and other cosmologies and categorical systems (Latour 1993). In these perspectives, the constitution of modernity legitimates the subjection of others to scientific rationality and ordering; to repression, control and exploitation. These understandings of modernity are important and they have fundamentally enhanced our understandings of history, colonialism, government and power. However, they have contributed to a reluctance to strive beyond critique, to break from the abstract and actively engage in the social process of reordering (Fraser 1989; Cooper 2005; Murray Li 2007: 9). Habermas acknowledges these various dimensions of the modern in his brief essay on the political implications of postmodernism (1985 [1983]), but he makes an important point. Rejection of the project of modernity outright jeopardizes the opportunity for social and political transformation; the issue for him was not to reject the capacity of government to contribute to improvement outright, but to seek ways in which government can achieve this less repressively. Social scientists and philosophers after Foucault have all but denied that this is possible, seeing in government and in governments only the potentiality of repression, subjection and power. If change for the better cannot be enacted institutionally because of the inherent problems of governance, power and the state, then, Habermas suggests, we risk immobilization in the quagmire of a profoundly conservative present (1987).

Anthropology has found addressing the future particularly problematic. The tendency to deconstruct facilitates the critiques of power for which the discipline is regarded. Reconstruction is beyond the scope of the current anthropological endeavour, as attitudes to governance as power mean that the only legitimate position for anthropologist to adopt in relation to reimagined futures is as an activist, critic or supporter of social movements. This as much as anything explains the absence of anthropologists from policy communities within and outside international development: a fear of contributing to the inherent repression entailed in the project of governance. This absence in the example of the OVC perpetuated misleading representations of the OVC as subject to specific risks and vulnerabilities due to HIV and AIDS. It also contributed to the kinds of mystifications about community and mutual assistance which have legitimated the current normative advocated response to the social effects of the pandemic.

Despite the emphasis in some recent anthropology on social transformation, anthropology has prioritized the repressive rather than the emancipatory potential of forms of social organization and power (Scott 1998). Ethnographic accounts of transformation privilege the view from below, the perceptions of social movements, the role of resistance and subalternity (Ortner 1995). Such studies are enormously important. They provide an insight into processes of change and remind us that government is often repressive, damaging, unfair. However, they detract from the potentiality in governance to bring about significant and positive social change. Often this dynamic for change is the result of conflict between elites and social movements, between above and below. Often it is the consequence of activism and political competition. It may also be the result of coups and revolutions. Ultimately the power to effect change on a wide scale in relation to achieving the improved welfare and security of millions of people in low income countries is vested in state structures and systems of government. Anthropology, like other social sciences, contributes to the perpetuation of powerful development categories even where it does not actively construct them by not engaging critically in the policy processes which sustain them and give them power (Mitchell 2002). In refusing to engage with government we may be missing an opportunity to contribute responsibly to the global processes of reordering, leaving the field to economics and allied disciplines which foster the social dislocations accentuated through pro-market policies.

Notes

1. Earlier versions of this chapter were given at the 2005 American Anthropological Association Annual Meetings in Washington D.C. in a parallel session on 'Calculating Compassion' co-organized with Erica Bornstein, and at seminars at the Universities of Cambridge, Liverpool, Brunel and Sussex in the U.K. Additional research was supported by the U.K. Economic and Social Research Council through the research programme of the Global Poverty Research Group. I am extremely grateful to David Mosse, Virginia Domuinguez, Georgina Born and to seminar participants for helpful comments on this chapter.
2. These practices and institutions include for example workshops, seminars, handbooks, manuals and toolkits, the training and reproduction of development professionals with specific competencies, and the national and international meetings, many of which are factored into the development calendar (such as UN summits, annual international meetings, the MDG review or, at a national level, Medium Term Expenditure Frameworks and reviews of poverty reduction strategies). For an account of the globalization of local development practices in Tanzania through professionalization and workshops, see Green (2003).
3. On the agency of artefacts see also Latour (1990) and Latour and Woolgar (1986).
4. UNICEF 2004.
5. `Vulnerability' in this context is a specialized development term, conveying susceptibility to worsening outcomes along various poverty axes.
6. Our agency organized its advisory teams by disciplinary profession as well as sectorally. Some kinds of expertise were sectoral and professional, e.g., health and economics,

mapping onto the health sector and the economy, whereas some, for example, social development, were 'cross-cutting'. For further detail on how professional advice was organized in the U.K. aid agency see Green 2002 and 2005; Eyben 2000.

7. As in Austin's classic work on 'How to Do Things with Words' (1976).

8. Of course, evaluation visits, project and programme reviews, appraisals and so on are also types of meeting.

9. See also Harper for the importance of 'meetings that count', in the workings of the IMF (1998: 232).

10. This was also important for mobilizing visions across the policy community, through time and space (cf. Latour 1990: 26–31).

11. The notion of 'keyword' seems to owe its origins to Raymond Williams (Shore and Wright 1997: 19).

12. Normative advocated response here refers to what agencies and multilateral agreements say should be the response to specific issues, or should be the response for some people (as in 'three by five', three million people on anti-retroviral drugs by 2005, or the prevention of mother to child transmission). This is very different from actual responses, which are constrained by multiple factors: funding availability, 'capacity', politics and so on. For accounts of failures in AIDS responses in Africa in the context of political and institutional constraints, see Allen 2004; Baylies 2000b; Putzel 2004; and Campbell 2003.

13. Despite the emphasis on traditional and community based structures in relation to 'care and support', property and access to services are considered to fall within the ambit of distinctly non-traditional patterns of entitlement and inheritance.

14. Because children and the disabled, in the representation of entitlements and need, are one of the few categories not expected to be productive in themselves, but to depend on the production of others. For a fuller discussion of the constitution of legitimate need and the moral limits of acceptable dependency, see Fraser & Gordon 1994.

15. For a description of a similar process in relation to the establishment and consolidation of 'civil society' in Africa, see Eriksen 2001. Eriksen shows how what starts out as a development category supported by spend comes to determine social reality, as people organize themselves around funding availability to form civil society organizations, to fill the (created) gaps in state service provision and to form lobbying coalitions around policy frameworks.

16. Including indicators to assess the level of national planning for the OVC category. See for example the UNICEF *Guide to Monitoring and Evaluation of the National Responses* (2005), UNICEF ESARO's 2004 review of national plans, and USAID's *OVC Policy and Planning Effort Index* (2004).

17. Note how the link between lack of access to education and assumed adult risk of HIV go together in this policy reasoning chain. The education lobby is very strong in the AIDS sector in international development, probably because of the long associations of education in development thinking with instrumental outcomes in relation to reproductive behaviour and infant mortality, and also because of the conceptual place of 'education' in the prevention strategies which have constituted the normative advocated response to HIV and AIDS to date. For an excellent account of the failure of prevention programmes in South Africa, see Campbell 2003.

References

Ainsworth, M. and D. Filmer. 2002. 'Poverty, AIDS and Children's Schooling. A Targeting Dilemma', *Policy Research Working Paper 2885*, Washington D.C.: World Bank.

Allen, T. 2004. 'Introduction: Why Don't HIV/AIDS Policies Work?', *Journal of International Development* 16: 1123–27.

Anderson, L. 2003. *Pursuing Truth, Exercising Power. Social Science and Public Policy in the 21st Century*. New York: Columbia University Press.

Apthorpe, R. 1997. 'Writing Development Policy and Planning Analysis Plain or Clear. On Language, Genre and Power', in C. Shore and S. Wright (eds), *The Anthropology of Policy. Critical Perspectives on Governance and Power*. London, Routledge, pp. 43–58.

Austin, J. 1976. *How to Do Things With Words*. Oxford: Oxford University Press.

Baylies, C. 2000a. 'Editorial: Special Issue on AIDS', *Review of African Political Economy* 86: 483–86.

———. 2000b. 'Overview: HIV/AIDS in Africa: Global and Local Inequalities and Responsibilities', *Review of African Political Economy* 86: 487–500.

Bebbington, A., S. Guggenheim, E. Olson and M. Woolcock. 2004. 'Exploring Social Capital Debates at the World Bank', *Journal of Development Studies* 40(5): 33–64.

Bicego, G. et al. 2003. 'Dimensions of the Emerging Orphan Crisis in Sub Saharan Africa', *Social Science and Medicine* 56: 1235–47.

Block, F. and F. Somers. 2003. 'In the Shadow of Speenhamland: Social Policy and the Old Poor Law', *Politics and Society* 31(2): 283–323.

Bowker, G. and S. Star. 1999. *Sorting Things Out. Classification and its Consequences*, Cambridge, MA: MIT Press.

Bray, R. 2003. 'Predicting the Social Consequences of Orphanhood in South Africa', *African Journal of AIDS Research* 2(1): 39–55.

Briggs, L. 2003. 'Mother, Child, Race, Nation: The Visual Iconography of Rescue and the Politics of Transnational and Transracial Adoption', *Gender and History* 15(2): 179–200.

Bujra, J. 2004. 'AIDS as a Crisis in Social Reproduction', *Review of African Political Economy* 102: 631–38.

Campbell, C. 2003. *Letting Them Die. Why HIV/AIDS Prevention Programmes Fail*. Oxford: James Currey.

Cooper, F. 2005. *Colonialism in Question: Theory, Knowledge, History*. Berkeley, C.A.: University of California Press.

Cooper, F. and R. Packard. 1997. 'Introduction', in F. Cooper and R. Packard (eds), *International Development and the Social Sciences: Essays on the History and Politics of Knowledge*. Berkeley, C.A.: University of California Press, pp. 1–41.

Craig, D. and D. Porter. 1997. 'Framing Participation: Development Projects, Professionals and Organizations', *Development in Practice* 7(3): 229–37.

Douglas, M. 1986. *How Institutions Think*. Syracuse, C.A.: Syracuse University Press.

———. 1996. *Natural Symbols*. London: Routledge.

Durkheim, E. and M. Mauss. 1963. *Primitive Classification*, translated by Rodney Needham. Chicago: University of Chicago Press.

Eriksen, S. 2001. 'The State We're In: Recent Contributions to the Debate on State-Society Relations in Africa', *Forum for Development Studies* 28(2): 289–307.

Eyben, R. 2000. 'Development and Anthropology. A View From Inside the Agency', *Critique of Anthropology* 20(1): 7–14.

Farmer, P. 1999. *Infections and Inequalities. The Modern Plagues*. Berkeley, C.A.: University of California Press.

Ferguson, J. 1990. *The Anti Politics Machine: "Development", Depoliticization, and Bureaucratic Power in Lesotho*. Cambridge: Cambridge University Press.

———. 1997. 'Anthropology and its Evil Twin: "Development" in the Constitution of a Discipline', in F. Cooper and R. Packard (eds), *International Development and the Social Sciences*. Berkeley, C.A.: University of California Press, pp. 150–75.

Ferguson, J. and A. Gupta. 2002. 'Spatializing States: Towards an Ethnography of Neoliberal Governmentality', *American Ethnologist* 29(4): 981–1002.

Foucault, M. 2002. 'Governmentality', in *Power: Essential Works of Foucault 1954-1984*. London: Penguin, pp. 201–22.

Fraser, N. 1989. *Unruly Practices: Power, Discourse and Gender in Contemporary Social Theory*. Cambridge: Polity Press.

Fraser, N. and L. Gordon. 1994. 'A Genealogy of Dependency: Tracing a Keyword in the US Welfare State', *Signs* 19(2): 309–36.

Goldman, M. 2005. *Imperial Nature. The World Bank and Struggles for Social Justice in the Age of Globalization*. New Haven, C.T.: Yale University Press.

Green, M. 2002. 'Social Development: Issues and Approaches', in U. Kothari and M. Minogue (eds), *Development Theory and Practice. Critical Perspectives*. Basingstoke: Palgrave, pp. 52–70.

———. 2003. 'Globalizing Development in Tanzania: Policy Franchising through Participatory Project Management', *Critique of Anthropology* 23(2): 123–43.

———. 2005. *Strengthening National Responses to Children Affected by HIV and AIDS: What is the Role of the State and Social Welfare in Africa?* Wilton Park Background Paper, UNICEF/Wilton Park.

———. 2006. 'International Development, Social Analysis … and Anthropology? Applying Anthropology in and to Development', in S. Pink (ed.), *Applications of Anthropology: Professional Anthropology in the Twenty-first Century*. London: Berghahn Books, pp. 110–29.

———. 2007. 'Delivering Discourse. Ethnographic Reflections on the Practice of Policy Making', *Critical Policy Analysis* 1(2): 220–34.

———. (2009) Doing Development and Writing Culture: Knowledge Practices in Anthropology and International Development. Anthropological Theory 10 (1), 1-23.

Groves, L. 2002. 'A Vertical Slice. Child Labour and the International Labour Organisation. A Critical Analysis of the Transformation of Vision into Policy and Practice', Ph.D. Thesis. University of Edinburgh.

Grzymala-Busse, A. and P. Jones Long. 2002. Re-conceptualising the State: Lessons from Post-Communism', *Politics and Society* 30(4): 529–54.

Gupta, A. 1998. *Postcolonial Developments: Agriculture in the Making of Modern India*. Durham, N.C.: Duke University Press.

Habermas, J. 1985. (1983) 'Modernity – An Incomplete Project', in H. Foster (ed.), *Postmodern Culture*. London: Pluto, pp. 3–15.

———. 1987. 'The New Obscurity: The Crisis of the Welfare State and the Exhaustion of Utopian Energies', *Philosophy and Social Criticism* 11: 11–18.

Harper, R. 1998. *Inside the IMF. An Ethnography of Documents, Technology and Organisational Action*. San Diego, C.A.: Academic Press.

———. 2000. 'The Social Organization of the IMF's Mission Work. An Examination of International Auditing', in M. Strathern (ed.), *Audit Cultures. Anthropological Studies in Accountability, Ethics and the Academy*. London: Athlone, pp. 23–53.

Horowitz, M. 1996. 'On Not Offending the Borrower: (Self?)-ghetttoization of Anthropologists at the World Bank', *Development Anthropologist* 14 (1 & 2): 1–12.

Kahn, J. 2001. 'Anthropology and Modernity', *Current Anthropology* 42(5): 651–80.

Lambert, H. 2006. 'Accounting for EBM: Notions of Evidence in Medicine', *Social Science and Medicine* 62(11): 2633–45.

Latour, B. 1990. 'Drawings Things Together', in M. Lynch and S. Woolgar (eds), *Representations in Scientific Practice*. Cambridge, M.A.: MIT Press, pp. 19–68.

———. 1993. *We Have Never Been Modern*. London: Harvester Wheatsheaf.

———. 2005. *Reassembling the Social. An Introduction to Actor Network Theory*. Oxford: Oxford University Press.

Latour, B. and S. Woolgar. 1986. *Laboratory Life. The Construction of Scientific Facts*. Princeton, C.T.: Princeton University Press.

Law, J. 1994. *Organizing Modernity*. Oxford: Blackwell.

Lewis, J. 2000. *Empire State Building. War and Welfare in Kenya*. Oxford: James Currey.

Madhavan, S. 2004. 'Fostering Practices in the Age of AIDS: Continuity and Change', *Social Science and Medicine* 58: 1443–54.

Mitchell, T. 2002. *Rule of Experts. Egypt, Techno-Politics, Modernity*. Berkeley, C.A.: University of California Press.

Moore, S.F. 2001. 'The International Production of Authoritative Knowledge. The Case of Drought Stricken West Africa', *Ethnography* 2(2): 161–89.

Mosse, D. 2001. 'Social Research in Rural Development Projects', in D. Gellner and E. Hirsch (eds), *Inside Organizations. Anthropologists at Work*. Oxford: Berg.

———. 2005a. 'Global Governance and the Ethnography of International Aid', in D. Mosse and D. Lewis (eds), *The Aid Effect: Giving and Governing in International Development*. London: Pluto, pp. 1–36.

———. 2005b. *Cultivating Development. An Ethnography of Aid Policy and Practice*. London: Pluto.

Murray Li, T. 2007. *The Will To Improve. Governmentality, Development and the Practice of Politics*, Durham, N.C.: Duke University Press.

Nyambedha, E et al. 2003. 'Changing Patterns of Orphan Care Due to the HIV Epidemic in Western Kenya', *Social Science and Medicine* 57: 301–11.

Nyangara, F. 2004. *Sub National Distribution and Situation of Orphans: An Analysis of the President's Emergency Plan for Aids Relief Countries*. Washington, D.C.: USAID.

Okongwu, A. and J. Mencher. 2000. 'The Anthropology of Public Policy: Shifting Terrains', *Annual Review of Anthropology* 29: 107–24.

Ortner, S. 1995. 'Resistance and the Problem of Ethnographic Refusal', *Comparative Studies in Society and History* 37(1): 173–93.

Packard, R. and P. Epstein. 1991. 'Epidemiology, Social Sciences and the Structure of Medical Research on AIDS in Africa', *Social Science and Medicine* 33(7): 771–94.

Pigg, S. 1992. 'Inventing Social Categories through Place. Social Representations and Development in Nepal', *Comparative Studies in Society and History* 34(3): 491–513.

———. 1997. 'Found in Most Traditional Societies: Traditional Medical Practitioners between Culture and Development', in F. Cooper and R. Packard (eds), *International Development and the Social Sciences*. Berkeley, C.A.: University of California Press, pp. 259–89.

Putzel, J. 2004. 'The Global Fight Against AIDS: How Adequate are the National Commissions?', *Journal of International Development* 16: 1129–40.

Riles, A. 2001. *The Network Inside Out*. Ann Arbor: University of Michigan Press.

Robertson, A.F. 1984. *The People and the State. An Anthropology of Planned Development*. Cambridge: Cambridge University Press.

Rugalema, G. 2000. 'Coping or Struggling? A Journey into the Impact of HIV/AIDS in Southern Africa', *Review of African Political Economy* 86: 537–44.

Scott, J. 1998. *Seeing Like a State. How Certain Schemes to Improve the Human Condition Have Failed*. New Haven, C.T.: Yale University Press.

Seidel, G. 2000. 'Reconceptualizing Issues Around HIV and Breastfeeding Advice: Findings from KwaZulu-Natal, South Africa', *Review of African Political Economy* 86: 501–18.

Shore, C. and S. Wright. 1997. 'Policy: A New Field of Anthropology', in C. Shore and S. Wright (eds), *Anthropology of Policy*. London: Routledge, pp. 3–39.

Stavrakis, P. 2002. 'The East Goes South: International Aid and the Production of Convergence in Africa and Eurasia', in M. Beissinger and C. Young (eds), *Beyond State Crisis? Postcolonial Africa and Post-Soviet Eurasia in Comparative Perspective*. Washington, D.C.: Woodrow Wilson Center Press.

Strathern, M. 2006. 'Useful Knowledge', *Proceedings of the British Academy* 139: 73–109.

Subbarao, K. and D. Coury. 2005. *Reaching Out to Africa's Orphans. A Framework for Public Action*. Washington, D.C.: World Bank.

Taylor, C. 2004. *Modern Social Imaginaries*. Durham, N.C.: Duke University Press.

UNAIDS. 2004. *HIV/AIDS and Education: the Role of Education in the Protection, Care and Support of Orphans and Vulnerable Children Living in a World with HIV and AIDS*. Geneva: UNAIDS.

UNICEF. 2003. *Africa's Orphaned Generations*. New York: UNICEF.

———. 2004a. *A Framework for the Protection, Care and Support of Orphans and Vulnerable Children Living in a World With HIV/AIDS*. New York: UNICEF.

———. 2004b. *Children on the Brink 2004. A Joint Report of New orphan Estimates and a Framework for Action*. New York, UNICEF.

———. 2005. *A Call to Action. The Missing Face of AIDS*. New York: UNICEF.

————. 2005. *Guide to Monitoring and Evaluation of the National Response for Children Orphaned and Made Vulnerable by HIV/AIDS*. New York: UNICEF.

UNICEF/ESARO. 2004. *The Rapid Assessment, Analysis and Action Planning Process for Orphans and Other Children Made Vulnerable by HIV/AIDS. Report of an Interim Independent Review of Country Plans.*

UNICEF/UNAIDS/DFID. 2006. 'Report of the Third Global Partners Forum on Children Affected by HIV and AIDS. Universal Access to Treatment, Prevention and Care'. London.

USAID. 2004a. *The OVC Policy and Planning Effort Index 2004: National Response to Orphans and other Vulnerable Children in Sub-Saharan Africa* (Draft).

Watts, M. 2003. 'Development and Governmentality', *Singapore Journal of Tropical Geography* 24(1): 6–34.

Wenger, E. 1998. *Communities of Practice. Learning, Meaning, and Identity*. Cambridge: Cambridge University Press.

World Bank Institute. 2005. 'OVC Toolkit For Sub Saharan Africa', available online at http://info.worldbank.org/etools/docs/library/164047/index.htm.

Chapter 3

RENDERING SOCIETY TECHNICAL

Government through Community and the Ethnographic Turn at the World Bank in Indonesia[1]

Tania Murray Li

This chapter is not an ethnography, insider or otherwise. Rather, it is a close examination of the documents produced by social development experts who use ethnography in order to devise and justify programmes of intervention. Programme documents, as Mosse (2004) has shown, routinely occlude the debates, doubts and dilemmas of development practitioners. Nevertheless, they are consequential: vast sums of money are spent and vast numbers of people are caught up in new ways of doing things, on the basis of the narratives experts construct to connect a specified problem to a proposed solution. These narratives are central to the practice Foucault termed 'government' – the attempt to act on actions, setting conditions to direct conduct along approved pathways. In the case of social development, the expert's aim is to 'get the social relations right'.[2] This is an extraordinary ambition. Tracking how it has been translated into programmes of intervention focused on 'community' is my focus in this chapter.

Government requires a rationale that identifies problems and links them to solutions in a systematic manner. Central to government is the practice I call 'rendering technical', a shorthand for what is actually a set of practices concerned with representing 'the domain to be governed as an intelligible field with specifiable limits and particular characteristics ... defining boundaries, rendering that within them visible, assembling information about that which is included and devising techniques to mobilize the forces and entities thus revealed' (Rose 1999: 33).

In the first part of this chapter I define 'government through community' and review some of the ways community has been rendered technical by development experts. The remainder of the chapter examines the operationalization of government through community by the social development team of the World Bank in Jakarta. Their work merits attention for several reasons. First, anthropologists are prominent among the experts in this team, and the team makes extensive use of ethnographic methods. They occupy the liminal scholar/practitioner niche David Mosse describes in his introduction to this volume, with its associated vulnerabilities. Second, their programmes are vast in scale: their flagship Kecamatan (subdistrict) Development Programme (KDP) has absorbed more than a billion dollars in loan funds, and clones have appeared from Timor Leste to Afghanistan. They are also vast in ambition, setting out to rearrange social relations at an extraordinary level of detail in tens of thousands of Indonesian villages. Third, their work is a striking example of a neoliberal approach to government that focuses on setting conditions under which people are encouraged to take responsibility for their own improvement by engaging with markets, learning how to conduct themselves in a competitive arena and making appropriate choices. Under such a regime, according to social theorist Nikolas Rose, the task of experts is:

> not a matter of 'freeing' an existing set of market relations from their social shackles, but of organizing all features of one's national policy to enable a market to exist, and to provide what it needs to function … All aspects of *social* behaviour are now reconceptualized along economic lines – as calculative actions undertaken through the universal faculty of choice. Choice is to be seen as dependent upon a relative assessment of costs and benefits of 'investment' in the light of environmental contingencies … And the paths chosen by rational and enterprising individuals can be shaped by acting upon the external contingencies that are factored into calculations. (1999: 141–42)[3]

Finally, the work of the social development team highlights the persistent quality of development as an 'antipolitics machine' that works by 'insistently reposing political questions of land, resources, jobs, or wages as technical "problems" responsive to the technical "development" intervention' (Ferguson 1994: 270). I will refer to this feature in passing, but my main focus in this chapter is not on what the development apparatus fails to do, but rather on the kinds of expert intervention that a governmental approach to community opens up.

Government Through Community

'[I]n the institution of community,' writes Nikolas Rose, 'a sector is brought into existence whose vectors and forces can be mobilized, enrolled, deployed in novel programmes and techniques which encourage and harness active practices of self-management and identity construction, of personal ethics and collective allegiances' (1999: 176). Government through community, Rose stresses, creates something new (Rose 1999: 176, 189). Community becomes a way of making collective existence 'intelligible and calculable'. Issues are 'problematized *in terms of* features of communities and their strengths, cultures, pathologies'. Solutions take the form of acting upon community dynamics (Rose 1999: 136).

At the heart of government through community is a paradox. Rose puts it thus: 'community is to be achieved, yet the achievement is nothing more than the birth-to-presence of a form of being which pre-exists' (1999: 177). Communities have the secret to the good life (equitable, sustainable, authentic, democratic – however the good is being defined), yet experts must intervene to secure that goodness and enhance it. To contain the paradox, attempts to govern through community often elide the situation that currently exists with the improved versions of community that are being proposed. The result of this elision is to make it unclear whether expert discussions of community refer to present or future forms. To complicate matters further, experts often locate the model for the perfected community in an imagined past to be recovered, suggesting that intervention is merely intended to restore community to its natural state. Alternatively, experts argue that they are not introducing something new, but are merely optimizing what is naturally present. Even when the object of desire – the authentic, natural community – is found to be intact, experts on community argue that it is vulnerable to degeneration because it lacks the capacity to manage change. It is the paradox of community that makes it an exemplary site for governmental intervention: experts do not direct or dominate, yet they always have work to do.

Although the theme of loss of community and the need to remake it appeared repeatedly in both metropoles and colonies from the nineteenth century onwards, Rose cautions that 'the community appealed to is different in different cases: differently spatialized and differently temporized' (1999: 172). In the governmentalization of community under neoliberalism in Euro-America at the turn of the millennium, he argues, the community referred to is 'not primarily a geographic space, a social space, a sociological space or a space of services, although it may attach itself to any or all such spatializations. It is a moral field binding persons into durable relations. It is a space of *emotional relationships* through which *individual identities* are constructed through their bonds to *micro-cultures* of values and meanings' (1999: 172, emphasis in original). It emerged as neoliberal regimes moved away from the idea that they had the responsibility or the capacity to define the good life and shape the citizenry according to an overall plan (1999: 135). Instead, populations were reimagined as forming so many natural communities – ethnic, religious, linguistic, territorial, professional, ideological, gendered, aged, and lifestyle based. Such communities were assumed to regulate the behaviour of their members according to their own values. As such, the task of government shifted. Experts were no longer to plan but to enable, animate and facilitate. They should devise appropriate constitutional frameworks for recognizing diverse communities, then set them free to find their own destiny within a strategic field Rose describes as autonomization and responsibilization (1999: 174, 178). In the same period, development regimes in the global south shared the frustrations of the Euro-American regimes described by Rose: the perceived failure of state planning, social engineering and the comprehensive management of political and economic life. This conjuncture stimulated interest in community as a self-generating formation capable of governing itself. Communities of various kinds were made up, autonomized and responsibilized.

Government through community requires that community be rendered technical. It must be 'investigated, mapped, classified, documented, interpreted' (1999: 175). It takes expertise to reveal a community's characteristics through specialized techniques. In the global north, favoured techniques in the 1990s were attitude surveys and focus groups, the latter used initially as a tool for market research. In the global south, beginning in the 1980s, the preferred technique for knowing 'local' communities and rendering them technical was participatory rural appraisal (PRA). This technique assumed, as it constructed, communities as bounded units. It invited 'communities' to reveal their geographies, histories, livelihood strategies and institutions in the form of maps, diagrams, charts and lists, using templates supplied by experts. The technique screened out the role of prices, laws and the repressive activities of military regimes. If these forces appeared at all, it was in the surreal and disembodied form of arrows pointing in from the edges of the village maps or diagrams taped to the walls of meeting halls after a participatory planning meeting. They could not take centrestage. Instead, PRA directed people to turn to 'their own' communities to solve their own problems, presumed to be preeminently local in origin. Its premise was that people who were stimulated to reflect on the (containerized, local) conditions of their lives would arrive at new understandings that *empower* the poor as social actors to embark on locally managed change' (Green 2000: 69, emphasis in original).[4] Through the same exercise, officials, development consultants and other high status outsiders were expected 'to gain satisfaction, fulfilment and even fun, from disempowering themselves and empowering others' (Chambers 1998: xvi). In PRA the process of consultation was itself the principal intervention. It was designed to foster new desires, new ways of thinking and acting. It simultaneously created communities, responsibilized them and emphasized their autonomy.

Groups were another form of community in the global south rendered technical in the 1990s. The exchange between two people chatting informally about a water distribution problem as they walk home from the fields, approaching the topic indirectly and in a joking manner because they are kin and want to avoid a fight, may be critical to the management of water in their village. However, informal practices of this kind, embedded as they are in finally calibrated and intimate relationships, can barely be described, let alone improved. To construct an arena of intervention, experts had to identity or create groups that could hold meetings and prepare plans. Only then could social forces be enrolled and calculations applied. In this spirit, groups were made visible, formalized and improved where they already existed, crafted where they were absent or resuscitated where they were disappearing. They could then be funded, counted, evaluated, licensed, legitimated and replicated on an industrial scale.

In 2001 observers enthusiastically announced 'remarkable advances in group formation' resulting in 'some 408,000 to 478,000 groups emerging with 8.2–14.3 million members in watershed, irrigation, microfinance, forest, and integrated pest management, and for farmers' research' (Pretty and Ward 2001: 209). They proposed a 'new typology' to describe the evolution of groups through three stages, and a scheme through which they could be evaluated and ranked according to their 'degree of maturity'. The latter was defined 'in terms of their potential for self-defining and self-sustaining activity'. This was a state to be brought about by combining the existing capacities of communities with 'inputs from government and voluntary agencies'. Thus groups were envisaged as natural, but 'institution building', 'local participation' and the upgrading of 'social capital' were matters for experts to arrange.[5]

Not all communities that were the subject of expert attention in the 1990s were spatially contained. Networks also became technical. Development experts examined transnational networks linking NGOs north and south, social movements and donors. They dissected the components of these networks and investigated their effectiveness, communications, hierarchies and tensions. They worried over how networking could be instrumentalized, accountability increased and the 'social learning' engendered through networks captured and replicated (see Brown and Fox 1998).

Following the collapse of the Soviet bloc in 1989 and the demise of some of the military regimes in the global south that had been backed by the U.S. in Cold War mode, civil society at large became the community of concern. Although critics of this approach argued that 'Successful civil societies develop their own systems and structures, norms and sanctions, over hundreds of years: by and large, they take care of their own strengthening' (Hulme and Edwards 1997: 277) civil society strengthening became a domain of expertise. The deficit of civil society, its putative absence, distortion or immaturity, had to be rectified. Civil society became a thing to be designed and promoted, 'grown from "the outside"' (Howell and Pearce 2000: 78), a project to be accomplished by training and capacity building. As civil society was rendered technical, it was bounded and defined. Its components were listed and prioritized according to both moral criteria – what was be supported or rejected – and instrumental criteria – which components of civil society had the capacity to be effective in pursuit of specified ends (Biggs and Neame 1996: 49; Howell and Pearce 2000: 80–81). Experts devised techniques for improvement and set them out in detail, manual style, complete with diagrams, lists, classificatory schemes, alternate strategies and instructions.[6]

Donor programmes to improve civil society were extraordinarily ambitious. Their target was not just delinquent components of the population (farmers, women, the poor, for example) but 'society' imagined as a whole. Experts constructed a model of society made up of three sectors – the state, the market and civil society – and set about reforming each of these 'sectors' internally and brokering the relations between them (cf. Lewis, Chapter 9 this volume). They made plans to create enabling environments, devise appropriate laws and regulations, facilitate dialogue and foster processes of consultation. They monitored the performance of the state apparatus and 'civil society organizations' to ensure they were accountable to their members, especially given the risk that donor funding would attract unscrupulous leaders (Bebbington and Riddell 1997: 110–11; Blair 1997; Edwards, Hulme, and Wallace 2000: 9). Yet in the attempt to optimize what naturally exists, the paradox of government through community re-emerged. There was a risk of governing too much – of creating something alien and inauthentic – a tension amply reflected in donor attempts to rebuild civil society in Indonesia after Suharto's resignation in 1998.

Optimizing Social Capital or 'Getting the Social Relations Right'

Post-Suharto, as donors initiated programmes to strengthen civil society, they stepped up their sponsorship of NGOs, renamed 'civil society organizations' (CSOs). Yet they soon became aware of the limitations of the 'NGO sector' as a vehicle for reform and diagnosed NGOs as unrepresentative and opportunistic – mere creatures of donor intervention. Further, New Order practices and perceptions also proved intransigent, as did New Order officials, many of whom still held key positions. To address the challenge of empowering the poor and creating a vibrant civil society, the World Bank's social development team took a different approach. It would not focus on the state apparatus or on 'civil society organizations'. Instead, it would focus on society at large, especially the rural poor in tens of thousands of villages. In so doing, it would link the reform agenda directly to the Bank's declared mandates of poverty reduction and good governance.

Poverty, the Bank team argued, was 'actively maintained by the difficult and almost non-existent access that communities have to higher level decision-making on development priorities and resources; the formal bottom up planning mechanism is ineffective and non-responsive to community needs; government gives neither incentives nor rewards for communities with good organizing performance' (World Bank 1999: 41).[7] Although the Bank's social development team did not suggest that inadequate planning and failures of governance were the only source of poverty, they were the only sources taken up as the basis for the team's very large and expensive anti-poverty programme. The exclusion of refractory relations – unequal relations of production and appropriation foremost among them – was intrinsic to the construction of communities as sites of intervention. Village welfare, the team declared, was linked to the 'ability to influence investment decisions and set community priorities' through 'deliberative institutions – public discussion and exchange' which enabled people to evaluate alternatives and make choices (World Bank 2002c: 13). One Bank study noted that villagers were relatively successful in solving problems of a social nature, especially those within their local arena, but 'economic factors are largely beyond villagers' control' (World Bank 2002c: 3). Taking the lead, it would seem, from villagers, the Bank team put unsolvable economic problems to one side and focused on planning.

The social development team's intervention into the minutiae of Indonesian village life was initiated in 1996, when Indonesia was selected as one of several sites in which to study social capital and test its impact on development. Members of the team were involved in promoting the concept of social capital at the Bank throughout the 1990s. For them social capital was a means to engage the attention of Bank economists and open a space for researching the social dimensions of development thus far neglected – an aspect taken up in Chapter 4 by Mosse in this volume. Responding to the work of James Ferguson and other critics who had stressed development's closed discourse and structure of knowledge, they were concerned to show that development discourse could be changed by reformers working within development institutions. Furthermore, a change in discourse could produce new policies and projects with better, pro-poor outcomes (Bebbington et al. 2002). They argued that their position 'in the belly of the beast' allowed them to translate new concepts into project design in ways that were not possible for outsiders (Guggenheim 2004: 34). Most significant for the purpose of my argument in this chapter was the way in which the concept of social capital enabled social development experts to constitute community as a terrain of technical intervention.

Drawing upon Robert Putnam's definition of social capital as the 'features of social organization, such as trust, norms, and networks, that can improve the efficiency of society by facilitating coordinated actions' (quoted in Wetterberg 2005: 3), Bank social experts used the concept to identify the social relations that animate communities – relations otherwise intangible and amorphous. These relations, they argued, could be measured according to various indices, correlated with desirable ends such as good governance and economic growth, and subject to econometric analysis. Social capital, in their version, had a feature consistent with the strategy of government through community I described earlier: it was naturally present, yet potentially deficient. Analysis of social capital thus enabled social development experts to identify a new task. They should create social capital where it was lacking, protect residual pockets of social capital from unwitting destruction, and experiment with deploying social capital to new ends.

In the early stage of World Bank thinking about social capital the emphasis was on quantity. Social capital became 'yet another "thing" or "resource" that unsuccessful individuals, families, communities or neighbourhoods lack' (Harriss 2002: 97). In later work, Bank social experts identified different kinds of social capital, tracked their distribution within and between social groups, and sought ways to promote the optimal balance. Social capital was parsed. It became linking, bonding and bridging capital. Some social groups were found to have too much of one and not enough of another. Too much bonding and not enough linking made social groups too tight – crime families, clans and ethnic enclaves were frequently cited examples. Bridging capital named the vertical links between poor people and the patrons, NGOs and officials who could help them (Woolcock 1998). The recognition that social capital, in the wrong quantities and combinations, had 'downsides' opened up the terrain of social relations to ever-more refined analysis and intervention.

For Putnam, social capital promoted 'the efficiency of society'. But efficient for what and for whom? Critics of the Bank approach to social capital argued that Bank experts defined efficiency primarily in relation to commerce. Improved social capital meant more trust and transparency, and better links between villagers and the markets from which they were purportedly disconnected.[8] John Harriss, for example, argued that Bank deployment of social capital served as a 'very convenient screen' for neoliberal market agendas, appearing to address social issues while leaving power relations and inequality intact (2002: 110). I concur with Harriss that the Bank's approach left fundamental power relations intact, yet I want to take this observation further to explore the terrain of governmental intervention social capital opened up. As I see it, the Bank's social development experts in Jakarta were not conspirators, pursuing a covert but dogmatic and singular goal. By optimizing social capital or 'getting the social relations right', they thought they could supply village infrastructure more efficiently, alleviate poverty, promote economic growth, foster good governance and enhance local capacities for conflict management – diverse ends that, separately and in combination, they thought would benefit the nation overall and the poor in particular. Theirs was a multifaceted agenda that took them deep into the minutiae of village life. It required the Bank to become ethnographic.

The Ethnographic Turn

The Bank team's empirical investigation of social capital in Indonesia proceeded through two studies, Local Level Institutions phase one (1996/97) and phase two (1998/99). The principal finding of these studies was that top down development under the New Order had caused a 'lamentable loss of traditional mechanisms of social control', especially at the village level (Guggenheim 2004: 37). However, the studies confirmed that autonomous local institutions continued to exist in Indonesian villages, and these institutions had the capacity to mobilize village resources for collective purposes. The strongest capacity was situated at hamlet level, where physical proximity, relative social homogeneity and kin ties created 'natural' communities. In contrast, capacities were weak at the village level, since the village was a standardized administrative unit that had been imposed under the New Order. Villages were often physically dispersed and socially fractured. Their administrators were oriented towards implementing top down policies and pleasing their superiors, New Order habits that continued to be intact in many rural areas in the period of reform (Evers 2000: 8).

According to the studies, the main groups active at the hamlet level were formed for religious purposes, social service or credit. Within their customary fields of operation, these groups 'set up special committees to plan out and implement projects and events, and often make regular work plans with their respective groups. They also raise funds, mobilize labour, carry out collaborations and mediate conflicts' (World Bank 1999: 15). These natural communities already undertook 'nearly the same range and scope of projects that government and development agencies' pursued. Furthermore, these communities had 'mechanisms that would allow members to challenge leaders and to call for reflective "breaks" should disputes remain unsettled' (Guggenheim 2004: 21). Thus, Indonesia's communities already had – or could have, with appropriate facilitation and incentives – everything good governance and village development required. The studies proposed that to rectify deficiencies, best practices already present in some villages could serve as models or guides for authentic, endogenous improvement.

The studies paid significant attention to the relationship between villagers and the state apparatus. They found this relationship troubled. They diagnosed that local capacity was undermined by distrust, by a disconnect between community and the state, and by the limited space for civil society involvement in the provision of services (World Bank 1999: 41). In particular, the routine procedures for vetting annual applications for village development funds were inept and unresponsive. Yet the studies discovered positive examples, confirming that 'effective groups could take advantage of project schemes that provided them with funds, clear accountability rules and the space to implement their own projects without interference'. Strong groups had strong leaders and they formed alliances with civil society groups operating at the district level. They were assisted by officials, the best of whom already played 'roles of conflict mediation, coordination, facilitation, and problem solving together with community leaders and village-based extension workers' (Guggenheim 2004: 22). That is, this improved model already existed. All the experts had to do was to document it, replicate it and make some adjustments.

The Bank's Local Level Institution studies should be read in relation to the discursive formation of which they were a part. They were part of a development discourse, that is, as James Ferguson pointed out, *sui generis*. Their purpose was not to increase the stock of scholarly knowledge, it was to diagnose deficiencies and delineate a technical field. The findings had a project telos. They were simultaneously the product of empirical research and blueprints for the KDP. Indeed, the first phase of the KDP was well into the planning stage before the findings of the first study were compiled, so the writing was in part a retrospective justification for interventions already underway. The problems identified were those for which the social development team had (or was attempting to devise) technical solutions. More specifically, as noted earlier, the governmental strategy that works through community requires that authentic, capable communities still exist or can be restored. It is this feature that enables experts to position themselves as midwives, assisting in the birth-to-presence of natural communities, rather than as ethnocentric outsiders imposing their views about how Indonesian villagers should live. For this reason the studies had to confirm the presence of actually existing community capacity. This finding, from the team's perspective, also set their initiative apart from standard rural development projects that failed to respect village ways (Guggenheim 2004: 22–23).

The tight relation between what the studies researched and the kinds of solutions they anticipated yielded the conclusion that the way for villagers to improve their condition was by reforming local level governance, beginning with improved planning and control of projects and resources close to home. The fact that villagers were indeed dissatisfied with the existing project planning system was confirmed through focus group discussions (World Bank 2002c: 63–64). The policy argument embedded in the KDP was thoroughly neoliberal in its ethos: it proposed that improved wellbeing was within the grasp of responsible communities that made appropriate choices.

The KDP

The design for the KDP responded to the problems identified by, and indeed already implicit in, the Local Level Institution studies. Its objective was not only to alleviate poverty but to inculcate habits of transparency, accountability, efficiency and the rule of law. These were the habits that empowered rural communities should adopt to govern themselves and should also demand of officials at supralocal levels. Yet popular demand for accountability, the team recognized, had to be created. Their ethnographic studies showed that too many rural Indonesians passively maintained New Order routines. They opted for stability, loyalty and customary standards of acceptable behaviour, including the diversion of a share of project resources to officials (Evers 2000: 47, 53). Their resistance to the abuse of power was indirect. It took the form of avoiding contact with official programmes and refusing to hold village offices or pay village fees (2000: 57). Yet, according to the team's studies, villagers behaved differently when they had contributed their own labour and resources to hamlet based collective endeavours or when they were given clear control over funds and had the right to decide on their own priorities (Evers 2000: 49; World Bank 1999: 51). The desire for accountability, the experts concluded, could be stimulated by project design and clear 'rules of the game', a central feature of the KDP (Evers 2000: 60).

The template for the KDP was simple. It provided block grants of U.S. $60,000 to U.S. $110,000 to subdistricts, where a committee adjudicated between competing proposals for infrastructure projects (local roads, water, irrigation) or for small enterprise credit proposed by groups of villagers.[9] A quota of the projects had to come from groups of women. Poorer subdistricts were given priority on principle and because the relative neglect of these subdistricts meant that modest infrastructure investments would yield high returns. The team considered the emphasis on common facilities to be pro-poor, because the poor would capture benefits in improved transportation, time savings and water quality. They would also benefit from millions of days of paid labour in construction projects, especially significant at a time of economic crisis. The evaluation of the KDP in phase one showed that it exceeded its material targets: 31,000 rural construction projects selected and managed by villagers were completed, at costs up to 23 per cent below the average for state-managed projects, and 25 million work days were generated (World Bank 2001: 6; World Bank 2002b: 6–8, 20–21). Targeting credit programmes to the poorest proved more problematic, because the KDP, following the practice of other microcredit programmes, insisted on lending only to viable enterprises with limited credit risk, who could pay market interest rates. Repayment of loans was also low (45 per cent) (World Bank 2002b: 8, 24).

As the social development team stressed, the innovations of the KDP lay not in its activities, rural infrastructure and credit, which were conventional, but in the mechanisms of project planning and delivery. Indeed, one observer who studied the project in 2002 concluded that the objective to raise rural incomes had actually been dropped, due to the difficulty of measurement and 'the primacy of the overarching objective – creating participatory institutions and processes' (Edstrom 2002: 2).[10] Every technical feature of the KDP was designed for a transformative purpose. Project funds were to serve as leverage. In order to access these funds, villagers had to subscribe to a very detailed set of rules that obliged them to form committees, hold consultations and interact with each other in new forums and new ways (World Bank 2001: 3). The rules were elaborated in manuals, checklists, information sheets and other documents. They were also presented verbally and reiterated constantly by the army of consultants and facilitators (over four thousand) hired by the project to work at the village or subdistrict level, and by selected residents – a man and a woman from each village who received training and stipends for their work on project implementation (Guggenheim et al. 2004: 9; Woodhouse 2005: 3; World Bank 2001: 13).

The Project Rules

There was a rather obvious tension between the KDP's claim to be building on the social capital naturally present in Indonesian communities and the detailed specification of nationally standardized KDP rules. As Guggenheim observed, 'KDP could not function without its operational manual, disbursement system, poverty targeting criteria, and innumerable "coordination teams" ... KDP villages twenty kilometres from Jakarta use the same formats, planning cycle, and facilitator structure that villages in the jungles of Papua do' (Guggenheim 2004: 38). How then did the KDP support 'local forms of organizing' and 'local adaptation and ownership' (Guggenheim 2004: 39, 40)? The claim came down to the way in which the KDP granted villagers responsibility and choice within the project framework.

The KDP's structures were designed to direct conduct. Neither the ends they sought to achieve nor the means were up for debate. The social development team argued that the KDP's detailed rules and constant monitoring were necessary because of the complexity of the social terrain they aimed to transform. Their ethnographic studies showed that villages had the potential 'to become self-managing actors in development programmes', but warned against overly romantic assessments. 'Most villages are not egalitarian, harmonious units, but conflictive and highly stratified entities with internal problems of exclusion, corruption, and conflict of their own.' In view of the high risk of elite capture, procedures must be designed to prevent it. The KDP set out to correct the deficiencies of past projects that 'simply "gave" resources to villages with no planning structure for negotiating through these problems' and watched 'their funds slip through village fingers with little return for the investment' (World Bank 2001: 4–5).

The routing of funds was key to the KDP's reversal of New Order-style business-as-usual development. The block grant funds were sent directly to a bank account in the subdistrict, cutting out the many layers of bureaucracy through which 'leakage' normally occurred. Villagers were informed about the exact funds potentially available to them and were encouraged to select projects from a menu of options. This procedure gave them autonomy, responsibility and choice (World Bank 2002b: 15). Each village that elected to apply for project funds had to present its proposal in the appropriate format and explain how it met the KDP criteria of being pro-poor. The subdistrict committee that adjudicated between competing proposals was comprised of villagers, facilitators and officials. Its task was to select the best proposals, those with the best plan, thereby rewarding 'performance'.

Once a proposal was accepted, villagers had to monitor to ensure that contracts for construction were awarded competitively and that materials met quality specifications. Transparency rules required project implementers at the village level to hold open public meetings to account for how the money was spent and to answer questions (World Bank 2002b: 54). There was a complaints procedure to handle breaches of the project rules. Independent NGOs and journalists were contracted to monitor the project and publicize its successes and failures. Their job was to draw attention to cases of corruption and to the efforts of villagers to get corrupt individuals convicted (Guggenheim 2004: 7). Sanctions were built into the project cycle, were well publicized and were followed through. Corrupt facilitators were fired, some officials went to jail, and 'non-performing' subdistricts were cut from the programme (Woodhouse 2005: 18). Through micropractices such as these the KDP set out to 'chip away at the fortresses of monopoly power and impunity' (World Bank 2002b: 54).

The anti-corruption strategy of the KDP was not an add-on – it was integral to the objective of the project (Woodhouse 2005: 1). Every step in the project process was designed to prevent corruption within the project and to establish new habits that would carry over into other arenas. The anti-corruption strategy occupied a seven page appendix in the KDP phase two project appraisal document (World Bank 2001). Corruption was also the subject of special ethnographic studies, case reports and experiments. It too was rendered technical and was parsed into components for remedial intervention.

Two approaches to corruption can be discerned in the KDP. One approach treated corruption as a problem of culture. The Bank's ethnographic studies showed that corruption was accepted as normal. Funds were routinely siphoned as a reward for public office (Evers 2001: 15–16; World Bank 2004). Villagers were driven to complain only when they deemed the balance inappropriate – when too much money was extracted from a project budget and not enough was shared with other claimants. This cultural norm, the experts argued, emerged historically in the distorted context of the New Order, when development assistance was understood as a gift. Villagers were told they should be grateful for gifts, however small, and not ask too many questions (World Bank 2002b: 52). When corrupt parties were confronted, KDP studies showed that villagers were mainly interested in having the money returned so the project could be completed. They were not interested in prosecution or other forms of punishment (Evers 2001: 14).

To the Bank's social development team, the finding that corruption was accepted by villagers highlighted a problem in need of correction. They proposed that KDP village facilitators should attempt to change defective cultural precepts through moral argument, explaining to villagers why corruption should not be tolerated. They should discuss corruption openly and consistently and 'shine a bright light' wherever it occurred (World Bank 2002b: 53). Nikolas Rose describes this strategy as 'throwing a web of visibilities, or public codes and private embarrassments over personal conduct', adding 'we might term this *government through the calculated administration of shame*' (Rose 1999: 73, emphasis in original). For the strategy to work, it is necessary to create the conditions in which a perpetrator does in fact experience shame. Such conditions, the Bank experts thought, might already exist in embryonic form. They tasked ethnographic researchers to identify 'key opinion makers, channels of information, and the forums where communities discuss among themselves local forms of anti-corruption action' (Guggenheim 2002: 4). Once these makers, channels and forums were identified, they could be optimized to achieve the results – transparency, empowerment – desired not only by outsiders, in this case the Bank, but also by communities already engaged in 'anti-corruption action' of their own. Ethnographic 'thick description' of corruption cases could also be used to reveal how social norms entered into incentive structures (Woodhouse 2005: 6).

In addition to researching the norms and practices already present, the Bank's corruption experts recommended teaching villagers techniques to reformat their local knowledge as a tool of surveillance. The KDP's village facilitators should be trained to map local power structures, record the names of key players such as village office holders and elite families, and list their kinship and other links. In this way, the practice of tracking power and making networks explicit – a standard research tool of anthropologists – would be devolved. Responsible villagers would learn to reveal to themselves how power works in their own communities and devise preemptive measures finely tuned to local circumstances. They should also forward information to subdistrict level facilitators, who could use it to reduce opportunities for elite manipulation and capture (Woodhouse 2005: 42).

The second approach to corruption in the KDP treated it as a problem of rational choice. From this perspective, corruption is not a personal failing. It is a rational response to a given structure of incentives and disincentives (Woodhouse 2005: 4–5). It occurs wherever the benefits of corruption outweigh the costs or, from the victim's perspective, the costs of protest outweigh the benefits. In this spirit, a Bank social research expert analysed the cost-benefit equations for each step of the project process for the different parties involved. Based on the findings, the consultant proposed adjustments to the reward structure to close loopholes, increase the risks and reduce the benefits from corrupt behaviour to the point where such behaviour would no longer be rational (Woodhouse 2005: 35–39).

Bank experts also worked on changing the cost-benefit equation from the perspective of the victims. Their studies showed that the victims of corruption often had quite complete knowledge about how, when and by whom project resources were stolen, but the costs of protest were too high for them to use the information. Costs included harassment or intimidation by the perpetrators or by police and other officials; being accused of giving the village a bad name, reducing prospects of receiving development funds in future; the cost of transportation to make repeated visits to the city to present information to the police and prosecutors; and time and energy spent in a legal process that few believed would produce any result. To change this equation, the Bank team experimented with the use of informal or customary settlement procedures, which they thought might be more effective and less costly for the complainant, both socially and financially (Evers 2001; Woodhouse 2005). Researchers also documented cases where 'poor people have been able to use the justice system successfully to defend their interests and rights'. From this analysis they identified the enabling conditions for successful village action and devised schemes to replicate them (World Bank 2002a: 4; World Bank 2004).

A few years into the KDP, and spurred by their success in devising schemes to intervene in community dynamics, the social development team turned their attention to an even more ambitious project: the management of the violent conflicts besetting the Indonesian countryside in the turbulent period after Suharto's resignation.

Conflict Management

For diplomatic reasons related to what Mosse calls the 'etiquette of the aid business,' it is difficult for donors to acknowledge violent conflict in which a ruling regime is implicated. I want to focus on a second problem: donors can only intervene in an arena they can effectively frame in technical terms and for which they can identify deficits they are equipped to fill. Officials, military men, militia bosses and gangsters operating as knowledgeable agents but seeking unacceptable goals such as plunder and domination are difficult to position as deficient subjects in need of guidance. Furthermore, changing the conditions that enable them to operate in these ways would require political interventions donors are not equipped to make. In contrast, villagers experiencing the confusion of rapid change can be positioned as deficient subjects, making rural communities a prime site for donor attention. In post-Suharto Indonesia, it was the social development team of the World Bank that led the field in rendering conflict technical and identifying points of interventions.

'Conflict', the Bank's social experts declared, is 'a necessary catalyst to, and an inevitable by-product of, development', especially where 'poverty and lack of opportunity underscore the need for change, and where, conversely, otherwise desirable periods of economic growth themselves become a force for realigning class structures and (potentially) re-imagining the basis for group identity.' Their task, as they understood it, was not to eliminate the source of conflict – economic growth that realigns class structures – but to devise techniques to manage conflict 'in constructive ways' (Barron, Smith and Woolcock 2004: 1). Since they viewed conflict as a normal social process, they focused their attention on social relations, especially the everyday social relations connecting and dividing groups of villagers. Their goal was to set conditions under which rational actors would be encouraged to channel collective energies into development activities and eschew violent mobilizations that undermined both security and economic progress. To this end, they sponsored a new set of ethnographic studies.

The team's ethnographies of conflict set out to examine the problem in a new way. Rather than focus only on the large scale violence in places such as Kalimantan, Maluku and Sulawesi, where thousands died and tens of thousands were displaced in 1998–2002, they highlighted the situation in the so-called 'non-conflict' or low intensity conflict areas. In Lampung, southern Sumatra, the studies found that conflict was pervasive, taking the form of vigilantism, banditry, lynching, extortion by armed militias and cycles of vengeance. They found that the outcome of violence in both the high intensity and low intensity cases was similar: conflict deepened ethno-religious segregation, caused the withdrawal of police, government services and development programmes, and created no-go zones in which there was no investment or economic growth. Unemployed youths, their studies showed, were prime candidates for recruitment into gangs and militias. A vicious cycle linked violence to economic stagnation. They also found that the triggers and pathways of violence were essentially the same in the low and high intensity provinces. Only the specifics of the conjunctures and levels of escalation varied. For the team, this finding pointed away from a focus on the unique causes of exceptionally serious violence towards a focus on endemic problems within rural society, problems of a kind that experts in social development could diagnose and resolve.

A second key finding of the Bank ethnographies was that structural factors alone did not account for violent outbreaks. Ethnic diversity and economic inequality were present everywhere in Indonesia, the Bank researchers argued, but they did not always result in violence. Some conflicts escalated while others did not, for reasons that should be explored. Furthermore, they proposed, explanations of violence that focused on structural factors such as ethnicity were out of touch with contemporary social theories that treated identities as constructed and dynamic. Through careful examination of the perceptions of parties involved in violent conflict as victims, perpetrators or potential mediators, they tracked how group boundaries were realigned as a conflict escalated. It was a finding that suggested a point of intervention: if escalation could be prevented, so could the hardening of boundaries.

Third, the Bank studies described violent incidents in ways that helped to pinpoint when and how intervention to prevent the escalation of conflict might be effective. As they explored violent incidents through case studies, they parsed their elements and framed them in technical terms. There were contexts, components, triggers, sequences and pathways. There were matters of leadership and recruitment. There were alternate outcomes – resolution, stalemate, escalation. This template of factors, derived inductively from case studies, was used to test variables and correlations through econometric analysis (Barron, Smith and Woolcock 2004: 7).[11]

Finally, the Bank conflict studies built on the earlier research on Local Level Institutions and the experience of the KDP. They identified existing social capital and local mechanisms for dispute resolution that could be supported, enhanced and replicated. They studied innovative practices that villagers had devised for themselves. The research was intimately linked to the proposed governmental strategy which was to work through community. Once again, the approach seems counterintuitive: if communities already held the secrets to overcoming violence (or poverty, for that matter), why did they need Bank assistance? Yet community, as I pointed out earlier, has uniquely inviting qualities as a governmental terrain. Its virtues are inherent, but are located in a past to be recovered or a future to be accomplished through expert intervention.

To explain why communities were both capable and deficient, the studies introduced a temporal before New Order/after New Order distinction. They argued that communities were previously less prone to conflict, because customary norms were agreed, rules were enforced and there were respected leaders capable of mediation.[12] These conditions no longer existed due to the mixture of populations and attenuation of custom brought about by migration, and by the New Order's deliberate displacement of customary institutions in favour of standardized, national institutions. Yet the New Order's standardized national institutions had not taken hold. There was no functioning, impartial justice system (police, courts) to which aggrieved parties could turn. The result, the studies found, was confusion. There were formal and informal rule systems that overlapped and conflicted. Rules were differently interpreted, poorly enforced and easily manipulated. For the Bank experts, confusion emerged as a significant cause of conflict and a point of intervention: the solution was to craft coherent rules to restore what was naturally present and supply something new to meet the needs of the time.

Crafting Interventions

Inevitably, since the World Bank is in the business of lending funds, there was a project telos to Bank sponsored research on conflict. The research was intended to provide 'a concrete platform from which to identify a range of possible entry points for crafting more effective local level conflict resolution mechanisms' (Barron, Smith and Woolcock 2004: 10). The strategy, drawing implicitly on game theory and what Mosse calls the 'new institutionalism', was to establish conditions and provide incentives to encourage individuals to make peace their choice.[13] More explicitly than in the studies for the KDP five years earlier, the language of the Bank ethnographies of conflict anticipated a strategy of this kind. They explored the 'rules of the game' – the laws and norms of engagement between individuals and groups; the 'dynamics of difference' – how ethnic and other differences were constructed, mobilized and strategically deployed; and the 'efficacy of intermediaries' – their capacity to resolve conflicts, make decisions and enforce rules.

As research moved into project-design mode, the claim to be merely assisting in the birth-to-presence of that which already existed was revealed, once again, to be contradictory. Local knowledge and practice should be nurtured, the experts argued, but also adjusted through the 'application of general democratic principles of conduct' (Smith 2005: 99). 'Outside technocrats' should not be the ones to determine new rules or resolve disputes. Instead, 'spaces, incentives, and resources need to be created and sustained by a range of actors that make it possible for disputants to craft resolutions that all sides can own, uphold and enforce' (Barron, Smith and Woolcock 2004: 33). The role of the Bank would be to supply the 'mediating institutions' and the 'meta-rules', or at least the 'minimum standards' for meta-rules that villagers would craft within the space the Bank's programme would provide (Barron et al. 2004: 27). The initiative to alter patterns of conduct, the experts stressed, must come from below. Where opposing sides desired to settle their differences, they needed 'the resources – human, financial, and administrative – to seek a resolution'. The human resources might already exist within communities or there might be a need for outside facilitators of high moral and professional repute, fully trained in the latest conflict mediation methods (Barron et al. 2004: 24–25). Mediators must earn legitimacy by 'demonstrated evidence of incrementally more significant accomplishments'. All parties must uphold agreements and be accountable for their actions (Barron, Smith and Woolcock 2004: 29, 30). In social life as in the marketplace, the experts insisted, only good performance should reap rewards. Bank-supplied incentives in the form of KDP-style block grants would be used to add weight to the protagonists' own cost-benefit analysis. Rational actors would stop fighting when the costs of conflict outweighed the benefits (see Tajima 2004: 26, 39). At that point, all that was needed was the appropriate mechanism.

Grafting conflict resolution onto the KDP had risks, as Bank experts acknowledged. Competition between groups over scarce resources was the source of many conflicts, yet they proposed to use more competition – well crafted, managed and 'facilitated' competition – as the solution.[14] Nevertheless, the chain of reasoning linking diagnosis to remedy was persuasive enough for the Bank to approve the Support for Poor and Disadvantaged Areas Project (SPADA) running from 2005 to 2010 with a loan of U.S.$104 million. Confirming the boundaries it drew around its technical domain, the SPADA appraisal document observed that there was no 'revolutionary solidarity' in the Indonesian countryside – hence, presumably, there was no point in thinking about revolution. Instead, it observed that 'conflicting loyalties divide local groups into violently opposed factions, thus creating fertile ground for the resumption of conflict at what often appears to be minor provocation' (World Bank 2005: 7). For the design team, the important triggers of violence and the ways to forestall it were located inside rural society. While recognizing that feelings of social injustice were widespread, they had no proposal to transform the material roots of those feelings. Rather, the proposal was that the SPADA would transform the feelings themselves, replacing them with feelings of trust, cooperation, (healthy) competition and empowerment. Monitoring in the SPADA would also be technical: 'tracer methodologies' would be used to track the effects of training interventions on 'changes in knowledge, attitude, and performance at periodic intervals'. Household surveys would evaluate impacts on social capital and attitudes towards conflict and violence, together with economic and other indicators (World Bank 2005: 31).

Conclusion

In this chapter I have explored the practices through which social experts set out to govern through community, devising interventions to reconfigure social relations in calculated ways. The Bank's social development team in Jakarta had very specific objectives in mind. Through their programmes they would build civil society, alleviate poverty, manage conflict and transform a corrupt and ineffective state apparatus by pressure from below. Their proposed transformation was simultaneously the return to authentic Indonesian ways and the realization of expert design. Natural communities required expert attention to make them complete. Improvement required that communities were rendered technical, the processes running through them were parsed and dissected, and points of intervention were identified. Furthermore, the experts argued that they must be bounded to set aside refractory political economic processes too difficult to render technical and rearrange. The Bank social development experts were fully aware of the limitations presented by their positioning on the 'practitioner' side of the scholar/practitioner divide. They acknowledged that their interventions did not 'replace in any way the need for a more fundamental restructuring of state-society relationships in Indonesia' (Guggenheim 2004: 33). Yet they proposed no strategies to accomplish that 'more fundamental restructuring'. Instead, they focused on the conduct of villagers and their capacities to plan and demand better 'development'.

The processes excluded from the KDP's field of intervention were evident in the documents – in the diagnosis of problems and solutions – and also from what was not in the documents. The voluminous documentation of the KDP included no discussion of how empowered rural subjects might come to demand not only better infrastructure projects or better governance, but access to land, fair prices and fair wages. Despite its promising title, the KDP study entitled *Village Justice in Indonesia* did not discuss how the poor might change the structures of inequality that surround them. In true liberal mode, it focused on procedural matters such as villagers' access to 'the justice system' and, more specifically, the measures needed to help poor people prevent corrupt officials from stealing project funds (World Bank 2004). Justice became a matter of distinguishing the legal from the illegal, the accountable from the corrupt, the plan that was 'pro-poor' from a plan that would benefit the rich, the deserving poor from those whose failure to perform made them ineligible for assistance. The exclusions of 'social development' also shaped the team's approach to conflict management. To point this out is not to suggest that there was a hidden agenda for which the programme's rationale was merely a mask. The Bank's social development team was very explicit about its aims and I take the team at its word. The limits of the programme stemmed not from deficits in their research capacity or understanding, but rather from the requirements of their institutional location: to render problems such as poverty and violence technical and manageable, and act on them by means of expert prescription.

My main focus in this chapter has been to highlight the extraordinary scope, scale and intensity of the field of intervention opened up by the approach I have labelled 'government through community.' Under various rubrics – community driven development, the enhancement of social capital, the restoration of authentic local traditions and the promotion of choice – experts have constructed a technical field in which they are licensed and enabled to intervene in the minutiae of peoples' lives. Neoliberalism does not mean less intervention: it means intervention thought about and constructed along different, more subtle lines. For the anthropologist-as-expert it is a heady moment in which their success at constituting an arena of intervention is mixed with the anxiety of knowing full well the limits of expert schemes. How they handle this predicament personally and professionally is a problem taken up in several chapters of this volume.

Notes

1. This chapter is based on a close reading of documents prepared by the social development team at the World Bank in Jakarta in the period 1996–2004. For an 'insider' account by the anthropologist who was a key architect of this programme, see Guggenheim 2004. For updates on the project, which has continued to grow and evolve, see the World Bank website in Jakarta. I offer further reflections on the World Bank programme and my own position both inside and outside the development apparatus in Li 2009 and 2010. Thanks to Duke University Press for permission to use extended excerpts from *The Will to Improve: Governmentality, Development, and the Practice of Politics* (2007, Durham, N.C.: Duke University Press). Funds to support research and writing related to this chapter were provided by the John D. and Catherine T. MacArthur Foundation programme on Global Security and Sustainability and by Canada's Social Science and Humanities Research Council. Special thanks to Scott Guggenheim for being a thoughtful and engaged interlocutor.
2. This expression appeared in Woolcock 1998: 187.
3. Rose calls this formation advanced liberal.
4. Green provides a useful critical analysis of empowerment and participation in theory and practice.
5. For these authors, the neoliberal agenda to promote entrepreneurship through group formation was explicit. They argued that the purpose of support was to make groups independent, because 'creating dependent citizens rather than entrepreneurial citizens reduces the capacity of citizens to produce capital' (Pretty and Ward 2001: 220).
6. For a striking example see Blair 1997.
7. See also (Evers 2000: 11, 15; World Bank 2002c: 36).
8. See Fine 1999, Hart 2001, Watts 2001 and especially Harriss 2002 for critiques of the Bank's use of social capital.
9. Block grants had been used before, under the New Order and during the 1997–98 crisis, but without such tight control (Guggenheim 2004).
10. Guggenheim et al. (2004: 6) still listed poverty alleviation as the KDP's prime objective.
11. See also Barron and Madden 2002; Madden and Barron 2004; Smith 2005; Tajima 2004; and Welsh 2003.
12. Smith (2005) describes past customary regimes in Kalimantan in these terms. Madden and Barron (2004: 67) describe the attenuated mediation skills of villagers.
13. On methodological individualism in Bank social science, see Harriss 2002; on the crafting of institutions, see Agrawal 2001.
14. The risks are described in Smith (2005) and Tajima (2004: 27). Bank social experts planned a controlled study of the risks and benefits of using KDP-style mechanisms for conflict management (Barron et al. 2004).

References

Agrawal, Arun. 2001. 'Common Property Institutions and Sustainable Governance of Resources', *World Development* 29(10): 1649–72.

Barron, Patrick, Rachael Diprose, David Madden, Claire Smith and Michael Woolcock. 2004. *Do Participatory Development Projects Help Villagers Manage Local Conflicts? A Mixed Methods Approach to Assessing the Kecamatan Development Project, Indonesia*. Washington, D.C.: World Bank.

Barron, Patrick and David Madden. 2002. *Beyond Structural Factors: The Importance of Culture in Conflict Resolution in Indonesia*. Cambridge: Kennedy School of Government, Harvard University.

Barron, Patrick, Claire Smith and Michael Woolcock. 2004. 'Understanding Local Level Conflict Pathways in Developing Countries: Theory, Evidence and Implications from Indonesia', Washington, D.C.: World Bank, *Social Development Papers, Conflict Prevention and Reconstruction No. 19*.

Bebbington, Anthony and Roger Riddell. 1997. 'Heavy Hands, Hidden Hands, Holding Hands? Donors, Intermediary NGOs and Civil Society Organisations', in D. Hulme and M. Edwards (eds), *NGOs, States and Donors: Too Close for Comfort?* New York: St Martin's Press/Save the Children.

Bebbington, Anthony, Michael Woolcock, Scott Guggenheim and Elizabeth Olson. 2002. 'Exploring Social Capital Debates at the World Bank', *Journal of Development Studies* 40(5): 33–64.

Biggs, Stephen and Arthur Neame. 1996. 'Negotiating Room to Maneuver', in M. Edwards and D. Hulme (eds), *Beyond the Magic Bullet: NGO Performance and Accountability in the Post-Cold War World*. West Hartford, C.T.: Kumarian Press.

Blair, Harry. 1997. 'Donors, Democratisation and Civil Society: Relating Theory to Practice', in D. Hulme and M. Edwards (eds), *NGOs, States and Donors: Too Close for Comfort?* New York: St Martin's Press/Save the Children.

Brown, L. David and Jonathan Fox. 1998. 'Accountability within Transnational Coalitions', in L. David Brown and Jonathan Fox (eds), *The Struggle for Accountability: The World Bank, NGOs, and Grassroots Movements*. Cambridge, M.A.: MIT Press.

Chambers, Robert. 1998. 'Foreword', in J. Blackburn and J. Holland (eds), *Who Changes? Institutionalizing Participation in Development*. London: Intermediate Technology Publications.

Edstrom, Judith. 2002. 'Indonesia's Kecamatan Development Project. Is it Replicable? Design Considerations in Community Driven Development', Washington, D.C.: World Bank. *Social Development Paper No. 39*.

Edwards, Michael, David Hulme and Tina Wallace. 2000. 'Increasing Leverage for Development: Challenges for NGOs in a Global Future', in D. Hulme and T. Wallace (eds), *New Roles and Relevance: Development NGOs and the Challenge of Change*. Bloomfied, C.T.: Kumarian Press.

Evers, Pieter. 2000. *Resourceful Villagers, Powerless Communities: Rural Village Government in Indonesia*. Jakarta: World Bank.

———. 2001. *Legal Assistance Program for KDP Communities: A First Assessment of the Legal Assistance Pilot Project in Central Java and North Sumatra (August–October 2001)*. Jakarta: World Bank.

Ferguson, James. 1994. *The Anti-Politics Machine: 'Development,' Depoliticization, and Bureaucratic Power in Lesotho*. Minneapolis: University of Minnesota Press.

Fine, Ben. 1999. 'The Developmental State is Dead – Long Live Social Capital?', *Development and Change* 30: 1–19.

Green, Maia. 2000. 'Participatory Development and the Appropriation of Agency in Southern Tanzania', *Critique of Anthropology* 20(1): 67–89.

Guggenheim, Scott. 2002. *Proposal to the Norwegian Trust Fund for Environmentally and Socially Sustainable Development*. Jakarta: World Bank.

———. 2004. *Crises and Contradictions: Understanding the Origins of a Community Development Project in Indonesia*. Jakarta: World Bank.

Guggenheim, Scott, Tatag Wiranto, Yogana Prasta and Susan Wong. 2004. *Indonesia's Kecamatan Development Program: A Large-Scale Use of Community Driven Development to Reduce Poverty*. Jakarta: World Bank.

Gupta, Akhil. 1995. 'Blurred Boundaries: The Discourse of Corruption, the Culture of Politics, and the Imagined State', *American Ethnologist* 22(2): 375–402.

Harriss, John. 2002. *Depoliticizing Development: The World Bank and Social Capital*. London: Anthem Press.

Hart, Gillian. 2001. 'Development Critiques in the 1990s: Culs de Sac and Promising Paths', *Progress in Human Geography* 25(4): 649–58.

Howell, Jude and Jenny Pearce. 2000. 'Civil Society: Technical Instrument or Social Force for Change?', in D. Hulme and T. Wallace (eds), *New Roles and Relevance: Development NGOs and the Challenge of Change*. Bloomfield, C.T.: Kumarian Press.

Hulme, David and Michael Edwards. 1997. 'Conclusion: Too Close to the Powerful, Too Far from the Powerless?', in D. Hulme and M. Edwards (eds), *NGOs, States and Donors: Too Close for Comfort?* New York: St Martin's Press/Save the Children.

Li, Tania Murray. 2007. *The Will to Improve: Governmentality, Development, and the Practice of Politics*. Durham, N.C.: Duke University Press.

———. 2008. 'Social Reproduction, Situated Politics, and *The Will to Improve*. *Focaal: Journal of Global and Historical Anthropology* 52: 111–18.

———. 2010. 'Revisiting *The Will to Improve*', *Annals of the Association of American Geographers* 100(1): 233-235.

Madden, David and Paddy Barron. 2004. 'Violence and Conflict Resolution in "Non-Conflict" Regions: The Case of Lampung, Indonesia', Jakarta: World Bank. *Social Development Paper No. 2*.

Mosse, David. 2004. 'Is Good Policy Unimplementable? Reflections on the Ethnography of Aid Policy and Practice', *Development and Change* 35(4): 639–71.

Pretty, Jules and Hugh Ward. 2001. 'Social Capital and the Environment', *World Development* 29(2): 209–27.

Rose, Nikolas. 1999. *Powers of Freedom: Reframing Political Thought*. Cambridge: Cambridge University Press.

Scott, James C. 1998. *Seeing Like a State: How Certain Schemes to Improve the Human Condition Have Failed*. New Haven, C.T.: Yale University Press.

Smith, Claire. 2005. 'The Roots of Violence and Prospects for Reconciliation: A Case Study of Ethnic Conflict in Central Kalimantan, Indonesia', Washington, D.C.: World Bank, *Social Development Papers, Conflict Prevention and Reconstruction No. 23*.

Tajima, Yuhki. 2004. *Mobilizing for Violence: The Escalation and Limitation of Identity Conflicts: The Case of Lampung, Indonesia*. Jakarta: World Bank.

Watts, Michael. 2001. 'Development Ethnographies', *Ethnography* 2(2): 283–300.

Welsh, Bridget. 2003. 'Mobbing for Justice: Variation in Vigilante Killings in Indonesia', Jakarta: World Bank. Seminar Presentation, 15 December 2003.

Wetterberg, Anna. 2005. *Crisis, Social Ties and Household Welfare: Testing Social Capital Theory with Evidence from Indonesia*. Jakarta: World Bank.

Woodhouse, Andrea. 2005. *Village Corruption in Indonesia: Fighting Corruption in the World Bank's Kecamatan Development Program*. Jakarta: World Bank.

Woolcock, Michael. 1998. 'Social Capital and Economic Development: Toward a Theoretical Synthesis and Policy Framework', *Theory and Society* 27: 151–208.

World Bank. 1999. *Local Capacity and its Implications for Development: The Case of Indonesia, A Preliminary Report*. Jakarta: World Bank.

———. 2001. *Second Kecamatan Development Project: Appraisal Document*. Jakarta: World Bank.

———. 2002a. *Idea Note, Justice for the Poor: Program for the Reform of Legal Institutions in the Local Environment*. Jakarta: World Bank.

———. 2002b. *Kecamatan Development Program Phase One: Final Report 1998-2002*. Jakarta: Ministry of Home Affairs (Community Development Agency), KDP National Secretariat and National Management Consultants, World Bank.

———. 2002c. *Social Capital, Local Capacity, and Government: Findings from the Second Indonesian Local Level Institutions Study: Overview Report*. Jakarta: World Bank.

———. 2004. *Village Justice in Indonesia: Case Studies on Access to Justice, Village Democracy and Governance*. Jakarta: World Bank.

———. 2005. *Support for Poor and Disadvantaged Areas: Project Appraisal Document*. Jakarta: World Bank.

Chapter 4

SOCIAL ANALYSIS AS CORPORATE PRODUCT

Non-Economists/Anthropologists
at Work at the World Bank in Washington, D.C.[1]

David Mosse

Introduction

A considerable literature now deals with the disciplining, depoliticizing or governmentalizing nature of development policy, including its sociological concepts (e.g., Ferguson 1990; Harriss 2001; Li 2007). The claimed universal applicability of ideas such as participation, civil society, empowerment or social capital has been criticized, as have the political acts or external impositions legitimized by these terms. However, rather less attention has turned to the social and institutional work that policy ideas do at their point of formulation; to the institutional processes which reveal how the framing of policy-relevant concepts is socially embedded in highly localized processes, significantly shaped by the positions and interests of particular professional groups. To address this issue, this chapter turns to the World Bank and to its non-economist professionals.

International organizations, and especially international financial institutions such as the World Bank, have become important players in developing social and environmental standards and in promoting compliance with these (Sarfaty 2003: 1792). As Galit Sarfaty puts it, the Bank is not only an important 'interpretive community' for public international law, but also possesses a degree of 'norm-generating autonomy' (2003: 1792). '[I]ts own operational policies become de facto global standards among other banks as well as institutions engaged in project finance' (2003: 1792), and inform policy making in client countries (St Clair 2006: 79). Even those non-governmental organizations (NGOs) and lobby groups critical of the World Bank who protest over controversial projects such as the Narmada Dam in India or the Three Gorges Dam in China regard its standards as 'a minimum floor that any environmentally and socially sensible project should meet' (as Friends of the Earth put it in a press release, cited in Sarfaty 2003: 1793). The Bank is, of course, well known for its investment loans financing big infrastructure to which such standards apply. It is also well known for its development policy loans (formerly 'adjustment loans') in which lending is conditional upon policy and institutional change linked to wider goals of neoliberal reform and, more recently, poverty reduction (that is, through the Poverty Reduction Strategy (PRS) process). Combining World Bank commitment to neoliberal policies of growth through participation in global markets with the notion that market imperfections can be dealt with by manipulating social institutions – allowing the state and a degree of managerialism back into international development – has opened up further areas for global social policy making to which Bank social scientists contribute.

It is in this context that anthropologists at the World Bank's Washington, D.C. headquarters describe their responsibilities broadly in terms of the social aspects of development and social analysis contributing to social development goals. However, the discipline was first institutionalized within the Bank differently, as a concern with safeguarding vernacular social and cultural realms and local livelihoods against the threats from growth-driven development and its technical interventions, particularly its large scale infrastructure projects – dams, roads and the like.[2] Interest in access to employment or income, generating community capacity or social capital, participation, empowerment, reaching the poorest and (to these ends) getting social analysis into the system followed.[3] Today anthropologists at the Bank are involved in norm-setting both in relation to investment loans – through the social and environmental 'safeguard policies' – and in relation to policy based lending through various tools of social analysis. No longer construed simply as the protection of vulnerable local groups from the side-effects of growth-driven development, the norm-setting of Bank anthropologists embraces conceptual work on the social goals of development – equity, empowerment and social cohesion – as well as on the means to achieve them, including participation, citizen engagement or consultation within frameworks of economic growth. And the non-economist social scientists represented by anthropologists now include sociologists, political scientists and human geographers, among others – a broad group who, for the sake of brevity I will continue to refer to as 'anthropologists' (making reference to the social science discipline most clearly distinguished from economics: see Bardhan 1989; Bardhan and Ray 2008).

Anthropologists at the World Bank are, however, acutely aware of a contradiction between their professional responsibilities and the exigencies of the organization which constantly threatens their sphere of practice and influence. Their structural vulnerability in an 'economics fortress' (Cernea 1995: 4) means that while pursuing social development goals they have simultaneously to attend to their own 'system goal' of protecting professional space.

The purpose of this chapter is to bring these points together and show how globally influential social development policy ideas and norms are generated by small networks of experts in an international institution, whose thought work also has to serve to protect professional space. Of course, World Bank 'anthropologists' do not think or act in isolation. They are part of transnational epistemic communities. Their ideas draw on and develop concepts from elsewhere – often broader intellectual movements such as the shift to participatory development or the idea of social capital – as well as taking on a life of their own outside the Bank. But by turning an ethnographic eye on how social development knowledge is produced at the Bank's headquarters and on the work of a specific group of expert actors, it is possible to see the importance of local social relations and internal organizational dynamics in the framing of global policy norms. Put differently, systems of relationships that are internal to organizations or epistemic communities become externalized as global policy ideas: cosmopolitan goals arise from village politics. The case I am focusing on is the micropolitics of disciplinary relations at 1818 H Street, Washington, D.C., the headquarters of the World Bank.

Between October 2003 and March 2004, I undertook 'fieldwork' of a kind in the offices and corridors, the coffee shops and canteens, the meetings and seminars of the World Bank headquarters, mostly whilst a Visiting Fellow in the Bank's development economics research group (DECRG).[4] What follows are some preliminary reflections on the position of the growing number of non-economic social scientists – 'anthropologists' – at the Bank, leading specifically to the suggestion that the marginality of this professional group in an bureaucracy dominated by economics shapes the modes of social science analysis at the Bank and the kind of social policy ideas that are generated.[5] My particular focus will be on the work of social development advisers (SDAs), many of whom might not identify themselves primarily as anthropologists but who do see themselves as responsible for 'the social' in development. The wider argument, then, concerns the relationship between policy making 'thought work' and the 'system goals' of professional survival in a large bureaucracy (cf. Heyman 1995; Quarles van Ufford 1993).

One would think that things could not be better for social scientists at the World Bank. In their short history they have increased in number from a single anthropologist appointed in 1974 to around 150 trained anthropologists among Bank staff in 2004,[6] and from an initially narrow focus on *ex post* evaluation or mitigating social costs (such as forced displacement) to the present role of shaping, *ex ante*, the Bank's policy-based and investment lending. When in 1996 the Bank's President, James Wolfensohn, promoted the concept of the 'knowledge bank' and the agency was reorganized for knowledge management creating 'knowledge-based communities' and thematic networks (King and McGrath 2004: 56), social scientists could come together for the first time as a professional group 'anchored' in the Bank's Social Development Department, but with a large network spreading across other sector and regional departments, including the Operations and Evaluation Department (OED, now the Independent Evaluation Group, IEG).[7]

Why then was the experience conveyed to me, as I chatted over cappuccinos, one of a significant professional marginalization of anthropologists? Why did anthropologists feel peripheral? And how did this affect their 'thought work' and the framing of social development concepts?

Social Development and Institutional Marginality

It is clear that the World Bank is an organization dominated by economists and economics paradigms (St Clair 2006). The framing goals, the definition and the measurement of development success all derive from economics frameworks and the discipline is privileged in the Bank's career structure and in its streams of promotion. Partly because anthropologists' historical route to influence was through environment-resettlement issues and 'safeguard policies', the Social Development (SD) 'family', in which anthropological expertise is concentrated, is located within the Environmentally and Socially Sustainable Development (ESSD) network (now the Sustainable Development Network) along with fields such as water resources and infrastructure, which some regard as a strategically poor location at a distance from economists in the influential Poverty Reduction and Economic Management (PREM) network.[8] While several SD staff, including the head of the unit at the time of this research, are economists, there are tellingly only three non-economists (out of eighty-three full-time research staff) in the Bank's prestigious research department, where I was lodged. Anthropologists are also under-represented in the career-building operational parts of the Bank.

In the Bank headquarters, the demand and institutional support for ethnographic knowledge or social analysis is limited.[9] Anthropological expertise is scattered across the organization in a way that fails to produce a critical mass. Bank anthropologists have nothing equivalent to the strong positive loops linking research, sector boards and programmes that Bank economists enjoy (at least research economists in the DECRG); and their perspectives or pragmatic innovations are poorly represented in the outputs that present the public face of the World Bank. The prominence of high profile economics research in publications and websites occludes their intellectual concerns and pragmatic innovations (Bebbington et al. 2004). This under-representation and misrecognition of what they do weakens the ability of Bank anthropologists to explain their work and to engage constructively with external critics or interest lobbies, who then refuse to collaborate with them. Bank anthropologists, it seems, have few friends. While a career in the World Bank can place a research economist at the centre of his or her academic discipline, the same career can virtually disqualify an anthropologist academically. While Bank research economists continue to collaborate with academic colleagues in top university departments (whose concepts and models they brought with them into the Bank) and to publish in the same peer-reviewed journals, anthropologists have to reinvent themselves and acquire new perspectives, methods and skills.[10] They experience profound professional disjuncture.[11]

The intellectual life of anthropologists at the World Bank is shaped by the organization's operational exigencies as much as by the dominance of economics and the relative weakness of their internal and external networks. The jointly staffed and managed IDA (International Development Association) and the IBRD (International Bank for Reconstruction and Development) – both constituent parts of the World Bank Group – have the primary mandate of making and recovering loans. For the operational staff running the Bank's international programme, performance depends upon preparing, appraising and delivering a portfolio of viable loans. Sector departments commit to prepare projects identified in a three-year Country Assistance Strategy, and operational staff (Task Managers) have to meet targets against which administrative budgets (and reputations) are allocated. The pressure is considerable and short term. As one task manager explained, although in theory the Bank has a three-year cycle, the administrative reality is that it is delivery within any twelve-month cycle that is critical. Only a few task managers (anthropologists among them) are able to carve out a space for innovation or to reconcile the desire for attention to the complex social relationships of development with the relentless demands and short term pressures of meeting lending targets, managing a pipeline of projects, maintaining clients and avoiding a 'delivery crunch'.

The operational staff I spoke with in 2003–4 experienced such pressure as intensifying in recent years as the Bank's lending volumes decline with globally low interest rates and rising private sector investments. As one manager put it, 'the portfolio is sinking like a rock'. Finding World Bank credit less attractive, many of its biggest clients (such as India and China) today need the Bank less than it needs them and are newly intolerant of restrictive policy, burdensome appraisal and safeguard processes or fiduciary procedures – 'they want options not [policy] menus or blueprints' and simpler, faster operating procedures which private investors or competitor donors such as the ADB (Asian Development Bank) can offer.

Yet, at the same time, operational staff face increased pressure for rigour in conforming to internal appraisal procedures and in complying with 'safeguard' policies (some shareholder investment may in fact be conditional on the Bank meeting its commitments on environmental and other safeguards). These are enforced through monitoring by a Quality Assurance Group (QAG). An 'unsatisfactory' QAG grading reflects poorly on task managers and departments, but the demand for rigorous procedure gives no let-up on the time pressure on loan preparation. Indeed, the reverse is the case. When Bank managers recently (in 2003) received the results of a survey that showed a correlation between QAG 'problem' projects and the length of time to approval, time and delay were themselves indicators of inefficiency, rather than of institutional complexity which was, of course, more likely.

Now, since anthropologists visibly exert influence through their policy network by building social development concerns into the Bank's operational directives – *inter alia* on involuntary resettlement, critical habitats, environmental assessments or indigenous peoples[12] – they can be seen by those responsible for the 'real work' of negotiating loans as part of the problem, adding neither knowledge nor workable solutions but hoops to negotiate. Anthropologists are part of a system of centralized directives and upward accountability that task managers perceive as inappropriately influencing project design (budgets and components) and rendering projects hard to negotiate 'in country' and difficult to implement. Loans still have to meet criteria of economic returns and finding in-country support for Bank social development concerns can be hard. Even if there is backing from local civil society organizations (e.g., for themes of accountability or rights), getting these past nationally recruited donor 'governance advisers', let alone government, is difficult.

Recent rhetoric on partnership or 'local ownership' has not reduced the accountability of operational managers for centrally driven designs that are hard to deliver. As some see it, the 'top level opens up policy ideas, the networks [e.g., SD] push forward ideas, and they are in the middle having to do the business – negotiating and getting the loans out, keeping the money moving, making profits'. 'It's a struggle to get the process going', said one Task Manager, 'but in Washington people are not interested in that; their eyes glaze over, their interests is in the success of models.' Managers can be heard grumbling that SDAs mistakenly imagine that operational people are not already well aware of the social issues their programmes face; that SDAs rarely offer workable solutions; and that their frameworks only add to the complexity of existing safeguard policies and fiduciary procedures.

However, if anthropologists make the negotiation of projects more difficult downwards (or externally) with clients, their intellectual efforts are essential to negotiating them upwards (or internally) in the Bank. After all, task managers have to turn loans into products that can be sold internally and that will be positively evaluated. In order to produce 'success', projects need to be able to articulate central policy models and to define programmes that will be well judged by the Operations and Evaluation Department (OED). Indeed, when 'PY' took up his initial task manager post, one of the first things his manager got him to do was an Implementation Completion Report (ICR) so that he would understand clearly what was required of a successful project; then he could turn to design. Regardless of the operational context, institutional definitions of success prevail. It is here, some operational managers explained, that anthropologists (SDAs) help to stabilize complex situations, give recognizability and credibility, defend innovation and sustain representations such as 'empowerment', 'social capital' or Community Driven Development (CDD) through their conceptual work and its models, metaphors or worldviews that, as Heyman in another context puts it, can be 'sold upwards as rationales for resource requests and downwards as justifications for orders' (1995: 269). However, the processes that add ideas so as to recruit supporters and to sell a project internally also create, as one research economist put it, 'Christmas tree projects', decorated with glittering policy keywords that are difficult to execute. The most successful policy models are those that appear to reconcile this contradiction, helping move the money faster (and therefore satisfying the shareholders' view of performance) while also handling the external environment (the Bank's potential supporters and critics). At various times, concepts such as 'privatization' or 'social funds' have attracted support for this reason. CDD is currently successful as an approach (in winning internal support) because it hits several policy targets simultaneously – participation, poverty reduction, local governance and decentralization. It is good for public relations, demonstrating the kind of development the Bank should be doing, has top level support, offers delivery efficiencies and the possibility of big budgets and lending at scale (e.g., Guggenheim 2006).[13] At other moments, social development ideas fail to deal with inconsistencies between operational demands and policy goals; they become redundant or are experienced as weakening or failing. Anthropologists have to be alert to a constantly shifting policy field.

The point is that the exigencies of the World Bank reproduce a disjuncture between the operations part of the organization and its knowledge networks, between institutional practice and authorized knowledge, and that anthropologists both experience and reproduce this gap. They find their ideas facilitating processes of internal legitimation while having limited influence either on operations or on research. While World Bank social scientists may articulate their aim, as one put it, 'to make the complex simple while making the simple complex', their position in the organization conspires to prioritize the upward selling of ideas for policy coherence (and viable organizational relationships), while passing contradictions downwards to underanalysed practice. Their conceptual work does not explore the particulars of donor practice and the contradictions which are the everyday experience of staff, but is constrained by a wider knowledge system that emphasizes universal over contextual knowledge, a knowledge system that is deductive and oriented to general predictive models, and that constantly organizes attention away from the contingencies of practice and the plurality of perspectives (cf. King and McGrath 2004) (and which therefore marginalizes anthropology as a critical and ethnographic discipline).

Other factors also serve to limit learning and protect dominant paradigms: first is the prioritizing of information from the Bank's own experience ('"empirical" means proven from our practice', is how one staff member put it); second is the institutional marginality of evaluation (and the OED/IEG) and outputs such as the End of Project Reports; third are the small, invisible, subliminal pressures and disincentives to raising problems that act on staff; the risk of being labelled as a 'non-team player' or 'non-operational', and an awareness of the influence of heterodox opinions on relationships with bosses, on postings or promotions. As one Bank anthropologist put it, 'You can't take a stand too many times and build a career'. Correspondingly, there are high rewards for loyalty and long service. Bank staff are subject to the vulnerability of the overpaid in an overstaffed organization – held captive by high salaries, lifestyles, work permits and commitments to children's education, they pass remarks about 'golden handcuffs' (cf. Goldman 2005: 4). These seemed to me quite pervasive perspectives among my Bank interlocutors, although an individual's sense of intellectual freedom appeared to depend considerably on the style of particular managers. Fourth is the disciplining effect of the Bank's Time Recording System through which all professional staff have to give a quantified account of their activities so as to allow the allocation of costs for programme development. The output orientation here fosters the manufacture of knowledge products, while the time-cost calculation of Bank staff means that, as one put it, 'I'm too expensive to do fieldwork'. Indeed, social research is often undertaken by consultants who (some suggest) are easier to manipulate. The system of 'cross-support' that requires Bank researchers to sell a third of their time to operational departments demands policy marketability and policy 'resonance' rather than independent critique (see Broad 2006, who reviews other 'paradigm maintenance' aspects of Bank research culture).[14]

No wonder, then, that there is widespread scepticism about the Bank's transition to 'plurality and openness' and its new role as 'knowledge broker', not just from external commentators (King and McGrath 2004; Mehta 2000), but also from its own employees. For example, David Ellerman, formerly a Bank senior economist, argues that the Bank 'remains a bureaucracy in which loyalty and right thinking are valued from staff and clients' and that the capacity for organizational learning is in contradiction with the promotion of official views, 'branded knowledge', 'best practices' and 'funded assumptions' – being a church and protecting an orthodoxy (King and McGrath 2004: 94–95, citing Ellerman 2002).

However, what struck me during my stay at the Bank in Washington, D.C. was not consensus and compliance, but the high degree of self-criticism and scepticism regarding official narratives and development recipes among my predominantly social development interlocutors. As one put it, 'while the "golden handcuffs" are powerful incentives to conform, there are, in the hearts of most people, I think, strategies for resistance and rebellion'. I was intrigued by how many people represented their work in terms of a tactical battle against the system. But this was not a battle that could be conducted openly. There was no authorized space for (self-)critical analysis and reflection. The complaints about editorial control or of 'a relentless and multi-layered pressure to keep a positive spin no matter what' were testimony to the presence of both internal challenges and constraints, indicating a clear view on the parameters that defined social development staff's own strategic options. And it is to these strategies that I want now to turn to show how the tactics of internal battles of dissent in fact serve to reproduce the Bank's knowledge system while shaping knowledge products for 'global' social policy.

Anthropologists as Bureaucratic Entrepreneurs

Anthropologists at the Bank are acutely sensitive to their institutional context – their vulnerability in the face of operational constraints and dominant economics paradigms. The optimists among them will say that the Bank is an organization constrained by size rather than ideology, and that size opens up 'structural holes' which can be used by bureaucratic entrepreneurs to innovate and influence.[15] The pessimists will say that the size of the holes in this 'Swiss cheese' organization is shrinking rapidly. As 'entrepreneurs', anthropologists in the social development knowledge network have two tasks. First, they have to develop and sell products – 'business lines', packages of concepts, models, methods or tools[16] – to their clients, who for the most part are the hard-pressed operational teams. Some spoke to me of having to provide 'off the shelf ideas' to assist those who might say, 'Hey Peter, we want to figure out how we can take account of social capital in our programme; how we can test the strength of trust in government institutions'. Second, they have to make institutional space for themselves and create 'systematic room for social knowledge' (Cernea 1995: 13). Their knowledge products – social analysis, CDD, social capital and empowerment – have to meet certain criteria. They have to be simple frameworks that are accessible to managers; they have to define fields of intervention and be instrumentally important (to effectiveness in poverty reduction), to 'have traction', be widely applicable, predictive and prescriptive, measurable ('if you do it you've got to measure it') and subject to empirical testing and econometric analysis. And they have to be visible.[17] As Cernea puts it, anthropologists have to pay their way 'in the coin of knowledge of recognisable organisational utility' (1995: 6). Operational managers live in a zero-sum world in which resources (not least time) for social development products have to be diverted from other things; these therefore have to be justified in terms of efficiency. There have to be answers to questions such as what is the added value from investing in 'empowerment?' What new areas of investment will social capital (or CDD) open up? New concepts need supporters with a stake in them. As a Bank consultant trying to understand the system put it to me: 'In this wildness

I am trying to work out how to influence. By stealth? By patronage? By collaboration? By transparency? Even working out who to email is a political act' (November 2003). Success comes with entrepreneurial flair.

As well as being compatible with the operational exigencies of programme managers, the Bank's social development products also have to be consistent, first with the ruling economic paradigms which define 'soundness', 'robustness' and respectability; and, second, with the legal definition of the organization's mandate set out in its 'Articles of Agreement'.[18] The two conditions are related in that giving social development ideas a 'sound economic basis' is the means to depoliticize social development approaches which have to comply with the Articles and be negotiable, both with the Bank's clients, who may resist what are construed as internal political matters, and with those on its Board who represent client government perspectives (World Bank 2004b: 19).

Two examples illustrate the way in which anthropologists have to comply both with the ruling economics paradigms and with the legal definition of the World Bank's mandate. The first concerns the idea of 'social capital'. In their interesting self-history of the negotiation of the concept of social capital, Bank anthropologists (Bebbington et al. 2004) have themselves revealed the stages by which a conception of the social as networks and relations was reshaped in the metaphor of 'capital' through a series of epistemological and methodological concessions to a culture of 'economics' in the Bank. The economistic notion of social as capital has received critical attention in the literature on the grounds that it encourages a depoliticized analysis of power relations and social institutions, leading to conservative system-sustaining interventions (Harriss 2001; Fine 1999). However, the rise of social capital in the Bank in the late 1990s (as well as its more recent decline, superseded by notions of governance)[19] reveals not the power to depoliticize the social world, but rather the structural inequality of economists and non-economists in the World Bank, and the tactical compromises of the latter professional group, who constantly have to persuade those with power (task managers, vice-presidents and regional budget holders) that social relations are important to development. 'Social capitalists' in the Bank argue that these concessions to economics reasoning are strategic – social capital is a Trojan horse, a 'gateway to get people in the Bank to think about context'. There has, however, always been scepticism outside and increasingly inside the Bank about the feasibility of exerting influence over economists through discursive frameworks (such as social capital) which, after all, are themselves the product of the power relations that produce the dominance of economics in the first place. The experience of social capital is illustrative of 'anthropological' approaches that have been 'buried at a high level'.[20]

The second case concerns the way in which the custodians of the Bank's concept of 'empowerment' were trying to consolidate this as an institutionally viable operational concept. At a World Bank-DFID workshop I attended in March 2004 on 'Power, Rights and Poverty Reduction', a Bank Vice-

President noted that 'we have made our peace with empowerment'.[21] Indeed, the Bank has specialists, websites and a comprehensive handbook devoted to the theme.[22] However, mention of power (as in rights or political structures) crosses 'an invisible barrier into politics',[23] contravening the Bank's Articles of Agreement, and has to be excised from Bank publications reviewed by its legal department. The same is true of 'rights'. When I was in Washington, D.C., the draft of the SD group's first Strategy Paper was returned by the legal department with all reference to 'rights' and 'rights based approaches' excised. As one social development adviser explained, the problem is not only that the concept of rights is essentially political, but also that, since rights have infinite value and so involve infinite costs to maintain, they do not fit within an economics framework, whereas 'empowerment' allows some 'wriggle room';[24] it allows gradation and measurement, and is permitted in relation to, say, capacity, accountability or identity, or as the vague outcome attributed to PRS national planning. Still, as empowerment or social accountability ideas push up against the rights/politics barrier, the contradictions of policy and institution are only too clear. Some commentators on an early draft of this chapter emphasized recent (post-2005) changes in the perspective on power and rights in the Bank, especially with the framing of the World Development Report (WDR) 2006 on Equity and Development, and Paul Wolfowitz's (the next President) stress on governance and anti-corruption. Questions of rights, power and politics have indeed recently become the focus on debate in the Bank. However, as McNeill and St Clair show in their discussion of the WDR 2006 (in Chapter 5 of this volume), the Bank continues to subordinate an intrinsic to an instrumental understanding of rights and equity. Human rights may be a legitimate consideration for the Bank, but only 'where they have economic ramifications or impacts'; rights and respect for civil liberties, where linked to the performance of government projects.[25]

In conceptualizing power as 'empowerment', anthropologists again consent to instrumentalize it as a variable correlated with the achievement of poverty reduction and development effectiveness. One SDA asserted, 'For our audience we need a reductive framework'. As Tania Li (2007, this volume) points out, social capital and empowerment (and perhaps in some frameworks, rights and equity too) become ideas used to imagine society for measurement and improvement. They allow a conceptualization of society in terms of deficiencies (and surpluses) and a mode of diagnosis that allows the expert design of technical interventions for social reorganization; invariably at the local or community level through neoliberal (or neo-traditionalist) models of self-help, self-organization and 'responsibilization' (Li 2007, this volume; Rose 1999). But my point is that such conceptions are also – perhaps more urgently – necessary (and so organized) to protect the existence, position and identity of a professional group within the Bank as an organization. Here, SDAs find franchizable ways to make the social calculable and subject to technical intervention (despite their own doubts) because this is a precondition for their continued existence as a professional group. In other words, ideas of empowerment and social capital may tell us something about how social development experts think, but they say more about the structures of institutional power to which they have strategically to adapt.

So, the Bank's anthropologists have to choose their language carefully if they are to sell 'the social'. Their conceptual work is not only shaped by the need to manufacture products, but it also aims to mobilize existing support; to 'raise the floor rather than raise the ceiling'[26] in order to pursue the second task of creating institutional space by building constituencies and legitimacy. Here, the work of a concept like CDD is strategic rather than conceptual or practical; it is a type of symbolic capital, important for whom it brings together rather than what it says. An idea like CDD deliberately obscures differences (e.g., between older approaches of social funds or community based development) to build a critical mass of support around a simple message – 'if communities control the budget and make decisions efficiency is improved' – in order, for example, to argue with the fiduciary parts of the organization and thus ensure that rules of procurement are revised or relaxed.[27] But to become a 'community of practice', CDD has to become a known item, a brand name so that the sense of uncertainty or risk associated with innovation in the Bank is reduced.

Of course, brand names function better when endorsed by celebrities and senior people, which is why anthropologist staff confessed to analysing Bank president Jim Wolfensohn's speeches to find any mention of key 'social' themes. These are the strategies of a professional group that is marginal and vulnerable, whose work is largely externally resourced through trust funds set up by donor governments (especially Scandinavian) hoping to steer the agenda rather than from core Bank resources; people who cannot rest from making alliances, building constituencies, creating space and making visible or manufacturing products, on whose marketing success their careers and survival depend.[28]

It happened that during my stay in Washington, D.C. (in late 2003), social development staff were debating how to consolidate their brand name as an explicit SD strategy; something that would be needed, as one put it, 'because there may be a reorganization of the boxes in the Bank; and if you don't have a strategy paper, you don't have a box, so you might disappear'.[29] Drafting the Strategy Paper proved to be an intriguingly complex yet critical process.

First, the strategy had to consolidate support by embracing a wide range of quite different approaches among Bank social development staff themselves. There were significant demarcations, for example, between those who favoured clarifying a distinctive SD professional space through specialization around products such as social capital or CDD, and those who argued for the synergies of getting social analysis into the policy mainstream; between those who saw social development as a form of 'cross-sector support' (offering its products and technical advice to others) as against those who preferred a focus on designing and managing distinctive SD project approaches (such as CDD) and creating operational domains where SD ideas could work unfettered and produce pilot project exemplars. Further differences separated *ex ante* approaches focusing on the design of interventions from *ex post* approaches that aimed to track reform processes through public expenditure reviews, citizen report cards or the media to monitor policy commitments to accountability; or the preference for shaping reform through positive analysis versus using the power of veto to resist. These and other differences (reflecting *inter alia* personal backgrounds and career paths into the Bank) would not be resolved but rather contained within the official Strategy Paper. While trying to create clarity of purpose, the drafters of the SD Strategy Paper knew that innovation in the Bank is not created conceptually but tactically. Keeping many people and perspectives on board, giving people a stake and the painfully slow process of building alliances required strategic vagueness and conceptual ambiguity. One commented that a brilliant analytical paper would instantly provoke resistance and set people against it.[30]

Second, the SD Strategy Paper marked another level of strategic accommodation among 'anthropologists' in the Bank in face of a new vulnerability – an awareness that the size to which the SD department had grown under the Wolfensohn presidency was not justified by the scale of investment in 'social development'; that a 'return to essentials' and a renewed interest in big-spending infrastructure projects was in the wings. Staff spoke of a 'closing window' and of existing on 'borrowed time'.[31] They anticipated a 'push back' against sophisticated regulations and pointed to the desire of the Operating Policy and Country Services (OPCS) to modernize, simplify and speed up policies and procedures that was supported by client governments and by managers under the rubric of 'Client Responsiveness'. For a professional group whose influence had been underpinned by operational rules and procedure, the new interest in simplifying and flexibility was a threat. In response, the draft SD Strategy Paper put new emphasis on anthropologists' 'upstream analytical work' allied more closely with the Bank's core policy goals such as sector reform, and on the work of anthropologists with economists in mainstream neoliberal dialogue on the creation of opportunities for investment through broadbrush sector or country-level assessments feeding into Poverty Reduction Strategy Papers (PRSPs) or Bank Country Assistance Strategies (CASs).

In this way, the growing operational pressure (to keep up loan portfolios) would present opportunities rather than threats to social development staff able to make rapid assessments, mould reform agendas and improve investment choices in a way that constituted a tactical move of space making for social development in the Bank. The earlier emphasis on safeguards and sector-focused models was regressive. On the one hand, anthropologists had been too reliant on the power of veto; their view of people as victims and their focus on 'high risk civil society' – the protestors and public interest litigators – had separated them from the mainstream. On the other hand, their sector based sociology had lost popularity. The irrigation sociologists' specialist interest was buried in rural development, and their products such as user groups (which had long been a staple of irrigation, education and other investments) had been the subject of critical evaluations. Anthropologists were no longer to be looking up from the village or 'lobbing bombs' from a disciplinary enclave, but were sitting at the same table in the smoke-filled rooms in which macrobudgeting and the like took place.[32] And the diversification of the social development group beyond anthropologists/sociologists to include economists was itself a survival-oriented adaptation. There was no less need to develop and sell SD products, but the new product – Integrative Country Social Analysis (ICSA) and Poverty and Social Impact Assessments (PSIAs) – were oriented upstream to appeal to country managers rather than operational teams and project task managers, towards 'unpacking growth' into desirable social change and monitoring the process – a 'mapping approach' that 'follows the money' (as explained to me) – rather than just *ex ante* project design. Still the question raised at the SD board meeting (in this case in relation to ICSAs) remained: 'It is complex; is it sellable?'

Third, as an instance of tactical space making, the draft Strategy Paper shifted from the previous view of 'social development' as a means – serving the existing development goals through sector-focused sociology or 'risk mitigation' – to an end view in which 'forward looking' social analysis defines what constitutes a better society and works for positive social change (as noted) to make societies more 'inclusive', 'cohesive' and 'accountable' – the three 'pillars' of social development for the Bank (World Bank 2004b).[33]

Such strategic accommodations and brand making are not without their internal detractors. Some expressed fear over what was regarded as a loss of anthropologists' 'functional agenda' and sociological skill – whether of the sector-focused sociological research on irrigation, fisheries and forestry, or the work on displacement and resettlement – that grew historically in the shadow of major investment lending (Cernea 1991; World Bank 1996). They decried the loss of clear arguments backed by ethnographic evidence or the critical edge and influence that was associated with the high profile Inspection Panels exemplified in the Narmada (India) controversy, when the senior management, the President and the board had no choice but to listen to what anthropologists had to say because of their evidence and because powerful political constituencies in recipient and donor countries – NGOs on Capitol Hill – demanded it.

Some were concerned about a value-laden, managerial perspective and the ends-oriented macroengineering of social outcomes.[34] Others feared that as social analysis goes 'upstream', it becomes not just more visible, but more readily proscribed as 'political'. Yet others had sympathy with outsiders who reflected pessimistically on the various discursive strategies that have been used to influence policy in the past or who regard hopelessly unrealistic social goals as part of an 'enabling environment' for continuing structural adjustment, merely adding capacity to the 'anti-politics machine' (Ferguson 1990). Some regional SD departments then tried carving out conceptual spaces of their own; for example, in South Asia, where SD staff were developing a higher risk approach by moving away from both the 'traditional' safeguards approach and the new normative mainstreaming towards a social analysis that focused on the functioning of institutions, paying attention to the underlying informal systems and interests (e.g., patronage and incentives in government systems) and to the analysis of failure and of institutional arrangements in which the Bank was itself implicated. But in the climate of pragmatic accommodation these advocates of critical analysis were unpopular 'blockers', 'analysing things to a standstill', and their efforts to 'fight the system' were dismissed as naïve, sometimes through the personal narratives of their colleagues who could say that 'I too was a critic when I joined the Bank and thought that I would change things from inside by revealing the wolf behind the sheep's clothing, but now I am a decision maker' (SDA interview).

Finally, there was an opinion that was doubtful of the value of explicit policy statements as a vehicle for influence or survival in the Bank at all. For such pragmatists, concealment from policy, innovation at distance and the documentation of success are the means to work towards social development ends. Their point was that, in the main, documents do not push policy frontiers forwards; effective policy making is after the fact. They point to innovations, for example, the promotion of identity cards for electoral regulation, which if framed as explicit policy/design would have been rejected as political by the Bank's legal department. Some noted that bureaucracy can hold a policy paper hostage but is powerless to control pragmatic innovation. A policy which builds upon seven years of practice easily acquires legitimacy, and less through documentation than by arranging educational or 'fact finding' field visits for World Bank Board members and executive directors. The CDD work in Indonesia (the Kecamatan Development Programme) under the programme leadership of the anthropologist Scott Guggenheim is a case in point (Guggenheim 2006). The preparatory 'local institutions studies' for this project contributed significantly to the negotiation of the idea of social capital in the Bank in the late 1990s, and the Programme itself has probably pushed further than any other to turn ethnographic methods to operational ends. In doing so, 'thick description' is used instrumentally to diagnose and monitor corruption and increase transparency (but see Li 2007, this volume). On the one hand, this is a remarkable governmental application of social science (whose politics being confined to the community exists 'below the radar screen' of Indonesian officials who fail to see the 'democratization initiative masquerading as an anti-poverty project': Barron et al. 2006). On the other hand, strong internal resistance to identifying World Bank operations as in any sense political (even while it is understood that in practice they routinely put the organization in breach of its Articles), means that secondary analytical work is still needed to establish the 'sound economic basis' of such work in Washington, D.C.

Conclusions

This chapter has examined the way that policy ideas are shaped by the institutional exigencies of the bodies within which they are formulated. I suggested that policy ideas have social or institutional work to do. They are fashioned so as to protect the interests of professional groups operating within particular organizational contexts. In particular, the chapter argued that World Bank 'anthropologists' define social development concepts so as to manage their structural vulnerability in an 'economics fortress' (Cernea 1995: 4) and to attend to their own 'system goal' of protecting professional space. Tactical concessions push the analytical work of Bank non-economists towards instrumental and economistic formulations that not only remove the possibility of ethnographic insights into the nature of the contradictions of development itself, but also contribute to the knowledge system that perpetuates separation of the corporate world of policy rationality from the contingencies of practice.

The dilemma that I have highlighted endures. It was again brought to light in a recent assessment of World Bank 'social analysis' (Ladbury and Kuehnast 2007). This concluded that in theory Bank social development experts engage in three types of 'social analysis': developing standardized products (CSA, PSIAs, etc.); responding to operational problems (in-country); and producing academic research framed by social theory. In practice, however, the emphasis has to be on the first, the development of social analysis 'products' through which SD experts secure the 'corporate visibility' that is crucial to professional survival. But the dilemma is that social development's upwards-oriented 'corporate products' have little value or practical influence in operations (because of limited engagement with country-level staff or due to being ill-matched to the shorter timeframes of development policy lending). Meanwhile, anthropologists' less visible country-level work aimed at operational solutions is too slow, low profile and country-specific to contribute to their system goal of survival. Much the same is said today of formerly central work on social safeguards, which being country-contextual has lost out to 'upstream work on policy' and so has fallen to the bottom of the social development knowledge hierarchy. Meanwhile, the structure of incentives and demand around knowledge at the Bank continually work against the promotion of theoretically informed critical empirical (perhaps ethnographic) social research and the recruitment of the relevant skills into the organization.

One might suggest that 'anthropologists' at the Bank were subject to what Quarles van Ufford (1993) refers to as the organizational need for ignorance about what is going on locally, in order to save, protect and promote politically important notions, including their own products – whether participation, empowerment, social capital, CDD or 'social analysis'. Arguably, the more marginal a professional group, the more carefully its products have to be protected against attack (from operational people complaining of unusable complexity or from research economists complaining of analytical vagueness). Anthropologists in the Bank need strategies, concepts, boxes or crushproof cages to demarcate their institutional space; some even hold appointments – not to mention visas, school places – that came with the rise of key products (e.g., social capital or CDD), so that identities, reputations and careers are tied up with their continuing success. The institutional conditions of a large bureaucracy are such that innovators are turned into gatekeepers.

Through their need to reproduce their expertise, anthropologists at the Bank become part of a knowledge system that tailors its way of knowing the world to its own administrative rationality, leading, as Quarles van Ufford puts it, 'to an integrated discourse in which the capabilities of the administrative "machine" and the definitions of development constitute a single whole' (1993: 140). Quarles van Ufford's insights are extended by Mitchell's important *Rule of Experts,* in which he explains the role of experts and expertise (in modern Egypt) precisely as securing a sphere of rational intention or abstract design which appears external to (and generative of) events – through writing, models and maps that erase the personal, contingent, hybrid agencies, struggles, connections and interactions of actual practice (2002: 77). Experts are charged with effecting artificial separations between representations and reality so as to 'allow reason to rule, and allow history to be arranged as the unfolding of a locationless [policy] logic' (2002: 15, 36). Therefore, the disjuncture between policy and practice is not an unfortunate gap to be bridged between intention and action; it is a necessity, actively maintained and reproduced by knowledge systems that also incorporate anthropologists as social development experts.

Notes

1. A preliminary shorter version of this chapter appeared as 'Social Analysis as Product Development: Anthropologists at Work in the World Bank', in A. Giri, A. van Harskamp and O.Salemink (eds), *The Development of Religion/The Religion of Development*. Delft: Eburon, 2004.
2. It was work on resettlement in the context of major controversies and public relations disasters, in particular that surrounding the major Narmada dam project in India in the late 1980s, which gave anthropologists a higher profile in the Bank (Michael Cernea, pers. comm.).
3. In the Bank in 2003–4, 'anchor' staff were grouped into thematic teams reflecting these concerns, such as 'Participation and Civic Engagement', 'Community Driven

Development', 'Social Capital', 'Indigenous Peoples', 'Social Analysis', 'Conflict Resolution' (in the Social Development Department) and 'Gender', 'Empowerment' (in PREM – Poverty Reduction and Economic Management).

4. In October–December 2003, I was a DECRG Visiting Fellow, and in March 2004 I participated in a World Bank/DFID workshop on power and empowerment. Unless otherwise stated, all quotations are from conversations with World Bank staff with whom I interacted. I am grateful to the DECRG for the research fellowship and to many World Bank staff in other departments for support and insights during my visit. For perceptive feedback on earlier drafts of this chapter, I am grateful, among others, to Gershon Feder, Paul Francis, Sarah Ladbury, David Marsden and Biju Rao. Of course, I alone am responsible for the analysis offered here.

5. To clarify further, I will use the label 'anthropologist' to refer to those working at the Bank with training in non-economics disciplines including sociology, human geography and political science, as well as social/cultural anthropology. Taken to include SD and gender staff/consultants and others from the non-economics social sciences, these numbered as many as 446 people in 2003–4 (World Bank 2004a: 8).

6. The Bank appointed its first and sole staff anthropologist, Michael Cernea, in 1974 and by 1995 an in house corps of fifty to sixty anthropologists and sociologists represented 'the world's largest group of its kind' (Cernea 1995: 4). For a personal account of the way 'social issues' were first incorporated into the Bank, see Cernea and Freidenberg 2007.

7. SD units within the regional departments have a hierarchy of posts professionally linked to the SD advisory group 'anchor'.

8. Bank staff responsible for the gender theme took the strategic decision to ally with the PREM economists. The Bank's 'matrix' structure means that many staff in the SD family actually work in regional and other departments.

9. Outside of Washington, D.C. this can be less so, and there are isolated country programmes where ethnographic research has been incorporated into project strategies (Guggenheim 2006; Li 2007 and Chapter 3 this volume). Lack of interest characterizes the centre, and reportedly the Bank-IMF library cancelled its subscription to *American Ethnologist* a few years ago (around 1996).

10. The actual (and rather critical) judgement of academic economists on the work of World Bank research economists can be discerned from the recent report, 'An Evaluation of World Bank Research, 1998–2005,' prepared by a panel chaired by Angus Deaton, Professor of Economics at Princeton University (accessible via www.worldbank.org). This methodological review criticizes Bank economics research as unduly bending towards the organization's ruling policy regimes (Fine 2008).

11. This disjuncture is amplified by the effective exclusion of anthropologists from the Bank's prestigious research department and an opinion among several Bank economists (with whom I spoke) that did not hold the professional standing of non-economists in the Bank in high regard. Indeed, one of the most common arguments for not recruiting more sociologists or anthropologists into the DECRG was that it would be difficult to recruit individuals of appropriate calibre. A handful of Bank research economists in the DECRG are interested and well read in anthropology, and it is significant that the few recent initiatives to engage conceptually and methodologically with anthropology as a critical ethnographic discipline have come from this department rather than from social development. These arise from the perceived weakness of Bank anthropologists' ethnographic research and include the 'culture and public action' project (Rao and Walton 2004), and indeed my own short appointment as a visiting fellow.

12. See safeguard policies of the World Bank Operational Manual at: http://wbln0018. worldbank.org/Institutional/Manuals/OpManual.nsf/TOC1?OpenPage.

13. The over-positive evaluation of this favoured programme model has recently been sharply criticized by Robert Chambers among others (Kumar et al. 2005: 151–53).

14. Economists in the research department with whom I discussed these matters considered that social development staff were more vulnerable than themselves to pressure to bend

concepts and research to current policy models: the SD department is new and has grown fast, its senior people have left, an interpretive discipline (anthropology) lacks the means to sustain criticism or alternative glosses, and there is a high dependence on external consultants. Certainly, research economists could afford to be critical of the Bank's SD policy models, and it is from them that internal criticism of participation, CDD or social capital has recently emerged (Mansuri and Rao 2004). But while some high profile internal critics have been economists (e.g., Joseph Stiglitz, William Easterly), recent reviews have done much to strengthen the impression of the core policy-supporting nature of economics research at the Bank (Broad 2007).

15. Michael Woolcock. Presentation at *World Bank/DFID Working Meeting on 'Power, Rights and Poverty Reduction', 23–24 March 2004, Washington, D.C*: http://lnweb18.worldbank.org/ESSD/sdvext.nsf/68ByDocName/CurrentInitiativesPowerRightsandPovertyReduction.

16. Some of these are general obligatory tools (part of the operational directives for setting up loans), while others are context-specific (conflict analysis, gender analysis).

17. A dilemma expressed by SD staff is that the impact of SD is not directly visible. An early draft of the Bank SD strategy (October 2003) put it like this: 'Its subtle, multi-sectoral nature makes social development hard to see directly. However, its failure is glaringly obvious in civil strife, violence and war. Preventing such disasters takes constant effort, the sort of steady, quiet effort noticed primarily when it is withdrawn.'

18. Section 6 of Article 5 states that Bank shall not 'interfere in the political affairs of any member; nor shall they be influenced in their decisions by the political character of the member or members concerned. Only economic considerations shall be relevant to their decisions' (available at www.worldbank.org).

19. The present-day demise of social capital at the Bank is as revealing of the character and politics of its HQ knowledge processes as was its rise. The social capital theme is peripheral on today's (August 2008) World Bank website and is no longer a major and active item under social development.

20. Jonathan Fox commenting at the World Bank/DFID Working Meeting on 'Power, Rights and Poverty Reduction', 23–24 March 2004, Washington, D.C.

21. Working Meeting on 'Power, Rights and Poverty Reduction', 23–24 March 2004. DfID and the World Bank, Washington, D.C.: http://lnweb18.worldbank.org/ESSD/sdvext.nsf/68ByDocName/CurrentInitiativesPowerRightsandPovertyReduction.

22. As with social capital, the many volumes and inches of websites devoted to the theme may be an indicator not of the power of a concept, but rather of the political weakness of its advocates and the struggle to achieve respectability for ideas which still command little support internally.

23. SD Strategy Paper, October 2003 draft, p. 10.

24. Comment at Working Meeting on 'Power on 'Power, Rights and Poverty Reduction', 23–24 March 2004 (see note above)'.

25. Citation from Senior Vice-President and General Counsel Roberto Danino's 'Legal Opinion on Human Rights and the Work of the World Bank' (27 January 2006). For this and a general summary statement on the current position on human rights, see the Bank's website: www.worldbank.org.

26. Participant comment at Working Meeting on' Power, Rights and Poverty Reduction', 23–24 March 2004 (see note above).

27. The ambiguity of such policy concepts also gives them immunity to falsification through the testing of causal relations (Mansuri and Rao 2004).

28. The marginality of social development here amplifies what are in fact quite general institutional processes in the Bank. Even larger 'mainstream' groups such as agriculturalists are constrained to promote the new 'products' of their club (Gershon Feder, pers. comm.), and economists too have to adapt to a shifting policy field and reinvent or package their ideas (Biju Rao, pers. comm.).

29. Or, as another experienced SD staff member put it, 'Social Development are the new kids on the block – and may be the first to go'.

30. Critics, research economists among them, regard such a position as symptomatic of the intellectual weakness of 'social development types' in the Bank, their own failures of networking and research being blamed on the fact that others do not take them seriously.
31. These were somewhat prophetic statements given the stress, under Wolfowitz's presidency, on governance, corruption and infrastructure, which may not be routed through social development and which is now brought under the same umbrella as infrastructure, and departments such as environment and rural development.
32. Comment by a senior SD manager.
33. Those drafting the Strategy Paper suggested that these 'pillars' summarized a view from staff of what they already did in practice; it was an aggregate self-representation.
34. SD staff who had worked in European traditions of public social policy admitted that they might be more comfortable with ideas of social engineering than their Anglo-American colleagues. But one of these Europeans, the Director of SD, has himself expressed concern about an international institution without democratic governance (unlike the UN, voting rights in the Bank are not one member, one vote) trying to 'design the global social policy' (online 'discussion with Steen Jorgensen on Social Dimensions of Development Effectiveness, 11 May 2004: http://discuss.worldbank.org/chat/view).

References

Abramson, David. 1999. 'A Critical Look at NGOs and Civil Society as Means to an End in Uzbekistan', *Human Organisation* 58(3): 240–50.

Anders, Gerhad. 2005. 'Good Governance as Technology: Towards an Ethnography of the Bretton Woods Institutions', in David Mosse and David Lewis (eds), *The Aid Effect: Giving and Governing in International Development.* London and Ann Arbor, M.I.: Pluto Press, pp. 37–60.

Bardhan, Pranab. (ed.). 1989. *Conversations between Economists Anthropologists: Methodological Issues in Measuring Economic Changes in rural India.* Delhi: Oxford University Press, Delhi.

Bardhan, Pranab and Isha Ray. (eds). 2008. *The Contested Commons: Conversations between Economists and Anthropologists.* Oxford: Blackwell.

Barron, P., R. Diprose and M. Woolcock. 2006. 'Local Conflict and Community Development in Indonesia: Assessing the Impact of the Kecamatan Development Program', *Indonesian Social Development Paper No. 10.* Jakarta: World Bank.

Bebbington, A., S. Guggenheim, E. Olson and M. Woolcock. 2004. 'Exploring Social Capital Debates at the World Bank', *Journal of Development Studies* 40(5): 33–42.

Broad, Robin. 2007. '"Knowledge Management": A Case Study of the World Bank's Research Department', *Development in Practice* 17(4): 700–8.

Cernea, Michael M. (ed.). 1991 *Putting People First: Sociological Variables in Rural Development,* 2nd ed. Oxford: Oxford University Press.

———. 1995. 'Social Organisation and Development Anthropology', *Environmentally Sustainable Development Studies and Monograph Series No. 6.* Washington, D.C.: World Bank.

Cernea, Michael and Judith Freidenberg. 2007. '"Development Anthropology is a Contact Sport." An Oral History Interview with Michael M. Cernea by Judith Freidenberg', *Human Organization* 66(4): 339–53.

Ellerman, David. 2002. 'Should Development Agencies Have Official Views?', *Development in Practice* 12(3–4): 285–97.

Ferguson, James. 1990. *The Anti-politics Machine: Development, De-politicisation and Bureaucratic Power in Lesotho.* Cambridge: Cambridge University Press.

Fine, Ben. 1999. 'The Development State is Dead – Long Live Social Capital?', *Development & Change* 30(1) 1–19.

———. 2008. 'Social Capital and Health: The World Bank through the Looking Glass after Deaton', Draft Paper for Presentation on 12 March 2008 at the Seminar for School of

Oriental and African Studies/London International Development Centre.

Foucault, M. 1991. 'Governmentality', in . Burchell, C. Gordon, and P. Miller (eds), *The Foucault Effect: Studies in Governmentality*. Chicago: University of Chicago Press, pp. 87–104.

Goldman, M. 2001. 'The Birth of a Discipline: Producing Authoritative Green Knowledge, World Bank Style', *Ethnography* 2(2): 191–217.

———. 2005. *Imperial Nature: The World Bank and Struggles for Social Justice in the Age of Globalisation*. New Haven and London: Yale University Press

Guggenheim, Scott. 2006. 'Crises and Contradictions: Understanding the Origins of a Community Development Project in Indonesia', in A. Bebbington, S. Guggenheim, E. Olson and M. Woolcock (eds), *The Search for Empowerment: Social Capital as Theory and Practice at the World Bank*. West Hartford, C.T.: Kumarian Press.

Harriss, John. 2001. *Depoliticising Development: The World Bank and Social Capital*. London: Anthem Press.

Heyman, Josiah McC. 1995. 'Putting Power in the Anthropology of Bureaucracy', *Current Anthropology* 36(2): 261–87.

King, Kenneth and Simon McGrath. 2004. *Knowledge for Development? Comparing British, Japanese, Swedish and World Bank Aid*. London: Zed Books.

Kumar, Nalini, Anju Vajja, Barbara Pozzoni, George Garner Woodall. 2005. The Effectiveness of World Bank Support for Community-based and Driven Development: An OED Evaluation. (Independent Evaluation Group Studies) Washington, D.C.: World Bank, http://www.worldbank.org/oed/cbdcdd.

Ladbury, Sarah and Kathleen Kuehnast. 2007. 'Review of Social Analysis Practice within the World Bank', Draft for discussion July 2007.

Li, Tania. 2007. *The Will to Improve: Governmentality, Development, and the Practice of Politics*. Durham, N.C.: Duke University Press.

Mansuri, Ghazala and Vijayendra Rao. 2004. 'Community-based (and Driven) Development: A Critical Review', *World Bank Research Observer* 19(1): 1–39.

Mehta, Lyla. 2000. 'The World Bank and its Emerging Knowledge Empire', *Human Organisation* 60(2): 189–96.

Mitchell, Timothy. 2002. *Rule of Experts: Egypt, Techno-politics, Modernity*. Berkeley, C.A.: University of California Press.

Mosse, D. 2005a. *Cultivating Development: An Ethnography of Aid Policy and Practice*. London and Ann Arbor, M.I.: Pluto Press.

———. 2005b. 'Global Governance and the Ethnography of International Aid', in David Mosse and David Lewis (eds), *The Aid Effect: Giving and Governing in International Development*. London and Ann Arbor, M.I.: Pluto Press, pp. 1–36.

———. 2006. 'Collective Action, Common Property and Social Capital in South India: An Anthropological Commentary', *Economic Development and Culture Change* 54(3): 695–724.

Quarles van Ufford, Philip. 1988a. 'The Hidden Crisis in Development: Development Bureaucracies in between Intentions and Outcomes', in P. Quarles van Ufford, D. Kruijt and T. Downing (eds), *The Hidden Crisis in Development: Development Bureaucracies*. Tokyo and Amsterdam: United Nations and Free University Press.

———. 1988b. 'The Myth of Rational Development Policy: Evaluation versus Policy Making in Dutch Protestant Donor Agencies', in P. Quarles van Ufford, D. Kruijt and T. Downing (eds), *The Hidden Crisis in Development: Development Bureaucracies*. Tokyo and Amsterdam: United Nations and Free University Press.

———. 1993. 'Knowledge and Ignorance in the Practices of Development Policy', in M. Hobart (ed.), *An Anthropological Critique of Development: The Growth of Ignorance*. London and New York: Routledge.

Randeria, S. 2003. 'Cunning States and Unaccountable International Institutions: Legal Plurality, Social Movements and Rights of Local Communities to Common Property Resources', *Archives Européennes de Sociologie / European Journal of Sociology* 44(1): 27–60.

Rao, Vijayendra and Michael Walton. (eds). 2004. *Culture and Public Action*. Stanford, C.A.: Stanford University Press.

Rose, Nikolas. 1999. *Powers of Freedom: Reframing Political Thought*. Cambridge: Cambridge University Press.

Sarfaty, Galit A. 2003. 'The World Bank and the Internalization of Indigenous Rights Norms', *Yale Law Journal* 114: 1791–818.

St Clair, Asunción Lera. 2006. 'The World Bank as a Transnational Expertised Institution', *Global Governance* 12: 77–95.

World Bank. 1996. 'Resettlement and Development: The Bankwide Review of Projects involving Involuntary Resettlement 1986–1993', Environment Department Papers No. 32. Washington, D.C.: World Bank.

———. 2004a. An OED Review of Social Development in Bank Activities Washington, D.C.: World Bank.

———. 2004b. 'Social Development in World Bank Operations: Results and the Way Forward', Social Development Department, Discussion Draft, 12 February 2004.

Chapter 5

THE WORLD BANK'S EXPERTISE

Observant Participation in the World Development
Report 2006, Equity and Development[1]

Desmond McNeill and Asuncion Lera St Clair

> 'Cognition is the most socially-conditioned activity of man,
> and knowledge is the paramount social creation.' (Fleck 1935,
> p. 42, quoted in Douglas 1986: 12)

Introduction

In this chapter we examine the challenge faced by the World Bank in
addressing issues concerning ethics and human rights. We show how
institutional forces in the organization constrain how it thinks and speaks
about such matters. More specifically, we analyse the World Development
Report (WDR) 2006 on Equity and Development – both the product and
the process – and the parallel discussions concerning the World Bank's
activities in the human rights field. This chapter therefore complements
others in this volume, demonstrating how expert knowledge in the World
Bank, and in this case especially economic expertise, shapes or 'frames'
ideas (Bøås and McNeill 2003) and thereby also action.

This case study is part of a larger comparative research project in which
we examine activities within the arena of ethics and human rights in the
World Bank and three other international organizations: the United
Nations Development Programme (UNDP), the United Nations
Educational, Scientific and Cultural Organisation (UNESCO) and the Inter-
American Development Bank (IDB).[2] The WDR 2006 is well suited to our
purpose, not only because it demonstrates so clearly the tensions that arise
in applying economic expertise to issues of ethics and justice, but also
because we have 'insider knowledge' of the process, having been quite
closely involved. This also raises ethical and methodological problems,
which we address at the end of the chapter.

In order to understand the significance of expertise in the Bank, it is necessary to study how processes of knowledge formulation are themselves embedded within sets of social relations among professionals in the Bank, as well as relations between the Bank and others outside. As Mosse argues in Chapter 1 of this volume, expert knowledge must be seen in the context of social relations among communities of professional advisers, consultants, policy makers, aid administrators and managers inside and outside the Bank, also in relation to its organizational culture. Bank experts need audiences that legitimize their knowledge. In many cases, these audiences are other bureaucrats or actors that are dependent on funds provided by the Bank to carry out activities that have been defined and promoted by the Bank's experts, thereby generating a circular dynamic between the expertise, the audience and the legitimacy of that expertise (St Clair 2006a). Moreover, because of the need to maintain a sense of coherence in an organization that is highly heterogeneous and complex, new ideas and themes tend to be built upon older and well established Bank ideas and discourse; critical views are excluded, in a process of what Broad (following Wade 1996) calls 'the art of paradigm maintenance' (Broad 2006). Where disagreement arises, consensus is reached through internal negotiation and contestation processes; however, these are not transparent, but rather take place in closed door meetings. Ideas that are not suited to the tools of analysis and instruments of policy of the Bank (for example, the role of human rights in bringing about fair development processes) tend to be excluded.

By comparison with other development agencies, or even international organizations in general, the World Bank's knowledge has been subject to considerable critical study (Broad 2006; Bøas and McNeill 2003; Goldman 2005; Mallaby 2004; McNeill, 2005; Sridhar 2007; St Clair 2006a, 2006b; Stone and Wright 2006; Wade 2002, 2004; Woods 2006). This is not surprising – besides its financial power through lending and grants, the World Bank is more influential than any other agency in terms of exercising power over the development 'discourse', policy ideas and development policy agenda. Moreover, the Bank itself takes pride in its expertise, which it regards as one of the most important sources of its legitimacy as a global development institution. Its expertise is located primarily within economics, and the alleged scientific character of this discipline is used to support claims about the neutrality and importance of its ideas. Since its creation, the Bank has built up an impressive stock of data and research about developing countries. By defining development-related issues as predominantly economic, it has established and perpetuated its own legitimacy and credibility, and generated demand for the sort of knowledge in which it specializes.[3]

The annual WDR of the World Bank is the organization's flagship publication.[4] It serves the purpose of synthesizing and, where possible, advancing what the Bank regards as state-of-the-art development thinking on the topic selected for that year, for example, agriculture, poverty or sustainable development. It is perhaps the most important way in which the Bank seeks to display its dominant position in the field of development research and policy.[5] The WDR is very widely distributed and attracts considerable attention both from the media and from the community of development practitioners, as well as political leaders in the global south. In this chapter we take the World Bank's *World Development Report 2006: Equity and Development* (hereafter the WDR 2006) as our focus of attention.

The WDR 2006

The process of preparing the Report began in 2004, and we can begin our account with a workshop in Oslo in September 2004 which we coorganized, and which constituted one of the first consultations on the Report.[6] The workshop had a dual purpose. It was primarily a response to President Wolfensohn's request to the Nordic countries to help him build a case for the integration of human rights in the Bank's work. In addition, half a day was devoted to discussing the WDR 2006 outline and how the Report could better incorporate a human rights perspective. There were presentations from scholars working on the role of rights-based approaches to development, and development ethicists.

Particular issues on which participants sought to have influence were, first, what sort of evidence is relevant for asserting that equity matters and, second, whether the argument that equity does matter should be based on intrinsic or instrumental grounds. The following points (among a few others) are documented in the World Bank's own record of 'important comments' from the workshop.[7] First, as background, it was noted that 'The climate in the Bank with respect to the HR approach has changed; the current General Counsel thinks HR should be part of the Bank's discourse. This is a major change with respect to the past'. Second, on the intrinsic argument, it was noted that: 'We really ought to refer to the human rights approach when talking about why equity matters intrinsically. More than a hundred countries have ratified the various Human Rights covenants that sanctions economic, social, and political rights.' Third, as a comment on arguments presented that inequality matters instrumentally: 'We need to clarify instrumentally to what. Arguably the goal is poverty reduction (not growth per se), with poverty intended broadly. This links to [the] question of addressing WHY reducing inequalities, before addressing the WHAT to do and HOW TO DO IT questions.'

Three important issues raised at this workshop will form the main basis for the analysis in this chapter. The first is what empirical evidence is regarded as relevant for demonstrating that equity matters. The second is whether one adopts an intrinsic or an instrumental argument for why equity matters. The third is how the World Bank addresses human rights issues, both in this WDR and in the World Bank more generally. (Clearly, an intrinsic argument for equity is closely linked to a human rights approach.) These issues both exemplify the economic-technocratic nature of the Bank and give valuable insights into some aspects of the internal dynamics of development's regimes of truth and the dynamics that drive institutional knowledge processes, as well as the professional communities involved. The issues we address thus illustrate the context and social processes – both within and outside the Bank – that influence the form that the Report takes.

We may begin by briefly summarizing the structure and contents of the final published version of the WDR 2006.[8] It is divided into three parts: Part I considers the evidence on inequality of opportunity within and across countries; Part II asks why equity matters; and Part III addresses how public action can level the political and economic playing fields in both the domestic and international arenas. The Report demonstrates, convincingly and with a wealth of empirical data, that huge inequalities of opportunity exist in practice – both within and between countries. It addresses political issues more explicitly than has often been the case in WDRs and in World Bank reports more generally. The language is sometimes unusually strong for a WDR – referring to 'staggering inequalities' between countries and using the term 'elite capture' several times.

However, it also emphasizes continuity and consistency with previous reports and with World Bank policy in general. Thus, it links the overall argument for equity with the two pillars of Bank policy – 'opportunity' and 'empowerment' – set out in the *World Development Report 2000.* (There are two basic issues which repeatedly arise in WDRs and indeed in the work of the World Bank generally: 'equity versus growth' and 'state versus market'. In practice, the Bank's position on both tends to be ambivalent and formalized in these two 'pillars'.) Indeed, the 2006 publication clearly specifies: 'This is not intended as a new framework. It means integrating and extending existing frameworks: equity is central both to the investment environment and to the agenda of empowerment' (World Bank 2006: 3–4). Or, as Wolfowitz puts it in the Foreword:

> In my view, the evidence that equity and economic efficiency as well as growth are complementary in the long run helps to integrate the main two components of the World Bank's poverty reduction strategy ... This report shows that the two pillars are not independent from each other in supporting development, but instead are intricately linked with one another. (World Bank 2006: xi–xii)

In building the Report, Bank experts were, as discussed below, concerned with providing strong empirical evidence that equity matters. It is common for Bank staff to stress the importance not only of analytical rigour but also of reliable empirical 'evidence', with a preference for quantitative data. Empirical work, data and surveys in developing countries are strengths of the Bank, key characteristics of the identity of the institution as an 'expert bureaucracy' in development work, and also key elements of the way in which the Bank builds and sustains its legitimacy (St Clair 2006a). Yet, as critics have argued, such empirical evidence is based on the Bank's often privileged knowledge, or even results from social relations between those seeking to establish statistical data on client countries and the officials and actors providing it (Griffiths 2003; Harper 2000; Goldman 2005). In the following analysis, we begin with the issue of which evidence counts, before turning to the 'intrinsic versus instrumental' question and finally to human rights. In examining these issues we will pay particular attention to three significant phenomena: changes in the text over time – as the Report moves from outline, to draft, to final version; differences between the Report's summary overview and its longer main text; and incongruities within the text that are indicative of rewriting and compromise.[9] We shall give examples of each.[10]

First, regarding the relative merits of different types of empirical evidence, of particular relevance for our purpose is the debate on the significance attached to research from a relatively new branch of economics, namely 'experimental economics'. In brief, this involves testing human (economic) behaviour under 'laboratory' conditions – often with economics students as its 'guinea pigs'.[11] Even within the discipline there are those who criticize this method, or at least regard it as being as yet underdeveloped. Its attraction for economists is that it is seen as cutting-edge economic research. There was debate within the team (see below) as to how much weight should be attached to such evidence. At the public consultation in Dakar, Senegal, in January 2005, McNeill criticized this type of argument. As recorded on the World Bank website, he argued that 'on the intrinsic argument, the best literature to draw from may not be the behavioural economics literature. Other disciplines have been saying these things for a long time'. McNeill also made direct contact by email with the team, strongly arguing that experimental economics evidence should not be given a dominant place in the argument as to why equity matters. At one stage it appeared that findings from experimental economics would be given considerable weight, but in the final version of the Report this was in fact adduced as only one of several forms of evidence, along with reference to 'religions from Islam to Buddhism and secular philosophical traditions from Plato to Sen' (for more details, see World Bank 2006: 76).

The second, even more revealing question is whether the case for equity in development is made on intrinsic or instrumental grounds. This issue was raised at an early stage in the report process, at the workshop in Oslo (see above), and was taken up again at later stages. Although the World Bank staff generally appeared to favour an instrumental argument, it seems that the issue was still not fully resolved in the final version, and the persistence of differing views on this matter is evident both in incoherence in the Report, and in variation between the overview and the main text.

Bank experts relate first and foremost to economists, and need to position the notion of equity within the dominant rationality of economics and market relations. This favours an instrumental view (see McNeill 2003 on social capital and Sridhar 2007 on nutrition). But the notion of equity is ambivalent, having, as it does, an undeniable intrinsic meaning – as fairness and as a determinant of justice. For those involved in producing this WDR, it was impossible to avoid references to equity as an intrinsic value. Arguably, the Report is marked throughout by equivocation between the two meanings of the term 'equity'. The balance of arguments seems to be determined by the obvious tensions between the scientific rationale of economics and the cognitive premises of ethical (or intrinsic) values and arguments. It illustrates the difficulties that Bank experts have when stepping outside mere economic argumentation, including a fear of moving into a territory where the Bank may not have the best expertise.

Here it is instructive to distinguish between the main text of the Report and the overview. The draft Report is written by its main authors, with the support of their team, but it has to be approved by the Chief Economist and the President, and 'signed off' by the Executive Board. In the process it is likely to be modified and, if controversial, glossed. It is not unusual that, in such processes, more attention is focused on the executive summary, or overview, than on the much lengthier main text. Disagreements are therefore revealed both by incoherence in the main text, and by variations in emphasis, or even substance, between the main text and the overview. Examples of both can be found.

The relevant section of the Report is Part II: 'Why Equity Matters'. (It is significant to note that the title of this Part was changed during the process of consultations from 'Does Inequality Matter?', a title that led to a storm of protests from commentators, largely non-governmental organizations (NGOs).)[12] This contains very few explicit references to the word 'intrinsic'. It does, however, state that 'To the philosophical and legal arguments for equity … we add a final argument [the instrumental]' (World Bank 2006: 84). This wording seems to imply that the authors primarily emphasize intrinsic arguments, but a very different impression is given in the overview. Here, it is primarily instrumental arguments for equity that are emphasized. The intrinsic argument is mentioned, but is not predominant. For example: 'So a portion of the economic and political inequalities we observe around the world is attributable to unequal opportunities. This inequality is objectionable on both intrinsic and instrumental grounds. It contributes to economic inefficiency, political conflict, and institutional frailty' (World Bank 2006: 9). The latter argument ('It contributes to …') is, of course, purely instrumental. The issue is also addressed in Chapter 10 of the Report, which provides a good example of how the pursuit of compromise can lead to merely vacuous statements such as: 'Greater global equity is desirable for itself to all those who find equity intrinsically valuable'(World Bank 2006: 206).

In summary, the Report argues for equity on both intrinsic and instrumental grounds. In the main text, the former is more heavily emphasized; in the overview (subject to strict approval at the highest level) the instrumental argument predominates.[13] This predominance of instrumental argumentation can be seen as a way to avoid stepping into the territory of human rights-based analysis, an arena which the Bank has been reluctant to enter, under the presumption that this conflicts with its 'apolitical' mandate. It is to this issue that we now turn.

A month after the Oslo workshop, on 15 November 2004, Asun Lera St Clair was invited to present a summary of its main points at a consultation at the Bank headquarters. This was organized jointly by the World Bank's Social Development Department, the WDR 2006 team, and the U.K. Department for International Development (DFID) to discuss several background papers prepared for the WDR 2006 (with DFID and World Bank funding). Presenting the recommendations from Oslo, St Clair argued that here was a clear opportunity to bring human rights issues into the WDR 2006. Rather than avoiding the issue, a Bank report on equity could emphasize the need to combine policies for economic efficiency and social equality using historical and empirical examples, such as Scandinavian countries, where this approach had led to growth and low levels of poverty. St Clair gave examples discussed in the Oslo workshop, in which human rights approaches to education and health, or rights in relation to access to justice, were consistent with other ideas and proposals flowing from the Bank's work and with the notion of equity argued for in the WDR. However, her presentation warned of a possible depoliticization of human rights and the seemingly equivocal meaning of equity in the WDR draft, and of the likely tradeoffs between intrinsic and instrumental values. One of the conclusions of the Oslo workshop was that human rights should not be addressed by the Bank unless this was done well and in a way that was consistent with other UN agencies and their rights-based work; as a challenge for Bank experts to question the 'why' of development assistance, rather than only as a value-added issue.

In the sometimes heated discussion that followed, some argued vehemently that it was not the role of the Bank to address questions of human rights. Although this view is often based on an interpretation of the Bank's mandate (see below), the major concern appeared to derive from discomfort with the 'intrinsic' argument for equity, which does not fit well with the dominant economic perspective. One of the key cognitive values of economics is the notion of a tradeoff – whether in seeking to understand people's behaviour or to advise on policies. This leads to serious incompatibilities with the ethical argument for equity as an intrinsic value grounded in human dignity (whether having religious or secular foundations). By definition, anything that is intrinsic is non-tradable. As Amartya Sen and Thomas Pogge rightly argue, human rights ought to be seen as moral as well as legal issues. The moral ground of human rights is the equal moral worth of all human beings regardless of age, sex, country of origin, ethnicity, etc. (Sen 2005; Pogge 2007)

This intrinsic argument for equity is very different from the instrumental argument about equity as enhancing the efficiency or effectiveness of development programmes. It is difficult for economists to include intrinsic values in their analyses. The remedy is not necessarily a new economics (though some would certainly favour this), but to recognize the limitations of economics in this regard and also to draw on the cognitive and analytical tools of other disciplines (for example, ethics, but also other social sciences) in promoting development and poverty reduction. The problem, then, lies in the professional self-identity of the Bank staff and the expertise-based power derived from economics.

The draft outline WDR (July 2004) made clear reference to the links between an intrinsic meaning of equity and the role that human rights and rights-based approaches to issues such as health and education can play in actually moving towards equitable societies. In the section 'Towards equity in assets, incomes and agency', the outline states:

> In some of these areas, such as basic education and health, rights-based approaches may be valuable ways of achieving greater equity. The report would explore empirical evidence on whether such explicit pursuit of economic and social rights is effective in achieving improvements in well-being of poorer groups in these dimensions (see Drèze 2004 for an argument that such approaches can be useful in mobilizing public action in the cases of education and basic food in India). (WDR July 2004 outline: 18)

However, the final version of the WDR does not argue for such a link. Human rights references are tangential to the central points and are used simply to argue that an intrinsic meaning of equity is consistent with human rights covenants (see World Bank 2006: 7). In general, the WDR is very cautious in referring to moral arguments. For example:

> The international human rights regime testifies to the shared belief that all should have equal rights and be spared extreme deprivation. Some *even* argue that there is a powerful moral case for rich countries to take action, because of the huge disparities and *(arguably)* because they partly created and perpetuate global inequities. (World Bank 2006: 206, emphasis added).

In summary, the final version of this WDR (2006) reveals some of the tensions and limitations of a primarily economic analysis of equity and development.[14] This is due not only to the topic itself, but also to the particular set of circumstances at the Bank at the time of the production of the WDR, and the social relations between experts and bureaucrats and among various sections and departments in the Bank, as well as relations with others outside the Bank. It is to these that we now return.

The Authors and the Audience

Processes of knowledge production require audiences that legitimize their knowledge outputs. This is a common characteristic of all types of expertise, which always depends on the relations between cognitive authority and audiences (Turner 2004). The knowledge claims of experts cannot be legitimized simply by the fact that their audience recognizes that they are indeed expert. There are different types of audiences and legitimizing processes, and also different kinds of dynamics that may lead to very different relations between experts and the sources of legitimacy of their expertise. One of the main reasons that World Bank knowledge cannot be said to be 'objective, solid science' is because of the ways in which the Bank's documents build legitimacy and credibility (St Clair 2006a, 2006b). This process deserves close scrutiny. With the WDRs it starts with the choice of topic and authors. The 2006 Report was the first WDR under the direction of the new Senior Vice-President and Chief Economist Francois Bourguignon. It began under the presidency of James Wolfensohn, but was written largely under the presidency of Paul Wolfowitz (from June 2005). The Report was co-directed by Francisco H.G. Ferreira and Michael Walton, two economists well regarded in the Bank who had already collaborated on a report entitled *Inequality in Latin America and the Caribbean: Breaking with History?*, released in 2003, which was by Bank standards rather radical (Ferranti et al. 2004).

The team was, like most WDRs, entirely dominated by economists. In addition to Walton and Ferreira, all but two of the fourteen other core team members were economists. There were five advisors, four of them economists trained and currently employed in U.S.A. or the U.K.[15] The only non-economist was Arjun Appadurai, a professor of anthropology at the New School, New York, but he excluded himself from the task at an early stage due to other pressing commitments.

Responsibility for the WDR is located in the Development Economics Vice-Presidency (DEC). The DEC is now the largest development research body in the world and is entirely dominated by economists.[16] In an insightful article, Broad analyses in detail the mechanisms by which the DEC produces research that is biased towards the neoliberal paradigm, showing how 'research that has "resonance" with the paradigm is elevated and dissonant research is discouraged' (Broad 2006: 412).[17] Various other departments have an interest and an input into the WDR, depending on the topic (see below).

For whom is the Report written? In order to understand the WDRs – indeed, any such document – it is necessary to ask who the authors consider to be their audience and whose judgment they think matters. We may distinguish several audiences. Colleagues within the Bank are one important influence. Those who prepare the Report, even if they are not long-term Bank staff, have often absorbed the Bank 'culture'. They are accustomed to (often critical) peer review from colleagues and especially from fellow economists. They therefore need to show that the Report is rigorous, according to the criteria of that discipline. But this audience also serves to ensure consistency with other well-established views and general trends in the organization. If a Bank report does not satisfy key audiences within the Bank or its sister organizations, it would not have sufficient legitimacy. To varying extents, the authors also want to impress, or at least protect against criticism from, academic economists outside the Bank. They can do this by ensuring that their arguments are rigorous (even if doubts remain as to the accuracy of the data used) and by demonstrating their knowledge of new ideas within the discipline; that is, being at the research frontier. In this regard, the judgement of their work by advisers, for example, Angus Deaton, President of the American Economic Association, would carry considerable weight.

It is often stated that ministers of finance in developing countries are the target audience of the WDR. The implication is that the document is aimed primarily at governments in poor countries (the 'clients' of the World Bank) and especially at those who have both the power and the technical competence to make use of the Report. Such people are, of course, also politicians, but the implication is that they too will be convinced by sound economic arguments.[18] Another audience is constituted by the Report's outside commentators and critics: especially, since the late 1990s, NGOs, politicians on both the right and the left, and the media.[19] Most NGOs regard the Bank as a haven for neoliberals and Republicans, while the *Economist* magazine sometimes portrays the Bank as alarmingly socialist. It is, however, the NGOs that are usually the most detailed and outspoken in their criticism, and the Bank tries not to provoke this quite influential audience more than is necessary.

The Report must be approved by the President and 'signed off' by the Executive Board, who, in this sense, form the most important audience and should be placed at the top of the list. The President is likely to be particularly concerned about the main message of the Report and hence with the wording of the executive summary. The views of individual member countries may range from objections to the very fact that an issue (such as equity) is addressed at all to objections about specific 'boxes' or empirical examples in the Report which reflect badly on them. As already noted, these pressures can lead to real modifications in the Report as a whole, but may remain unresolved, leading to incongruities or inconsistencies in argument or to noticeable differences between the executive summary and the full text. In addition to these various audiences, there are others who may have some influence on the process and product, including bilateral donors (see below) and, depending on the topic, other departments of the Bank. In the case of the WDR 2006, the Social Development Department (SDD) and the Legal Department deserve particular mention.

The SDD has a weak position in the Bank. As Mosse argues in this volume, noneconomist social scientists in the Bank (note the significance of this standard Bank terminology) are 'a marginal group'. They occupy a threatened professional space and are seen as contributing little in practical terms. The number of such social scientists in the Bank has increased (Miller-Adams 2003).[20] However, Mosse argues in Chapter 4 of this volume that with this has come a change in their role, from criticizing to promoting what might be called a 'technocratic' application of their expertise. They are faced with a twin dilemma: whether to be 'critical' or 'constructive'; and whether to couch their expertise in the language of the dominant discipline of economics. Our experience in witnessing the process of building the WDR 2006 is an illustration of Mosse's claim that non-economist social scientists are preoccupied with protecting their own cognitive space, while having little power. To quote Mosse (2006): 'they make the organization work better without changing what it does, even contributing to the unreliable notion that the organization is knowledge-led'.

The topic chosen for the WDR 2006 provided the SDD with a good opportunity to become involved, but they felt the need to proceed with caution. At the seminar in November 2004, St Clair experienced resistance both from the SDD and DFID researchers, which she understood to be motivated by concerns that pushing the human rights issues too hard would have negative consequences for the text (which might actually be weakened) and/or for the department and the staff promoting the issue (which might be criticized for overstepping their boundaries).[21]

The Legal Department was important because of the particular interests of Wolfensohn and the Chief General Counsel, Roberto Dañino. In the past, the Bank had had a cautious and rather unclear policy regarding the role of human rights in the organization's work. Traditionally, the Bank interpreted its Articles of Agreement in narrow economic terms. In the early 1990s, when 'good governance' came on the agenda, the then General Counsel, Ibrahim Shihata, reinterpreted this mandate somewhat more widely, allowing for some inclusion of 'political' issues. He retired in 1998 and no significant changes were made under the acting General Counsels who served until Dañino, former Prime Minister of Peru, was appointed in 2003 and adopted a more proactive role with regard to human rights than his predecessors. Wolfensohn had indicated interest in further work on these issues (and had taken up the matter with the Nordic member of the Executive Board – see above) and Dañino was actively involved. In recent years, the Legal Department has not restricted itself to dealing with contracts and advising on the legal aspects of projects and policies; it has engaged in law as a 'sector', supporting projects concerned with improving the operation of courts and has addressed issues in connection with human rights, and has more recently supported research on access to justice. Among Dañino's initiatives was a new interpretation of the Bank's Articles of Agreement. He argued that there is no reason why the Bank should not demand from its clients respect for human rights; however, he fell short of committing the Bank as an institution to be subject to human rights law, because human rights law, he claimed, applies to countries rather than to multilateral institutions.[22]

In December 2005, the Legal Department organized its annual Legal Forum around the WDR 2006, under the title: 'Law, Equity and Development'. One of the papers presented was McNeill's 'Equity and Development: Is There a Place for Ethics?'. This led to a lively discussion about the role of ethics in the work of the Bank, which revealed that human rights were mostly viewed by participants as legal norms. More important was the presentation by Roberto Dañino, who for the first time set out his legal opinion on the role that the Bank has in following human rights norms.[23] This event, and the Counsel's opinion, were an important indication of Dañino's commitment to the issue. But Paul Wolfowitz, who took over as President of the Bank in mid 2005, showed limited enthusiasm for this agenda, and Dañino left the Bank in January 2006, to be replaced by Ana Palacio, former Foreign Minister of Spain and a good friend of Wolfowitz.[24] At the time of writing, the future direction of human rights thinking in the Bank is not clear. Although the Legal Department has been active in promoting the role of legal mechanisms in empowering the poor, access to justice and legal reform, we see no signs of the Bank drawing on the ethical dimension of human rights as guidance for knowledge and action, nor a serious attempt to tackle the role of socioeconomic rights in bringing about development and reducing poverty or addressing the likely incompatibilities between rights-based views and neoliberal open market policies. As we have argued elsewhere, the technocratic and bureaucratic expert knowledge of multilateral organizations creates a sort of 'social distance' from the realities of the poor, as well as a way to shift or avoid responsibility for a full integration of rights questions into their mainstream economic work (McNeill and St Clair 2006). As former Senior Advisor on Human Rights Alfredo Sfeir-Younis stated, it is crucial to address the role that economics and, in particular, economic values play in restraining the Bank from engaging more openly in human rights issues. It is impossible, he argued, to view economic issues, rights and the operationalization of policies as separate matters; what weave them together are precisely underlying values, and a focus on values is the most important way to mainstream human rights into economic development (Sfeir-Younis 2003: 3). The reconciliation between economic and human rights issues needs to occur at an institutional level. This, however, requires the existence of a powerful legitimizing audience for these value-related issues. But such an audience is not yet strong enough, even on the donor side, to which we now turn.

Aside from NGOs, a limited number of donor countries are perhaps the strongest group promoting human rights and value-based reflection in the Bank (although their efforts may be counteracted by other member countries). In addition to being represented on the Board, donor countries also have some power to influence the processes of building knowledge in the Bank through the provision of additional resources. In preparing WDRs and more generally, the Bank may obtain technical and financial assistance from bilateral development agencies through trust funds. And the bilaterals may be eager to provide this, especially where they feel they can influence the Bank in the promotion of issues they regard as important.[25] In the case of the WDR 2006, UK (DFID) financed a number of background papers prepared in collaboration with the SDD (a workshop on empowerment, 'Power, Rights and Poverty Reduction', also sponsored by the DFID, and referred to by Mosse in Chapter 4, was used as background material in the Oslo workshop, which was itself a means for the Nordic countries to help former President Wolfensohn push for a human rights debate in the Bank). Such influence is channelled through particular social relations. Often donor countries favour or insist upon their own nationals for staff positions at the Bank, and they establish close relations with their own compatriots or with particular staff members. Donor countries' political agendas and the themes they wish to promote also lead to a tendency to work with particular departments. In the case of Norway and the WDR 2006, relations were closer to the SDD than to the DEC.

In preparing the WDR 2006, the varying interests and perspectives of different actors – the SDD and the Legal Department, the DFID and researchers sponsored by the DFID and Norway – created tensions that were evident in the debates over how to build a case for equity. Economists from the DEC, for example, were not accustomed to engaging with lawyers as peers in this type of debate. In the end, however, our analysis suggests that the influence of the donor-led agenda had little impact and did not lead to the fundamental changes in processes of knowledge production needed for the integration of human rights in the analysis. In any event, it is clear that the social relations between these various actors affect the way in which arguments are built, global ideas are framed and decisions are taken. And these social relations also affect us, as researchers working together with the Norwegian government.

Observant Participation

Our knowledge of the WDR 2006, on which the observations in this chapter are based, and indeed our knowledge about earlier WDRs, has been obtained in part because of the access we have had as a result of our advisory work for the Norwegian government. Our own social position vis à vis the object and actors of our study raises both ethical and methodological issues. The ethical question is whether we have abused our position vis à vis either the Norwegian government or those in the World Bank with whom we have interacted. There are two methodological questions: one is whether our interpretation is biased by our 'insider' position; and the other is whether we have ourselves influenced the situation we are trying to understand. What is clear is that had it not been for role as researchers with a close relationship with the Norwegian Ministry of Foreign Affairs, the opportunity to participate so actively (and possibly even exert influence) would not have occurred.

In brief, our response is as follows. On the ethical question of whether we have somehow abused a position of confidence, our response is that we have been open about our role, attending meetings, workshops, conferences, etc. as researchers. As regards our use of the information thus obtained, we have avoided direct quotation and have not revealed our sources. Indeed, we have perhaps erred on the side of caution here. If we had operated as independent researchers, we could very likely have obtained and made more use of direct quotations which would have strengthened the credibility of our claims.

Regarding the methodological issue, as partial 'insiders' we are certainly not unbiased, but then no commentator can be, and we believe that our position has allowed us to see what someone further removed could not (for example, we participated in some of the meetings, rather than relying on other people's accounts of them). Whether this gives us a more 'correct' or 'true' understanding of events is for others to judge, but our views are not thereby invalidated. On the second methodological issue, we have reason to believe that we had some minor influence on the process of producing the WDR 2006. It would, however, be foolish to exaggerate our importance here. Although our involvement might have marginally modified the final version of the Report, it was certainly surely not sufficient to change the conclusions that we have drawn in this chapter regarding the forces that shaped the production of the Report.

Conclusion

It is only a slight exaggeration to say that the WDR is written by economists for economists. This creates a situation which both constrains and, by a circular process of self-reinforcement, validates the outcome. Critical comments by noneconomists, mainly outside the Bank, to some extent counter this tendency; however, there are also factors which reinforce it, for example, the fact noted above that an increasing number of ministers of finance in developing countries are economists trained in the same tradition as Bank staff, and are thus part of this self-reinforcing process in which the audience is itself shaped by the organization.

For professionals in development agencies, many types of expertise may, in principle, be of relevance, but (not only in the Bank) economics is certainly the most influential, both with regard to the macro (national policy) and microlevel (project assessment). Even if not necessarily neoliberal, mainstream economics exerts a powerful disciplining force, and it combines very effectively with the bureaucratic imperative to 'operationalize' the contributions of researchers, thus creating a powerful economic/technocratic nexus, the cognitive values of economics fitting very well the values of policy-making (Bøås and McNeill 2003; St Clair 2006b). Bank experts' understanding of the relationship between ethics and their work relates largely if not exclusively to the values associated with their professionalism: that is, objectivity, technical excellence and operational relevance. When asked who are the ultimate 'beneficiaries' of their work, staff tend to respond that they are the Bank's clients – whether seen as governments or the people themselves. As 'experts', they seek to satisfy the academic community of economists, but as Bank staff they are required to produce policy-oriented work that fits the institutional demands of that organization.

The decision by the new Chief Economist to choose 'equity' as the topic for his first WDR may be characterized as brave or perhaps foolhardy. By contrast with, for example, 'Infrastructure', this topic is clearly a challenge to the organization and to the discipline of economics which dominates it. The Report therefore provides a revealing case study. Our examination of the process and product demonstrates, we suggest, the power of (mainstream) economics in the Bank. It shows how economic expertise is a key element in maintaining the legitimacy of the organization and in determining what the Bank says and does at the same time as it constrains and even censors effective and coherent analysis. But clearly it is not 'economics' as such which has this power; what shapes the thoughts and words of the authors of the WDR is a complex set of social relations between people inside and outside the Bank. It is these that we have sought to analyse, with the benefit of our privileged knowledge of this case.

Notes

1. An earlier version of this chapter was presented at SOAS, 9 January 2008. We thank David Mosse and the audience for valuable comments.
2. We are very grateful to the Research Council of Norway for funding this research.
3. Under President Wolfensohn it laid claims to being 'the knowledge Bank' and set up the Global Development Network (Stone and Maxwell 2004).
4. For a useful analysis of WDRs over the years, see Mawdsley and Rigg 2003.
5. The Human Development Report, produced annually by the UNDP, is often seen as its major rival for international attention.
6. McNeill's first involvement was in fact his attendance at a meeting in Oslo in summer 2004, at which the initial outline of the Report was presented in the Ministry of Foreign Affairs.

7. The outline of the Report was completed in mid 2004 and the draft of the Report in March 2005. Numerous consultations were held during the preparation of the WDR 2006, as recorded by the World Bank on their website: http://econ.worldbank.org/ WBSITE/EXTERNAL/EXTDEC/EXTRESEARCH/EXTWDRS/EXTWDR2006/0,,conten tMDK:20232854~menuPK:477653~pagePK:64167689~piPK:64167673~theSitePK:477642,0 0.html. Retrieved 20 November 2007.

8. This section draws heavily on a paper presented at the World Bank Legal Forum in December 2006 and subsequently published by the World Bank (McNeill 2007).

9. Sometimes, changes in the structure of the Report may also reveal tensions between differing positions. In 2000/2001 there was much debate about the order in which chapters were presented – apparently of sufficient importance for this to be a factor in the resignation of the author (Sindzingre 2003).

10. The very definition of the term 'equity', which was adopted in the report at an early stage, represents a compromise, although not necessarily an incoherent position. The Report states that 'By equity we mean that individuals should have equal opportunities to pursue a life of their choosing and be spared from extreme deprivation in outcomes' (p. 2) This is a concept of equity as 'equal opportunity', but not irrespective of the final outcome.

11. The *Journal of Experimental Economics*, established as recently as 1998, states that it: 'uses experimental methods to evaluate theoretical predictions of economic behaviour'. The WDR 2006 refers to several works by Ernst Fehr at the University of Zurich, the Institute for Empirical Research in Economics and games such as the Ultimatum Game and the Repeated Public Good Game with Punishment. One of the works cited, 'The Nature of Human Altruism' (Fehr and Fischbacher 2003), provides details on how such experiments are carried out: 'the subjects were students from the University of Zurich and the Federal Institute of Technology of Zurich'; 'subjects receive a show-up fee of CF 10 (cUS$8) in all experiments'; 'Player A had an endowment of 100 points and could transfer 0, 10, 20, 30, 40 or 50 to Player B who had no endowment. The third party, Player C, was endowed with 50 points, and had the option of punishing player A after observing A's transfer to B.'

12. An online discussion of the Report's outline, available in French, English and Spanish, was held from 12 October to 19 November 2004. The discussion on this point was summarized as follows:
1. Should this WDR address intrinsic reasons why people care about various inequalities, or restrict its attention to instrumental reasons, such as their effect on the growth elasticity of poverty reduction?
Participants indicated that inequalities matter both because they violate basic human rights and because they hinder growth and poverty reduction and agreed that the WDR should address both reasons.

13. In the outline of the Report, produced at an earlier stage, these two are given equal weight: 'Inequalities of opportunities or of outcomes may matter for both intrinsic and instrumental reasons' (p. 10).

14. In a review essay, Roemer (2006), usually quite a critical commentator, commends the WDR: 'The Report marks a major step forward in the discussion of poverty and development. Economists have, far too frequently, lauded themselves on their discipline's being "value free" and eschewed any justice talk in favor of efficiency talk. This is, I believe, a mistake, and the publication in question makes a strong case against that narrow view.' We suggest, however, that the step taken by the Bank could have been a much bigger 'leap'.

15. Of these, two (Sir Tony Atkinson at Oxford and Angus Deaton, now President of the American Economic Association, at Princeton) are very highly reputed academic economists; one (Martin Ravallion) is among the most senior research economists in the Bank (currently Director of the Development Research Group); and one (Naila Kabeer) is a professor at the Institute of Development Studies, Sussex, and describes herself as a social economist.

16. The DEC 'seeks to increase understanding of development policies and programs by providing intellectual leadership and analytical services to the Bank and the development community': http://econ.worldbank.org/WBSITE/EXTERNAL/EXTDEC/0,,content MDK:20279993~menuPK:477172~pagePK:64165401~piPK:64165026~theSitePK:469372,00. html. Retrieved 8 February 2008.

17. The article does not deal explicitly with the WDR, but gives clear evidence, based on numerous interviews, of the processes by which dissonant voices are silenced – being characterized as 'idiosyncratic', 'iconoclastic' or 'disaffected' (p. 407). Ellerman, one of the few internal critics, is quoted as referring to pressures for 'bureaucratic conformity' from the 'thought police to the black sheep in the organization who are 'not on message' (p. 407; cf. Wilks 2004: 2–3). Stern, former Chief Economist, expresses the situation in the DEC more cautiously: 'there is the strong hierarchy and an atmosphere much more deferential than would be found in universities' (Stern 1997: 594).

18. An increasingly high proportion of such ministers were trained in economics in the U.S.A. or the U.K., and/or attended short courses organized by the World Bank Institute.

19. As already noted, it has become regular practice that a draft of the Report is made available to a wider audience for comment during the course of its preparation. For the 2000/1 Report this was a very major exercise, with posting on the Internet and considerable interaction with NGOs and other commentators. Perhaps because of the problems that arose with the WDR 2000/1, a rather less demanding approach has been followed subsequently.

20. There are also political scientists among Bank staff, but usually with close links to economics (rational choice theory, new institutional economics, etc., as was evident in the 1990s debate about 'structural adjustment and good governance'). In this regard, it is interesting that in their sources of evidence for equity, the WDR 2006 editorial team never sought to make links with social democratic theories and traditions in Scandinavia, such as the work of Stein Rokkan or more recently Stein Kuhnle (Kuhnle, Hatland and Hort 2003).

21. When what are seen as radical ideas are promoted in an organization such as the World Bank, it is a matter of fine judgement as to how much one can 'get away with'. The resulting self-censorship can be as effective as, and in some ways more pernicious than, censorship by others.

22. With regard to the Bank's human rights agenda, interest and support from at least some of the Nordic countries, notably Norway and Denmark, has been maintained. The most significant outcome was a planned human rights trust fund. However, some Board members were sceptical about such a fund and the planned signing was long delayed. Attempts to resolve the problem by finding a less controversial name proved difficult: neither 'the rule of law trust fund' nor 'the legal empowerment trust fund' were considered to be suitable. The final solution was a masterly compromise: it was to be called simply 'the Trust Fund'!

23. See http://www1.worldbank.org/devoutreach/october06/article.asp?id=386 and also http://web.worldbank.org/WBSITE/EXTERNAL/EXTSITETOOLS/0,,contentMDK:207 49693~pagePK:98400~piPK:98424~theSitePK:95474,00.html.

24. Ana Palacio resigned in 2008 and was replaced in December that year by a French lawyer and former judge, Anne-Marie Leroy.

25. For several years, until 2008, McNeill chaired the Reference Group for the TFESSD, a trust fund supported by Finland and Norway that 'provides grant resources for World Bank activities aimed at mainstreaming the environmental, social and poverty reducing dimensions of sustainable development into Bank work'. See: http://web.world bank.org/WBSITE/EXTERNAL/EXTABOUTUS/ORGANIZATION/EXTSDNETWORK /EXTUNITFESSD/0,,contentMDK:20639137~pagePK:64168427~piPK:64168435~theSiteP K:1633788,00.html.

References

Bebbington, A. et al. (eds). 2005. *The Search for Empowerment: Social Capital as Idea and Practice at the World Bank*. Bloomfield, C.T.: Kumarian Press.

Bøås, M. and D. McNeill (eds). 2003. *Global Institutions and Development: Framing the World*. London: Routledge.

Broad, B. 2006. 'Research, Knowledge, and the Art of "Paradigm Maintenance": The World Bank's Development Economics Vice-Presidency (DEC)', *Review of International Political Economy* 13(3): 387–419.

Douglas, M. 1986. *How Institutions Think*. Syracuse, N.Y.: Syracuse University Press.

Fehr, E. and U. Fischbacher. 2003. 'The Nature of Human Altruism', *Nature* 425 (October): 785–91.

Fehr, E. and U. Fischbacher. 2004. 'Third-party Punishment and Social Norms', *Evolution and Human Behavior* 25: 63–87.

de Ferranti, D., et al. 2004. *Inequality in Latin America: Breaking with History? World Bank Latin American and Caribbean Studies* 28989. Washington, D.C.: World Bank.

Fleck, L. 1935. *The Genesis and Development of a Scientific Fact*. Translation 1997. University of Chicago Press. Chicago. Fortes, Meyer (ed.) Quoted in Douglas 1986.

Goldman, M. 2005. *Imperial Nature: The World Bank and Struggles for Social Justice in the Age of Globalization*. New Haven, C.T.: Yale University Press.

Griffiths, P. 2003. *The Economist's Tale: A Consultant Encounters Hunger and the World Bank*. London: Zed Books.

Harper, R. 2000. 'The Social Organization of the IMF's Mission Work: An Examination of International Auditing', in M. Strathern (ed.), *Audit Cultures: Anthropological Studies in Accountability, Ethics and the Academy*. London: Routledge, pp. 21–53.

Kuhnle, S., A. Hatland and S. Hort. 2003. 'A Work-Friendly Welfare State: Lessons from Europe', in K. Marshall and O. Butzbach (eds), *New Social Policy Agendas for Europe and Asia*. Washington, D.C.: World Bank.

Mallaby, S. 2004. *The World's Banker: A Story of Failed States, Financial Crises, and the Wealth and Poverty of Nations*, New York: Penguin.

Mawdsley, E. and J. Rigg. 2002. 'A Survey of the World Development Reports I: Discursive Strategies', *Progress in Development Studies* 2(2): 93–111.

———. 2003. 'The World Development Report II: Continuity and Change in Development Orthodoxies', *Progress in Development Studies* 3(4): 271–86.

McNeill, D. 2005. 'Power and Ideas: Economics and Global Development Policy', in D. Stone and S. Maxwell (eds), *The Challenge of Transnational Knowledge Networks: Bridging Research and Policy in a Globalising World*. New York and London: Routledge.

———. 2007. 'Equity and Development: Is There a Place for Ethics?', in C. Sage and M. Woolcock (eds), *The World Bank Legal Review: Law, Equity, and Development Volume 2*. Dordrecht: Martinus Nijhoff Publishers.

McNeill, D. and A.L. St Clair. 2006. 'Development Ethics and Human Rights as the Basis for Global Poverty Reduction: The Case of the World Bank', in D. Stone and C. Wright (eds), *The World Bank and Governance: A Decade of Reform and Reaction*. New York and London: Routledge.

Miller-Adams, M. 2003. *The World Bank: New Agendas in a Changing World*. London: Routledge.

Mosse, D. 2006. Localised Cosmopolitans: Anthropologists at the World Bank. Paper for 'Cosmopolitans and Devlopment' panel. Association of Social Anthropologists Conference. 10–13 April, Keel University, U.K..

Pogge, T. 2007. *World Poverty and Human Rights*, 2nd ed. London: Polity Press.

Roemer, J. 2006. 'The 2006 World Development Report: Equity and Development', *Journal of Economic Inequality* 4: 233–44.

Sen, A.K. 2005. 'Human Rights and Capabilities', *Journal of Human Development* 6(2): 151–66.

Sfeir-Younis, A. 2003. 'Human Rights and Economic Development: Can They Be Reconciled? A View from the World Bank', in W. Van Genugten, P. Hunt and S. Matthews (eds), *The World Bank, IMF and Human Rights*. Nijmegen, The Netherlands: Wolf Legal Publishers.

Sindzigre, A. 2003. 'The Evolution of the Concept of Poverty in Multilateral Financial Institutions: the Case of the World Bank', in M. Boas and D. McNeill (eds.) *Global Institutions and Development: Framing the World*. London, Routledge, pp. 164–177.

Sridhar, D. 2007. 'Economic Ideology and Politics in the World Bank: Defining Hunger', *New Political Economy* 12(4): 499–516.

St Clair, A.L. 2006a. 'The World Bank as a Transnational Expertised Institution', *Journal of Global Governance* 12(1): 77–95.

———. 2006b. 'Global Poverty: The Co-Production of Knowledge and Politics', *Journal of Global Social Policy* 6(1): 57–77.

Stern, N and F. Ferreira, 1997. "The World Bank as 'Intellectual Actor'," in *The World Bank: Its First Half Century*. Washington, D.C., Brookings Institution.

Stone, D. and S. Maxwell. 2004. *Global Knowledge Networks and International Development: Bridges Across Boundaries*. London: Routledge.

Stone, D. and C. Wright (eds). 2006. *The World Bank and Governance: A Decade of Reform and Reaction*. London: Routledge.

Summer, A. 2004. 'Epistemology and "Evidence" in Development Studies: A Review of Dollar and Kray', *Third World Quarterly* 25(6): 1167–77.

Turner, S. 2004. *Liberal Democracy 3.0*. London: Sage.

Wade, R.H. 1996. 'Japan, the World Bank, and the Art of Paradigm Maintenance: The East Asian Miracle in Perspective', *New Left Review* 217: 3–36.

———. 2002. 'US Hegemony and the World Bank: The Fight over People and Ideas', *Review of International Political Economy* 9(2): 215–43.

———. 2004. 'On the Causes of Increasing World Poverty and Inequality, or Why the Matthew Effect Prevails', *New Political Economy* 9(2): 163–88.

Wilks, A. 2004. *The World Bank's knowledge roles: dominating development debates*, Bretton Woods Project, Bretton Woods Update No.40—May/June 2004. 28 May 2004.

Woods, N. 2006. *The Globalizers: The IMF, the World Bank, and Their Borrowers*. Ithaca, N.Y.: Cornell University Press.

World Bank. 2006. *World Development Report 2006: Equity and Development*. New York: Oxford University Press.

Chapter 6

WORLD HEALTH AND NEPAL

Producing Internationals, Healthy Citizenship and the Cosmopolitan[1]

Ian Harper

Introduction

In this chapter I consider two groups of professional health workers and draw links to the creation and circulation of authoritative knowledge. Both these groups, namely, expert foreign development advisers informing the directions of Nepal's health development processes, and locally-trained health workers who aspire to work in more 'developed' countries, have global imaginings and movement. I will use the idea of cosmopolitanism, space and place as a frame to tentatively start thinking through the conditions and circulation of people and knowledge in what might be broadly described as the field of 'world health'. I aim to juxtapose these two different – yet intersecting – sets of professionals to see how this sheds light on the political economy of knowledge production and circulation. My intention is not to look at the content of the knowledge per se (as in specific programmes like maternal child health or tuberculosis control), but rather to focus on aspects of sociopolitical conditions and relations within domains that are usually kept analytically separate.

I undertake this exercise with a sense of unease. As Mosse points out in Chapter 1 of this volume, stepping outside of the analysis of content to reflect on form or relationships can invoke anger and resentment from insiders. It can be construed as arrogant. It certainly raises the spectre of ethics, questions our allegiances and challenges the boundaries of the ethnographic project itself (Mosse 2006). I reflect from the margins of my own research, driven by a will to constantly question and analyse situations in new ways. This might be validated by the discipline of anthropology but it still makes me uncomfortable. In part this is because I am unable to overcome a sense that I am infringing boundaries, but it is also because the exercise is a form of brutal self-reflection. I too am an element of the development machinery, live comfortably when in Kathmandu; I am granted – and at times invoke – the label of expert, yet retreat to private spaces to escape the labyrinthine complexity of policy, its politics and practice. Lines of difference and distance, those which traditionally comprise the discursive edge of the anthropological endeavour, are being erased. For example, I was unsure whether to write 'they' or 'we' when referring to health development experts, although 'they' recreates the distance. I remain unsure where such directions of enquiry will end up. At the conference where this chapter was first presented, an angry participant deeply involved in development work asked what right did we think we had to be so critical of professional colleagues. Leaving that question unanswered here, I shall allow it to hover as a shadow over this attempted thinking through of the issues.

I start with an understanding of the cosmopolitan that draws on a sense of universal humanity, reflexive distance from one's own culture and relating to traditions other than one's own (Anderson 1998). The historic particularities of the making of such subjects are varied, but can include ideas of self-formation that are not just emergent from free will, but are also produced in situations where people have less agency (Robbins 1998). As such, the classic type of cosmopolitan, and the first I consider, is the foreign advisor providing advice and consultancy to the governments and workers in this development context. Trained in the metropolitan centres of Europe and America, their global movement is fairly unfettered. They frequently shift from country to country, bringing ideas and epistemologies – or at least the techniques, technologies and values for the development of health-related knowledge – from these 'centres' to the 'periphery', bolstered by global imaginings of development and its humanitarian underpinnings. These workers are prescribing the medical knowledge and policy conditions necessary to improve health-related behaviours and practices in order to develop healthy citizens within states – universalistic aspirations that reach beyond the boundaries of the state to speak for, and of, an 'international community'.

To narrow down the analysis, I will develop an argument focusing primarily on geographical space. I wish to link both the spaces where diseases and health are understood to those through which the knowledge of these are generated and circulate: that is, from hospitals and other organizational spaces to where advisors live, the offices they inhabit, and the conferences and workshops that are attended, interspersed with trips to the 'field'. Save a few notable exceptions, many experts remain largely isolated and thus marginal in these peripheries. I argue that the political economy of development and the consequent structural positions occupied by health development experts make it difficult to open up to other ways of being and knowing. In effect, their knowledge and practices remain for the most part closed and 'walled' off. While there are a range of disciplinary reasons for this, I argue in this chapter that a key component to this is facilitated by the geography and spaces within which the knowledge brokers move.

The second type of cosmopolitan I look at – the migrant health worker – is at face value less obviously cosmopolitan. These workers who trained in the 'peripheries' of the developing world now move (in ways that are frequently brokered and are often on the fringes of legality in particular countries) to developed settings where they work in healthcare. However, in practice, the Nepali health workers (to take my example) who land in the U.K. to work in a resource-constrained National Health Service or in private nursing homes and other health institutions actually open up far more readily to other epistemologies and ways of being. Their medical training means that they have already learned to understand their bodies and health in radically different ways from those of the settings in which they were brought up. The conditions of their international movement mean that they are more readily opened to other ways of knowing and being. This is largely a consequence of structural factors and the political economy of their movement and re-emplacement.

Spaces of Knowledge Production and Circulation: Medical and Expert

I have long suspected that much of the 'order' of development-related practice was aesthetic and emotional. The longest period I spent in Nepal without returning to the U.K. was about eighteen months, working in the east of the country in the early 1990s on a health project. Single, with no family, I had been living fairly simply in the hills. Returning to the U.K. for leave and gazing out of the window on to the order of the fields approaching Gatwick Airport was dislocating in the extreme. Walking outside on the pavements, I had forgotten how clean, aseptic, ordered and empty the country felt. As one colleague arriving from Nepal to the U.K. for the first time commented, looking out of the window of the car driving away from the airport, where is everyone? He found the lack of people walking the streets disorienting. Is there a relationship here between the aesthetic order of modern life in Britain and the attempts to impose development orders elsewhere?

The importance of space in the production of knowledge about Nepal continued to nag at me while researching in the confines of a mission hospital in the western part of the country.[2] Spending time within the compound of this hospital and then walking out of the guarded iron gates and into the street was to experience a similar sense of dislocation. The high wall surrounding the compound physically and symbolically demarcates the space inside from outside. The order inside the hospital too is striking: passing through the wards, one comes into the inner areas of the hospital grounds where can be found the tennis court, the neatly ordered places where people can stay and a quiet guesthouse with an extensive library of mainly mission texts. To shift from this to the street is thus a movement from the relatively controlled internal space of the hospital to one jostling with large numbers of people queuing to get a 'ticket cut' or waiting for their number to be called so that they can enter into the outpatients section and these internal spaces.

Impromptu bazaars are arranged outside, beside the walls, as vendors sell a variety of commodities to the hospital visitors. For several months during the monsoon of 1999, for example, a herbalist from a district several days' walk to the north sat here and sold a number of curing stones, barks and powders, many to counteract the perceived negative effects of modern medicines. I would squat next to him while those attending the hospital debated the efficacy of his cures and purchased his wares to add to their pharmacy-bought products. Another healer whose home was a short distance from the hospital told me stories of the failed cures of those who came out of the hospital and how these failures of modern treatment were cured by *lama-jhankris* (the generic term used locally for shamans and mediums in this area of Nepal). The possibility of being cursed or afflicted by the glance or touch of the envious – food being particularly susceptible – was increased in the hospital, I was told, making these practitioners even more necessary as people moved through this modern space. There were stories circulating of miraculous cures from India and of the power of Tibetan healers from the north.

Here, outside the walls and beyond the control of the mission medical management, was an entirely different order from that within the hospital walls. Exiting the hospital is thus a movement away from a place where the order and spaces of disease are delineated and determined. In the hospital the patients are abstracted from the disease, as Foucault ([1963] 1991) famously noted in the *Birth of the Clinic*. These are the spaces where diagnoses are made and treatments are implemented, where the recording and reporting practices are performed; in short, where a medical epistemology is developed and stabilized. Central to this is space and its control, in areas quite different from the geography where other orders and rationalities exist and circulate.

The high wall surrounding the hospital – adorned on the outside by political slogans from various parties – seemed to symbolize the effort to impose and stabilize this medical order. This wall was keeping people with their differing rationalities towards health and their 'misunderstandings' or 'beliefs' about health out. This exterior, conceptualized as 'cultural barriers', 'traditional healers' and the like, constitutes an outside potentially infecting the 'real' – that is, allopathic – understanding of bodies and health. Keeping the cacophony outside at bay from the facts and figures of diseases and their distribution seemed to me to be made easier by the presence of this wall. The epistemic constitution of disease through the varied practices of the doctors, nurses, technologies of diagnosis – blood tests, x-rays, ultrasounds and the like – recording and reporting strategies, doctors' meetings and the production of annual reports and morbidity figures seemed more robust when physically and metaphorically protected from this external intrusion.[3]

These sites for the production of medical knowledge within Nepal thus require this stability and 'walling off'. But this attempted separation occurs in other locations, as well as within nonmedical discourses, and has been commented on by others. In his angry polemic against developmentalism in Nepal, Nanda R. Shrestha focuses on the Fort Durbar, 'that magnificent little America situated right in the heart of Kathmandu, the medieval city of Nepal, striving to ride the wave of modernity' (Shrestha 1999: 11). In an old Rana palace it is situated below the royal palace and is surrounded by a huge wall, which was rebuilt and fortified in the wake of heightened security concerns post 9/11; heavily guarded, it occupies a large expanse of Kathmandu's most expensive real estate. For Shrestha, this space and the activities within it signify both America's security issues and their social separation from the everyday life of the people of Nepal. No Nepali can enter here uninvited. Likening it to the 'imperial geography' of colonial regimes, he suggests that this is a 'contemporary American practice of using space as a social separator from the natives' (1999: 12). As one American boasted to Shrestha, this is where 'the world of civilization' (1999: 15) was to be housed, and this space becomes for Shrestha a metaphor for the relations of American foreign policy framed through development discourses. He is astonished that this distance between Nepal and America is 'only one step away, separated by a brick wall; it was simply only a matter of whether one was inside or outside the Durbar' (1999: 15). He reflects on another advisor who lived in a bungalow outside of the capital and, in contrast to his Nepali coworkers, had greater control over his living and other spaces. His ability to call his Nepali coworkers into this space at any time, he reflects, 'performed a dubious task. In the relations of power and control, spatial proximity is a curse as it has a way of impinging on the freedom of those who rank low on the totem pole of power' (1999: 20). The Americans could spirit themselves away into their living spaces, whereas Nepalis could not – a 'tyranny of spatial proximity' (1999: 15). Importantly for us here, these spaces are where the exchange of development ideas takes place and networks are fostered and developed; they are spaces of power, then, where in an aid-dependent country like Nepal, particular framings of the country and its needs circulate and are reformulated.

Now in Kathmandu there is also a spatial dimension to where the development consultants and advisors live, although rapid urban development may on the face of it be making this less obvious. This was certainly the case in the 1970s when Justice (1986) was researching health sector policy. She argued that the very geography of place fed into the relationships and misunderstandings between expatriates and their Nepali counterparts. In a wide-ranging and important analysis, she also touched on how expatriates not only occupied some of the older Rana buildings or large modern houses, but also tended to live in more salubrious areas and in conditions of far greater luxury that they could afford at home. Concerned with their servants and gardens, the school needs of their children and the like, there was a tendency for expatriates to move in certain circles, to associate with other expatriates and to be somewhat removed from Nepali realities. The same is pretty much true today. When a close Nepali friend of mine asked why a young advisor working for a bilateral organization was living in such a large old Rana house, the reply was to please not deny them the one opportunity to live in a form of luxury they could never afford at home.

Hindman (2002) also suggests we should think through development in conjunction with consideration of activities not normally thought of as part of the official discourse. Her analysis of U.S. aid in Nepal explores how the contracting out of development expertise, and the associated movement of large numbers of people and their families, creates a particular type of knowledge and living conditions. We need, she suggests, to examine the private and domestic matters associated with aid workers as part of the analysis. The model that still predominates in Nepal, she argues, was one initiated in the 1950s, when a new approach to development was introduced which relied more heavily on technical experts brought in for particular tasks. Then staff members all shared accommodation in two large Rana palaces and developed a very limited set of social relations as a consequence. Her review of personal accounts of these early days reveals the importance of domestic matters in the life of projects: 'Projects end not because their mission is achieved but because a family decides to allow their daughter to be educated in the United States' (2002: 126). Hindman points out that, while questions of Nepali 'culture' (in the sense of private practices of consumption, recreation or informal social relations) are appropriately considered a part of aid projects, it is not appropriate to consider how the private lives of the expatriates in Nepal shape the way that development is done. The development agenda, she argues, is also a domestic agenda, requiring 'an approach to the role the expatriate spouses play, a vision of what families do and should do' (2002: 129). She further suggests that it is the vision of the everyday lives of expatriates that remains constant, as development ideas and discourses shift and change. 'Houses, schools, swimming pools, grocery stores were all built to sustain the life of the valuable scientist' (2002: 130) and to bring the comforts of home to Kathmandu. It is this, as much as the real life of the projects, that sustains the development era as it is. I find this argument compelling, having only recently lived for any length of time in the capital Kathmandu, where we find the greatest concentration of development expertise. Yet, as Mosse points out in Chapter 1, this management of the personal – family, security, etc. – is barely touched upon in the literature. Perhaps securing the home environment provides the very foundation for dealing with the complex and frequently undeniably stressful work that expatriates undertake. But such concerns have consequences. I know personally of one case in which there was an immense shift in focus of an international NGO's work after its director was rehoused in Kathmandu because their spouse felt unable to live outside the capital.

Now this geography of the domestic surely also produces a situation where, as Justice remarked, 'most foreigners … serve as their own reference group, remaining socially and culturally apart from the people they aim to serve' (1986: 41), as many of the Nepalis they work with are uncomfortable with the luxury. The distance that Justice describes enters into professional relationships as well, through a lack of understanding of the administrative systems which, despite superficial resemblances with those of the home countries of expatriates, actually 'functions on the basis of familial, patron-client, caste, regional, and ethnic loyalties' (1986: 41). Meanwhile, she argues, the administrative demands of donor agencies keep advisors in their offices, creating a further barrier to socializing with their Nepali colleagues. Not only do they drive or are chauffeur-driven to their offices, but in addition these buildings themselves foster particular kinds of relationships and contact with others (1986: 41). Increased security means that heavily guarded buildings, such as the UN building containing the WHO offices, are increasingly difficult to enter. USAID have even moved their offices into the newly built and very heavily fortified American Embassy. Visitors have to negotiate the tightly patrolled and closely monitored entrances to get inside.

Moreover, the professional work of expatriate advisers is focused primarily on the transmission of administrative order. Many work with counterparts in the Ministry of Health developing the correct recording and reporting formats for the practices that will produce the epistemologies to characterize health in Nepal. The institutions and organizations generate country profiles, epidemiological profiles and the like, and chart the distributions of disease and illness. Huge amounts of work and effort are geared towards the stabilization of particular framings of Nepal healthwise and the corresponding policy frameworks.

A personal anecdote may further help to illustrate the geographical sense I am trying to develop here. I was recently a member of an international review team looking at a health programme. Experts from various organizations, including the WHO, were housed in Nepal's most exclusive hotels and ferried around from site to site in UN vehicles. Because of UN rules and security issues, the travel arrangements were tightly controlled. In the assessment of the programme, it was not possible to deviate from assigned visits to selected, primed clinics. Even the suggestion that we could take taxis was vetoed on the grounds that those who worked for the UN were not allowed, for security reasons, to travel in anything other than the UN vehicles outside of the Kathmandu valley. This geography of travel assisted in the development of a particular framing and picture of the programme. This is something I have regularly observed in other areas as well over the years, when visitors are taken to the best health posts and sites of exemplary practice on their carefully prepared and orchestrated tours of development programmes.

In 2004 I visited the offices of the DFID (the U.K. Department for International Development) in Kathmandu to talk to a senior advisor about a piece of research I was conducting into the growth of the private sector in the training of health workers. As a British citizen, getting past the ex-Gurkha soldiers working as security guards on the gates was relatively easy. However, walking into the purpose-built DFID office is a shock; through the glass doors and into the quiet foyer, where your name is taken and you are asked to wait, there is an aesthetic of business and purpose that suffuses everything. My conversation with the advisor was immediately framed through a whole series of documents which I was given copies of: the 2002 Health Sector Strategy: An Agenda for Change (reform); The Tenth Plan (Poverty Reduction Strategy Paper 2002–2007); a Joint Review of the Nepal Health Sector Programme – Implementation Plan; and the Nepal Health Sector Programme Implementation Plan (NPSP – IP) 2004–2009. A number of these were headed with the stamp of the Nepal government and the Ministry of Health. Current political instability – along with frequent changes in government – have allowed reform agendas to be passed more easily, as a number of advisors I spoke to mentioned.

My point here is simply to note (perhaps obviously) that these documents and their production are of great importance to the world of health development and are necessary for its stability. As I was recently told by one advisor, 'conversation and meetings are fine, but they can never replace the need for documentation'. As Mosse (2005) has pointed out, much of the work of development is geared towards the epistemic stabilization of particular framings. Yet what I had difficulty squaring up to was the world depicted in these documents and the empirical reality I knew through ethnographic research and its particular methodology. For example, in a review of Public Private Partnerships (one of the three areas required for reforms in the health sector, the other two being decentralization and the provision of essential healthcare services), the problem reflected on was the requirement for stringent monitoring of the implementation of regulations and policies by the state. The government needed to plan and continuously monitor the services for which it was 'contracting out' the advice.

In this review of regulatory reforms by one of the burgeoning consultancy organizations that feed the need for policy research that oils the cogs of the development machine, a package of ten strategies was called for that enabled the policy and regulatory environment and allowed for the legal enforcement of regulations and policy controls. My difficulty was that these documents and their policy suggestions seemed to assume the ideal of a liberal state and worked with this ideal, ignoring the more ethnographic picture I had come to develop. There was barely any regulation in practice, for example, of the truly astonishing and spectacular proliferation of the private sector. In the wake of the Maoist insurgency, this lack of accountability has led to an increase in frequently direct and violent action against doctors and health workers perceived as having done wrong. In short, development documents' simulacra assumed a U.K.-like liberal state, even as certain groups were starting to think of Nepal as potentially a 'failing state'. As I gazed from the window in the DFID building I was left, once again, with a strong sense of the disjuncture between 'out there' and the truths circulating 'in here' and between organizations.

Other Spatial Considerations

The way in which health expertise and its social context is spatialized is thus part of the production of development orders in Nepal. In short, there is the overlapping of spatialities, epistemologies and identities. Thus, the geographical spaces where professionals are situated and through which they can move seem to me to be an important consideration in understanding development processes. This is in addition to the way that spatial dimensions are important in disciplines like epidemiology, whose purpose is to spatialize the distribution of disease. Since Foucault, 'panopticism' has been a key analytic concept in attempts to understand the relationship between knowledge and power. He has been reproached for his 'spatial obsessions', but showing that knowledge can be analysed using such metaphors as space, region, territory, domain, etc. allows one to 'capture the process by which knowledge functions as a form of power and disseminates the effects of power' (Foucault 1980: 69).

In the context of Nepal, it has been noted that the national space onto which development framings are mapped is also never neutral. Various groups as types of person are mapped on this geography. Pigg (1992), for example, has suggested that the ways that development is charted in school textbooks in Nepal is both geographic in orientation – it is the villager who is underdeveloped, not those in the urban areas – and racialized. The picture of those who are more developed appear to be of higher caste in features and dress, whereas those who are not are more Tibetan looking in appearance. The whole geography of development is charted across the terrain of habitat, livelihood, religion and race (1992: 501).

The term 'sanitary citizenship', introduced by Briggs and Mantini-Briggs (2003), is also useful in understanding who has access to the civil and social rights of citizenship. The programme of Direct Observation of Treatment, Short-course (DOTS), developed by the WHO for the management of tuberculosis and rolled out over much of the country over the last decade, illustrates this point.[4] As I sat in clinics observing and participating in this programme in western Nepal, the requirement that the taking of medicines has to be observed fed into a distrust of patients. The staff implementing the programme seemed to be stricter with those from rural areas or the more obviously marginal and poor; they were less trusted (similarly, early writings on barriers to tuberculosis control work published on Nepal highlighted cultural barriers and dependence on traditional healers, amongst others). The correct mode of behaviour – that prescribed by WHO experts and implemented through the national tuberculosis programme – gazes down gradients of authority and places the burden of compliance with prescribed behaviour firmly on the shoulders of the ill. However, health workers too need to understand tuberculosis and the need for direct observation (currently being reframed as 'patient support'). Then, at another level still, the adoption of DOTS itself is a WHO prescription for a healthy functioning state; does failure to implement this mean confinement to the realms of unsatisfactory membership of the world of the UN? As Keene (1998) has pointed out, the WHO has a certain vision of how the world should be organized when envisioning a world free from disease.

To be 'sanitary citizens', then, requires that prescribed modes of behaviour are adopted in relation to medical epistemologies. This question of right conduct can be understood as an aspect of Foucauldian 'governmentality', that is, the formation of particular subjects as a part of activities that 'mold human conduct in a way as to bring about individual and collective wellbeing' (Inda 2005: 10). These behaviours are being prescribed by constellations of organizations (some state, some 'international'), and the surveillance of the programmes of implementation are overseen by experts (myself included) based in Kathmandu and others who fly in to evaluate its epidemiological and other parameters. Tracking where we stay, what spaces we move through and how geography defines and constrains the framings developed should be the part of any analysis. Also at stake here is membership to particular ideas of global health and citizenship.

Journeying across Medical Borders: Nepali Migrant Health Workers

I turn now to another scenario as a counterpoint: that of the large numbers of health workers who now minister to the implementation of the health programmes, and their desires and movement. Take Ms X for example, whom I met and interviewed during research in 1999, as I moved among clinics and NGOs attempting to grasp how their workers understood health and local nonmedical healers. She was a young Brahman woman from a rural village in a district of west Nepal. Raised on a small farm, her father died when she was young and her maternal uncles took some responsibility for her local education. As a glance at the school curricula textbooks attests, here she would have started to develop a sense of what forms of behaviour are appropriate for the healthy citizen of Nepal: learning the nutritional value of certain foodstuffs; how to brush teeth properly; the importance of visiting a medically-trained health worker when unwell, etc. She did well in her School Leaving Certificate (SLC) and it was decided that she should enter into a nurse training course. She travelled to Maharajgunj Campus, one of the few state-run institutions available for this in the late 1980s, and qualified in the early 1990s. She showed me photos of her contribution to the demonstrations in the campus that in 1990 had led to Nepal's second experiment with democracy. Many people told me how high the expectations had been following this 'revolution', and for so many of the young and educated youths, like Ms X, this was a time of gazing to the future with bright hopes.

She worked in an organization whose remit was bettering the health of the people of Nepal. Along with her expressed hopes and desires, during our conversations it became apparent that she was using her understanding of science to filter the 'good' aspects of traditional and village practices from the 'superstitious' and harmful aspects. Like many I spoke to, she was particularly condemning of the traditional healers, known locally as 'lamas'. Villagers require more 'outside knowledge' and remain too traditional, she informed me. She and her colleagues were linked into circuits of knowledge and understanding that stretch beyond Nepal's borders, as they implement Nepal's adopted health policies. But these global imaginings are not restricted to the bringing in of outside knowledge, as they also feed intense desires to travel. As well as telling me about these programmes and the work involved in trying to change the hearts and minds of villagers, she told me of her desire to move to Kathmandu. And, as frequently happened, I was asked if there might be any possibilities of working in the U.K. as a nurse, and if I could help her to find something.[5]

In 2004, I spent six weeks in Nepal doing some preliminary research into the 'production' of health workers, part of a concern to grapple with how their training fed into their understanding of health-related issues. The gaining of mobility as workers pass through these modern health trainings is now increasingly an option for many young Nepalis. Since the late 1980s, the state's monopoly of the education of health workers in Nepal (doctors and nurses as well as primary healthcare workers) has shifted dramatically. In 2004, travelling around the streets of Kathmandu, aside from the increased security presence everywhere, another significant change could be noticed, namely the spectacular range and types of billboards advertising education. These are not just for institutions and courses in Nepal, but increasingly all over the world. If you believe the advertisements, it seems possible to study most subjects almost anywhere, at a cost. A whole range of intermediary trainings, institutions and brokers are now available to assist in transforming these desires into the reality of green cards and student visas. The pages of the press too are full of advertments for private educational establishments.

This broader and spectacular commoditisation of higher education also plays itself out in the health field. Visiting Bhagbazaar – an area in central

Kathmandu – in 2004 was to be confronted with a variety of new institutions advertising programmes to train people to take the entrance requirements for medical, nursing and health assistant courses. Many dozens, probably hundreds of such institutions have been set up. These enterprises are purely commercial in nature and have grown in response to the increase in the numbers of students hoping to get into health-related courses and subsequently overseas work.

In the decade up to 2004 nine new private medical schools opened in Nepal; another five were planned. From fieldwork in the summer of 2004, I estimated that over 40 colleges training nurses and over 120 technical training colleges training health workers had opened since the late 1980s, most in the mid 1990s. A considerable number are located in Kathmandu. These institutions are responsible for the production of Health Assistants (who receive a two and a half years of training), Auxillary Nurse Midwives (ANMs) and Community Medical Assistants (CMAs), trained for one year. Many of the students I met were from rural areas and their families had made great sacrifices to keep the education of their offspring going. They shared expensive and frequently overcrowded living conditions in the capital (many areas today in the capital are increasingly unaffordable for most Nepalis who do not have money from remittances or salaries supplemented by the development industry). Upon qualifying, more and more health workers practice in the many new private hospitals, pharmacies and clinics or obtain (simultaneously, if they can) lucrative jobs in the public sector (as part of Nepal's rapidly expanding middle class, for more on which, see Liechty 2003). Others, like Ms X, will seek employment within the development apparatus, bringing modern ideas and health-related practices to Nepal's populations.

The routes through this web of education and its class labyrinth are complex (for a summary of this with regards to nurses, see Harper and Adhikari 2006; Adhikari 2008). Community Medical Assistants (CMAs), for example, are those workers who are trained for one year after their SLCs in order to work in the health posts. Currently thousands are being produced by the mushrooming numbers of privately run institutions. Through this training many are coming to perceive of their own 'cultural' practices as superstitious and as barriers to the attainment of 'health', as Ms X did. But those interviewed in 2004 at one institution who had entered into the HA line – accessible from the CMA route – really wanted to proceed to the MBBS medical qualification. This was the route they had chosen; the way of having a crack at MBBS entry without the Intermediate Science Certificate (although some regulatory changes preventing HAs from entering medical schools had been introduced in 2000). The group of HA trainees I spoke to at one institution saw the MBBS as the ticket to overseas work. However, they were concerned with the increasing numbers of students being produced and the fact that the sheer numbers were now making this progression much more difficult.

The area where there has probably been greatest expansion in health training is the nursing sector. There was considerable media and public attention on nursing in 2004 in Kathmandu, most of it linked to the capacity of nurses to go abroad to work. This needs to be read, in part at least, in tandem with the broader public discourses around women going overseas. The sexual harassment and consequent death of one woman from Nepal in 1999 in Saudi Arabia initiated a wave of media protest around women being trafficked and exploited abroad. In the wake of this, for a while the government banned women from going abroad (not far from the surface of this was the whole discourse around the trafficking of women in relation to sex work). However, there followed in the media a flood of pieces about women's more positive experiences overseas and of the considerable contributions that these women were making to the economy through remittances.[6]

Journalist writings have also brought the issue of nursing to the fore. For example, in the Nepali language *Himal*, a piece entitled 'They are Waiting for British and American Hospitals' highlighted how women are now able to stand on their own two feet and have considerable earning potential around the world where other health systems are in crisis.[7] Another, in a special edition of *Saptahik* on education, asks in the title 'What is the Attraction of Nursing to Female Students?'.[8] It too concludes that the attraction seems to be linked to expansion in the possibility of working abroad. In three interviews I did with second year nursing students in Dhulikhel hospital in 2004, each stated, in answer to an open-ended question about where they would like to work, that going abroad was their main aim. When I asked why, the reply was the potential to earn money. Only one combined this with the desire to gain experience of more technologically advanced nursing practices. These emerging middle classes increasingly have their dreams and desires firmly fixed beyond the boundaries of Nepal. At Dhulikhel, the number of applicants for 40 places on a nurse training programme in 2003 was over 400, and by 2004 this had risen to over 800. Competition is intense. Thousands are surfing the net in Nepal looking at the entry requirements and exploring how to get a job overseas. An increasing number are managing to translate these desires into international migration. There are now an increasing number of nurses trained in Nepal working in the U.K., the U.S. and Australia.[9]

Now, those nurses from Nepal who travel to the U.K. have a quite different experience from the foreign advisors and consultants who live in large spacious houses in Kathmandu. These health workers, who end up in very small and frequently crowded flats in the less than salubrious parts of the towns and cities where they work, are not going to develop policy and restructure health sectors, develop training curricula for health workers or work at stabilizing the recording and reporting processes and practices.

Most will have to have a period of intensive supervised placement before being allowed to register with the Nursing Council. Yet, without this movement of nurses (and other health professionals), mostly from the developing world to the U.K., the British National Health Service (NHS) would in all likelihood quite simply collapse. At the same time, these migrant health workers become the intense focus of discourses of integration, the subject of questions ranging from competence in English through to cultural competence and nursing competence, as well as being the focus of concern about the brain drain from developing countries and the 'haemorrhaging' of health workers away from where they should be working (as a recent WHO report has suggested).

By Way of Conclusion: The Political Economy of Health Cosmopolitans

Throughout this chapter I have attempted to address the question of movement and power by reference to the political economy of space and the circulation of health workers. Hannerz suggests that the strength of certain cosmopolitan global imaginings comes from their connection to those from more economically powerful countries who try to make themselves feel as much at home as possible (Hannerz 1996). As I have argued here, this politics of space and place – both private and professional –tells us something of the politics of knowledge production, and how this knowledge and its circulation is closed off from other epistemologies and ways of knowing. It is the wall that becomes the significant metaphor here, for that of a 'walling off', so to speak, or boundary to the other. I thus argue that the production of development orders in Nepal is spatialized through the social and geographical contexts in which experts are located and through which they move. To understand this we need to reach beyond merely the professional spaces to all those inhabited by aid workers to analyse the framing, fortification and stabilization and then the circulation of certain epistemologies over and above others.

By contrast to the luxurious, more insulated life of the global expert working in Nepal, the migrant health workers' journey from the streets of Kathmandu through the sites of their training and abroad is quite different. They often end up in the smallest of apartments both in Kathmandu, then in the more marginal parts of the cities and towns where they work. They remain less protected, so to speak, as they work in the hospitals and clinics and become the objects of discourses of assimilation. They have to demonstrate competence in language and adequate knowledge of health-related practice to work at all.

However, to suggest a similar scenario in the opposite direction would be uncomfortable for many development experts; that is, that they should be subjected to cultural tests, language competencies or even forced to partake in the shamanic rituals of the hills of Nepal before being registered as competent. Into the gulf that opens up around the apparent absurdity of this suggestion fall the inequalities and unequal power relations fostered by current geopolitical and economic relations framed as development, inequalities that are experienced and reconstituted both epistemologically and spatially.

Notes

1. I draw on experience and observations from a number of visits to Nepal over the last eighteen years. Two main periods of research in particular are drawn upon: my Ph.D. research, the fieldwork for which was conducted between 1998 and 2000, funded by the ESRC; and a repeat visit to Nepal in June–July 2004 funded by the Heyter and Munro Trusts from the University of Edinburgh. During the latter period I researched the growth of private health worker training institutions. The first draft of this chapter was presented at the Association of Social Anthropologists conference in 2006, on a panel, Cosmopolitanism and Development, organized by David Mosse. My thanks also go to all the participants at this conference for their feedback and particularly to Professor Deborah James for her comments as discussant. Radha Adhikari has also provided insights and useful comments and feedback, especially on the section on nursing in the U.K.
2. For a more detailed analysis of this hospital and its role in changing broader understandings of health and illness in this part of Nepal, see Harper 2009.
3. There is much literature in science studies and medical anthropology on this coconstitution of disease (see, for example, Mol 2002 and the collected essays in Berg and Mol 1998).
4. DOTS is the WHO prescribed tuberculosis policy developed in the early 1990s and now adopted by most countries as the cornerstone of their tuberculosis control programmes. It consists of five elements: political and financial commitment; case detection through laboratories; standardized treatment with supervision; good provision of drugs; and a functioning monitoring and evaluation system (see http://www.who.int/tb/dots/whatisdots/en/print.html for more detail).
5. Ms X is just one of a great number of people who work in the NGO and other sectors. It is beyond the scope of the discussion here to chart the complex relationships that many of these workers have with the development advisors I have mentioned in the first part of this chapter, and how they assist in the further education and travel of these workers. Nonetheless, her story here is more than just a narrative device to link the two concerns of the chapter.
6. See for example a collection of articles published during a media campaign to promote a more positive image of female migration. Produced by the NGO Sancharika Samuha and UNIFEM (United Nations Development Fund for Women) 'Foreign Employment for Women: Challenges and Opportunities', published in 2003, Putali Sadak, Kathmandu, Nepal.
7. KC S. 2004. 'British and American Hospitals are Waiting …', translated from Nepali 'Pratchaya ma chhan British ra American Aspatalharu', *Himal*, June–July, 16–31.
8. Pariyar, G. 2005. Health and Nursing: Attractive Career (translated from Nepali Syasthaya and nursing; Aakarshak Kariyar, 39–41).
9. Radha Adhikari, a Ph.D. student in the School of Health in Social Science at the University of Edinburgh, is currently writing a Ph.D. dissertation that is looking in detail at issues around both the proliferation of nursing campuses in Nepal and how they are adapting to the desire for nurses to migrate, as well as at the migration process itself and the experiences of being a Nepali nurse in the U.K. The final paragraph of this section comes from fieldwork and insights she is developing for this research, and I thank her for allowing me to share these here.

References

Adhikari, R. 2008. '"The Business Nursing Complex": Understanding Nursing Training in Nepal', *Studies in Nepali History and Society* 13(2): 297–324, December.

Anderson, A. 1998. 'Cosmopolitanism, Universalism, and the Divided Legacies of Modernity', in P. Cheah and B. Robbins (eds), *Cosmopolitics: Thinking and Feeling Beyond the Nation.* Minneapolis and London: University of Minnesota Press.

Berg, M. and A. Mol. (eds). 1998. *Differences in Medicine: Unravelling Practices, Techniques, and Bodies.* Durham, N.C.: Duke University Press.

Briggs C. and C. Mantini Briggs. 2003. *Stories in the Time of Cholera.* Berkeley, C.A.: University of California Press.

Foucault, M. [1963] 1991. *The Birth of the Clinic: An Archaeology of Medical Perception.* London: Routledge.

———. 1980. 'Questions of Geography', in C. Gordon (ed.), *Power/Knowledge: Selected Interviews and Other Writings 1972 –1977.* New York: Pantheon Books.

Harper, I. 2009. 'Mediating Therapeutic Uncertainty: A Mission Hospital in Nepal', in M. Harrison, M. Jones and H. Sweet (eds), *From Western Medicine to Global Medicine: The Hospital Beyond the West.* New Delhi: Orient Black Swan.

Harper, I. and R. Adhikari. 2007. 'Urban Livelihoods, Nursing and Urban Health', in J. Adhikari and B. Gautam (eds), *Urban Livelihoods.* Kathmandu: Martin Chautari.

Hannerz, U. 1996. *Transnational Connections.* New York: Routledge.

Hindman, H. 2002. 'The Everyday Life of American Development in Nepal', *Studies in Nepal History and Society* 7(1): 99–136.

Inda, J. 2005. 'Analytics of the Modern: An Introduction', in J. Inda (ed.), *Anthropologies of Modernity: Foucault, Governmentality, and Life Politics.* Malden, Oxford and Carlton: Blackwell.

Justice, J. 1986. *Policies, Plans, & People: Culture and Health Development in Nepal.* Berkeley, C.A,: University of California Press.

Keane, C. 1998. 'Globality and Constructions of World Health', *Medical Anthropology Quarterly* 12(2): 226–40.

Liechty, M. 2002. *Suitably Modern: Making Middle-Class Culture in a New Consumer Society.* Princeton, C.T.: Princeton University Press.

Mol, A. 2002. *The Body Multiple: Ontology in Medical Practice.* Durham, N.C.: Duke University Press.

Mosse, D. 2005. *Cultivating Development.* London and New York: Pluto Press.

———. 2006. 'Anti-social Anthropology? Objectivity, Objection and the Ethnography of Public Policy and Professional Communities', *Journal of the Royal Anthropological Institute* 12(4): 935–56.

Pigg, S.L. 1992. 'Inventing Social Categories through Place: Social Representations and Development in Nepal', *Comparative Studies in Society and History* 34: 491–513.

Robbins, B. 1998. 'Introduction Part 1: Actually Existing Cosmopolitanism', in P. Cheah and B. Robbins (eds), *Cosmopolitics: Thinking and Feeling Beyond the Nation.* Minneapolis and London: University of Minnesota Press.

Shrestha, N.R. 1999. *In the Name of Development: A Reflection on Nepal.* Kathmandu: Educational Enterprises (P) Ltd.

Chapter 7

THE SOCIALITY OF INTERNATIONAL AID
AND POLICY CONVERGENCE

Rosalind Eyben

Introduction

For a long time I thought of myself as both an anthropologist and development bureaucrat. By leaving my increasingly bureaucratic job at the head office of the U.K. Department for International Development (DFID) in early 2000 to run its small country office in Bolivia, I hoped to revive the moribund anthropologist. I used to make regular visits of a few days to different parts of the country with no other purpose except, as I explained at the time: 'to deepen our knowledge of the work of social and economic institutions at the local level, to understand more about the lives of poor people and their communities and to consider the links between micro-level reality and macro-level policy and action.'[1]

I failed to persuade either my own colleagues or my counterparts in other official aid agencies to undertake similar 'reality checks'. I have since been part of a campaign to persuade staff of international aid agencies to take time out of their offices to spend a few days as participant observers in local communities in aid recipient countries. We have argued that such direct experience is essential for effective aid (Irvine et al. 2004).

Our campaign has had some successes. The report of the peer review of U.K. official development aid by the OECD Development Assistance Committee included the recommendation that 'staff currently working in headquarters ... spend more time visiting the field and country office staff to spend more time out of capital cities. Greater effort should be made in getting key staff closer to the development realities they support' (OECD 2006: 7). Members of staff from the Swedish aid agency, Sida, are now officially encouraged to undertake what have come to be called 'immersion visits'.

Yet, overall, the level of interest in getting closer to 'development realities' remains low. My colleagues in Bolivia were not an exception in their refusal to undertake such visits. It was not anxiety about difficult living conditions. Many of them tolerated these when undertaking tourist trips when on holiday. No, the reason they gave me was the need to give priority to spending time in government offices on 'policy dialogue' and on donor coordination in designing and spending official aid.[2]

One of those I failed to convince about reality checks was Mr A, the country representative of another government's aid agency. He preferred to spend most of his time in La Paz, the capital city. I have no recollection of him reading many reports and analyses about Bolivia as a possible substitute to going to see for himself. Yet he was an outstanding and highly influential personality in the local donor community. He worked very hard, taking the lead in donor coordination meetings, visiting key government ministries, attending official receptions most evenings of the week and, in the weekends, organizing picnics and parties for the donor and government staff he had been meeting throughout the week. Lack of interest in reality checks was not connected to an unwillingness to explore Bolivia; he and his wife loved making trips to sites of cultural and natural beauty. But even then he was keen to invite colleagues and their families to accompany him, organizing for example some twenty-five of us to go together with our families to a major cultural festival in another city in Bolivia. He coordinated our leisure activities as well as our professional practice.

Mr A did not do reality checks because his attention was focused on constructing and sustaining relations with other donors, government officials, politicians and other influential players for a harmonized and aligned international aid programme to Bolivia. I worked very closely with him. Our primary sources of knowledge were our common networks of relationships. These influenced my choice of consultants and analysts to inform me about the political and social situation. Because we sought a shared understanding of Bolivia's problems to agree on a common line to take with the government in policy dialogues, it was important to share these reports with others in the aid community. For example, I worked hard to persuade my donor colleagues that social and political exclusion was a significant issue. Mr A initially supported my efforts until – as I will explain later – I overstepped the limits. He supported me possibly not because he had any intrinsic interest in the matter, but because it was an aspect of his collegiality, an element in a certain kind of sociality necessary for constructing and sustaining a donor community as an essential component of policy convergence.

In this chapter I argue that the efforts to construct and sustain a donor community locally and globally are an essential component of a harmonized approach to aid. Expatriates in developing countries, including aid agency staff, have always tended to enjoy a shared social life with the picnics and parties that I describe later. It goes without saying that the particular political and cultural context in each aid-dependent country will affect the social lives of aid officials and the extent, for example, to which they mix with local elites (Crewe and Fernando 2006). Nevertheless,

I suggest that what I shall describe about Bolivia at the time I was there reflects a more general trend. The current normative imperative for donor agencies to work together has given these social events a new significance, leading to a greater integration of social life into everyday working practice, making the sociality of aid officials vulnerable to the systemic contradictions and discursive disjunctures in international aid practice (Mosse, Chapter 1 this volume).

I explore how the importance of 'being there' in the country related to working and socializing with each other and with a handful of Bolivian consultants and government officials, rather than getting to know the country and its people in any broader or deeper sense. The very frequent meetings (both formal and informal) between expatriate staff in donor agencies created a strong sense of local community, linking very tenuously and through a few select individuals to the wider 'local' of Bolivia. This donor community can be best understood as a local cell of a global, 'virtual' international aid community for which Raymond Apthorpe has coined the notion of 'Aidland' or 'Bubbleland' (Chapter 10 this volume). I then generalize from this account to propose that international aid staff in country offices belong to two overlapping communities of meaning and practice – the 'global' and the 'back home'. At times these different 'communities' impose conflicting demands on them, rupturing social relationships in the local cell. I illustrate my argument with two cases of strong disagreement and contention.

This chapter concerns the everyday social activities of donor staff in Bolivia in the period prior to the elections of 2005 when an indigenous leader, Evo Morales, became President and there was a radical change in government as well as in donor-recipient relations. Shortly after completing the final version of this chapter, I visited La Paz in January 2008 and interviewed former contacts about changes in donors' sociality in this new revolutionary context, and I briefly discuss these in a postscript.

Meanwhile, before introducing the reader to the social round of the donor community in Bolivia, some historical context is required to understand the nature of aid practice and the current retreat from local reality into Apthorpe's Bubbleland.

Aid Practices: A Historical Perspective

The Changing Character of Expertise

International aid, as we currently understand it, began in the 1960s when many colonies became independent. Although dams, roads and hospitals were built as part of development aid, much of the effort related to what was described as 'technical assistance'. In relation to British aid, with which I am most familiar,[4] in the mid-1960s there were, for example, 7,000 employees of the DFID's predecessor, the Overseas Development Ministry, resident in eastern and southern Africa (Soper 1966). What came to be called 'Technical Co-operation Officers' (TCOs) and their families tended to live in close-knit expatriate communities, albeit very small ones if they were living in rural areas. They were socially quite separate from the everyday lives of the local people. Nevertheless, the professional lives of the TCOs were significantly shaped by the local; they lived in the districts to which they were responsible for providing assistance. Right up to the early 1990s – when the practice of focusing aid in specific localities of a recipient country started to decline – there were technical cooperation staff working alongside government counterparts in provincial or district authority offices.[5] Aid staff were not concentrated in the capital city. They and visitors from the High Commission or London would spend much of their time going out in the country, looking at projects or meeting local leaders in the aid-receiving districts.

The original declared reason for deploying such a large body of TCOs was that recipient country expertise was absent. Thus, a complementary effort was to train thousands of professionals from aid-recipient countries to fill the gap in 'manpower'. As these countries developed their own cadres of professionals, the justification for TCOs disappeared. By the late 1990s they were almost gone, along with many of the localized projects which they managed. One of my first tasks on arriving in Bolivia in 2000 was to meet with the twelve remaining TCOs working on various agricultural and veterinary projects in the country to tell them that their projects were being shut down.

By the start of the present decade, TCOs had been replaced by two sets of people. The first were staff employed no longer as advisers to recipient governments but as aid administrators based in DFID country offices in the capital city and reporting back to London. The others were a growing number of specialized 'consultants' hired by the DFID to advise on the complex issues of designing and managing programmatic support. In both cases, knowledge of the 'local' became less relevant.

For some thirty or so years after colonies gained their independence, many of the staff working in bilateral and multilateral aid agencies had started their careers as colonial officers with a strong cultural tradition of going on field trips around 'their' districts, one that they sustained even when they were no longer TCOs but instead performed an oversight function at the High Commission or in the head office. As these officials retired in the late 1980s and early 1990s, this tradition faded. Kothari (2005) has traced the historical shift from the lives of colonial officers who spent most of their career in particular localities to those of development experts, recruited not on the basis of knowing about a specific country or region – which in any case could now be understood as the responsibility of national expertise – but because of certain technical knowhow that could be equally well applied anywhere. Not knowing much about any particular place facilitates a standardization of approach that a revival of reality checks might challenge.

The Age of Harmonization

One of the long-standing issues in the practice of international aid has been how each official donor (bilateral and multilateral) has designed and run its own projects so that the already overstretched recipient government has to relate with and seek to make some sense out of the overlapping and sometimes contradictory activities of dozens of separate donors. In the language of Aidland, 'harmonization' means donors trying to have common programmes and procedures, so that the recipient needs to communicate with only one single set of financing agencies. It is associated with certain ways of doing aid whereby donors coordinate negotiations with a government about its policies and agree to provide budget support for the implementation of the policies they favour, for example poverty reduction strategies or sector policies in education or health (Eyben 2007). Developing over the last ten years, it has resulted in a single global approach to aid, albeit one currently challenged by emerging nontraditional donors such as China.

Harmonization was facilitated by the delinking of aid practices from local knowledge. The retirement of the old cadre of colonial officers and the ending of the era of TCOs serendipitously coincided with the arrival of email, which provided the technology for standardization of practice. When in 1987 I started working in the DFID's head office, an exchange of letters between London and the regional offices in Africa took up to six weeks: two weeks for a letter to arrive from Nairobi, one to two weeks for me to reply and a further two weeks to get back to the desk of my correspondent. As an adviser trying to influence my colleagues in Nairobi, I found that most decisions had been made locally before I was even aware of what was happening. Today, although there are far greater numbers of aid agency staff posted in capital cities of aid-recipient countries than there were twenty years ago, the ICT revolution has led to their being more closely controlled today by their head offices. The greater control that head office can now exert on staff contradicts the current favoured discourse of the Paris Declaration on Aid Effectiveness. Context-specific responses are emphasized, including greater delegated authority to donor staff in country offices (OECD 2005). One size is no longer meant to fit all. Donor governments, and the multilateral organizations such as the United Nations Development Programme UNDP and the World Bank funded by these governments, are committed to greater aid effectiveness through the 'harmonization' and 'alignment' of aid delivery in support of poverty reduction strategies that the recipient country, rather than they, has taken the lead in developing. Yet these same harmonization efforts, whereby donors construct a common diagnosis concerning the perceived problems of each recipient country, combined with a rigorous discipline of seeking results against internationally agreed targets – the Millennium Development goals – may be actually reinforcing rather than diluting the 'one size fits all' approach.[6] New aid instruments of multidonor-financed direct budget support and sector-wide approaches require aid officials getting to know the patterns on the carpet of the Ministry of Finance and the small number of technocrats who work there – and these technocrats themselves move to and fro between jobs in the World Bank and in the Ministry of Finance in their country of origin.

Much more than before, head office members of staff working on a similar policy issue are in regular face-to-face and email contact with each other. A visit to the homepage of the OECD Development Assistance Committee will show the frequency of official meetings. Many other meetings, seminars and visits take place on a very regular basis, including through other groupings such as the Utstein Four[7] (in existence when I was in Bolivia) and as of writing 'the Nordic Plus'. Consultants and academics like myself also play a honey-bee role in communicating to staff in one head office the latest views and news from another head office or international meeting. These strengthened ties between head offices potentially narrow the room for manoeuvre of country office staff unless, as I will now go on to discuss, they can form their own local community that enables them to resist head office requirements by exploiting latent rivalries and differences between their head offices.

The Social Round

When I moved to Bolivia in early 2000, I discovered a rich fabric of donor sociality. This was constructed around both organized social events (formal, which were paid for from the office budget, and informal, which we paid for ourselves) as well as through encountering each other at the same shops and other public venues that we shared with the wealthiest 'white' Bolivians, referred to in Aymara as *k'ara*. Most aid staff, including me, lived in one of the several smart residential neighbourhoods in La Paz, renting houses from wealthy Bolivians from whose class came most of the government officials, consultants and leaders of donor-friendly NGOs that we met in our social round. Aid professionals were made to feel rapidly included within this element of Bolivian society, easily making a circle of friends through professional, sporting and cultural activities and with their children going to the same school – the German, American or French School – and using the sports clubs associated with these. Many *k'ara* had studied at American or European universities, and their professional knowledge and social interests were very similar to those of the donor community (Eyben and León 2005).

The relatively easy socialization between expatriate donor staff and the elite in Bolivia, as compared with other aid-recipient countries, may have placed an even greater barrier than elsewhere between donor staff and the mass of the population whose poverty-stricken situation was the reason for our presence. This socialization was also very visible. The Bolivian newspaper with the widest circulation in La Paz, *La Razon*, had a daily social/gossip column illustrated with photographs of the capital's elite at a round of luxurious parties and receptions. These pictures very frequently included donor representatives, who themselves were often the party givers and who had contacted the social editor of *La Razon* to ensure a press photographer would be present.

There were few businesspeople at donor-hosted receptions other than the odd visitor up from Bolivia's commercial capital in Santa Cruz. Many of the regulars were ministers, vice-ministers or heads of state organizations. Other guests had occupied such positions during a former administration and were now employed by aid agencies as consultants and advisers. Other guests were from the elite element of Bolivian 'civil society'. These were often kin to the politicians but were understood to be more radical, financed by international aid for playing the 'watchdog' role expected of them in the donors' liberal understanding of state-society relations. Like the consultants, NGO leaders were important sources of information and gossip, and several became close personal friends.

The first significant social event for a donor staff member newly arrived in the country was the welcome reception, usually hosted by the newcomer's immediate senior. In my case this was the British Ambassador, who identified the guests by selecting names from the Embassy's 'QBP list', that is, those invited to the annual Queen's Birthday Party (once in post, I developed my own networks and contacts who were in turn added to the QBP list, a matter to which the Embassy overall paid considerable attention). Then, when I had moved into my house, one I had carefully chosen because it had three interlinked reception rooms, I gave an informal housewarming party. Unlike the Ambassador's reception, the expressed purpose was enjoyment while laying the seeds for future friendships and relations of mutual confidence. I invited my immediate colleagues from DFID and the Embassy, all the bilateral and multilateral agency country representatives and those Bolivians whom I had already met and realized were significant for me in my role of influencing the government – 'policy dialogue'. Because the party was 'informal', I paid for it personally rather than from the official entertainment budget.

Backroom Coordination

At the start of the millennium Bolivia was a recognized 'pilot' in new approaches to aid such as basket funds (where several donors club together to fund a government programme) and harmonization (where donors agree to common procedures and recipient reporting requirements) as well as being among the first generation of countries taking a Poverty Reduction Strategy Paper to the World Bank and the International Monetary Fund (IMF). All these required that donor staff consult each other at frequent intervals to iron out any differences in approach and to agree on a joint line to take with the government. Such consultations took place at many formal meetings held not only in each other's offices but also at lunches of 'the likeminded' donors held in the private back room of a particular French restaurant, 'The Dumas', which was located close to most of our offices.

If one of us had a visitor from head office who was failing to understand the picture as seen from Bolivia and was causing difficulties, we would ask colleagues to meet the visitor not only at the customary cocktail party but also at a private dinner in our home or at 'The Dumas'. There, the task was to bring the head office visitor round to a different point of view concerning the realities of aid. The reverse could also happen. Soon after my arrival, along with other donor staff, I was invited to lunch at 'The Dumas' to meet an important visitor from the head office of one of our number. He turned out to be an old acquaintance of mine from my own head office days. In a hastily scribbled note, he asked me to dine with him privately that evening to advise him on how to handle his recalcitrant local man, who was refusing to follow the head office line.

Trust was important. On one occasion, I asked Mr A if he would help me influence the DFID to change its procedures. I drafted a letter that he then translated into his own language and sent to his boss at head office. The letter commented on how his DFID colleague (me) was being prevented by her head office from putting funds into a common donor basket, pointing out the irony of the situation, bearing in mind the rhetoric of harmonization that the DFID was espousing at global meetings. As he and I had hoped, his boss had the letter retranslated back into English and forwarded to his counterpart in London with a covering note that the U.K. did not appear to be practising what it was preaching to others. The letter's recipient was fighting his own internal battle on this same issue and used the letter as ammunition. Later, after both he and I had left the DFID, he admitted to me that he had suspected that I had been the author of Mr A's letter.

Real friendships as well as enmities developed among a relatively small group of people who communicated in a mixture of English and Spanish, and saw each other at meetings and at social events several times a week. On randomly opening my appointments diary for 2001, I find that in the space of thirty days from 8 January, when I returned to Bolivia from my Christmas holidays, I was out of La Paz for a total of three working days (a trip to the DFID office in Lima and a reality check to Potosí that I used a weekend for). The rest of the time was spent in La Paz, where I had only three meetings with recipients (one in the Ministry of Finance, one in the Ombudsperson's office and one in the Ministry of Health). All the other formal encounters were with international aid staff, including six lunches, four evening receptions and eleven meetings in our different offices.

Perforce we had to be nice to each other even when disputes over how to do aid became quite tense. Everyone had to be invited to particular parties – particularly those paid from our entertainment budget – even if working relations were difficult.

Leadership

A donor community is a political presence in any country. It seeks to influence change in that country through its intellectual and financial engagement with national and international actors and institutions. In that shared effort, there are intense internal political struggles. In Bolivia, authority and leadership within the community were primarily achieved through the capacity to exert patronage through networks of clients in and outside the recipient government as well as with fellow donors. Such capacity was only partly contingent on the size of the donor's budget; it also required access to information, social and political competence and prior reputation within the global donor network. Unlike the formal receptions where everyone was treated as theoretically equal, informal social occasions revealed this status differentiation. Country representatives from donor agencies with big budgets might find themselves excluded from the most prestigious yet informal events, should they be judged as having little political influence, boring and without a sense of fun.

The two clear leaders of the aid community were Mr A and the country representative of a multilateral organization, Mr B. Mr A was responding to his ministry's back-home interest in promoting the harmonization agenda. Mr B from the multilateral institution stood to gain in influence and authority – both with the recipient government and back at head office – the more that the bilateral donors and the other multilateral agencies agreed to a common framework of donor action, a framework that in most countries has resulted in his institution playing the leading role in managing policy dialogue and funds on behalf of the other donors.

Combined with a mutual commitment to making Bolivia known globally to be at the cutting edge of aid practice, Messrs A and B threw great parties. To their parties came all those invited, including not only the movers and shakers in the aid world but also the most important ministers, distinguished consultants (ex-ministers from the former administration) and newspaper editors. Their wives' contacts through school-based parents' associations or cultural activities in the world of art or theatre also brought to the parties certain people beyond the circle of aid relations. These guests appeared to be taking advantage of the invitation to provide a congenial locus for Bolivian wheeling and dealing beyond the concerns of Aidland. For our part, there was a touch of glamour in associating with the musicians and painters that Mesdames A and B had been cultivating.

This intense social life was noteworthy for the challenge the community faced in sustaining sociality with a fairly transient population. Most aid staff served between two and four years in the country. There was not only the need to integrate newcomers through welcome parties but also to maintain the social fabric when someone was departing. Thus, in addition to the formal farewell reception hosted by the Ambassador or other senior personage, there was the informal party hosted by one of the departing person's close donor friends. The party, involving skits, charades and generally 'taking the mickey' about key episodes in the departing colleague's life in Bolivia, was an opportunity for a collective laugh at the paradoxes and problems of our work, reinforcing a sense of donor community. I came to understand that the efforts at constructing and sustaining such a community are an essential component of a harmonized approach to aid, acting as a counterweight to the pressures on each country office from the demands from back home.

The Wider Picture

The Pressures of Back Home

Within our social life there were shared cultural values about 'back home' as being the ideal site of modernism where things work properly. It served as a reference to ideal models of how things should be done in recipient countries (Pritchett and Woolcock 2004). This shared culture informed much of the sense of belonging that I look at later with the notion of a global donor community.

The members of a local donor community are nearly all employees of large bureaucracies whose head office is back home in some other part of the world. Each of their bureaucracies has much in common, but also what we saw as notorious differences. These included, for example, the application of aid procedures that donor head offices struggle to harmonize against the objections of their respective national accounting offices. There may also be internal policy struggles between ministers and permanent civil servants or between sections of the ministry. These struggles back home are shaped by national characteristics of policy processes as well as by historically and contextually derived positions on certain topics (van Gastel and Nuijten 2005). It was a regular topic of interest and discussion within the local donor community to compare and contrast the political processes that characterized their different administrations. It was a relief to a frustrated official to complain about his or her head office over a drink with sympathetic colleagues from other aid agencies.

For those working for multilateral organizations, their bureaucratic 'back home' is Washington, Brussels or New York, where rules and values are constructed locally through self-reference (Mosse, Chapter 4 this volume). Struggles within the multilateral part of a local donor community can reflect strong disagreements between their respective head offices. The situation of those working for bilateral aid programmes is rather different. For them, 'back home' is directly connected via their head office with a government and the citizens whose taxes are paying their salaries. In some cases, donor staff saw the local representatives of 'back home' to be their diplomatic colleagues, staff from the Ministries of Foreign Affairs. While in many instances there was a coincidence of concerns, at other times the ambassador and foreign ministry colleagues would feel the need to represent their country's specific values and national commercial or political interests as distinct from aspiring to those global goals of international development that were the concern of the donor staff. Depending on time and place, the local head of the aid agency may be more or less independent of ambassadorial influence. At the time I was in Bolivia, the DFID's position as a separate department of state from the Foreign Office meant it had greater autonomy from the diplomatic perspective than was the case for many other aid agencies.

A head of the country office of a bilateral aid agency – or his or her equivalent, the development counsellor at an Embassy – may, out of a sense of obligation or enjoyment, participate in the kind of 'back home' nostalgic social life such as the St Andrew's night parties described by Rajak and Stirrat (Chapter 8 this volume). This had been the lifestyle of the now largely vanished TCOs mentioned earlier, each with their own national club where they mixed with other expatriates from the same home country. However, for those who have replaced the TCOs – the staff of aid agency country offices – spending too much of their social life within their own expatriate community, whether Dutch, British or German, would symbolically send the wrong signals about their commitment to the new aid agenda. In practical terms it would result in their not having invested sufficiently in the trust-based personal relationships required to take them through the rocks and rapids of negotiating a multidonor budget support facility.

For me the centrifugal force of back home was of secondary importance because my head office, like that of Mr A, emphasized donor coordination and harmonized approaches. For others, whose head offices were more ambivalent about harmonization or where broader national constituencies for aid were pursuing certain influential agendas, back home was likely to have a stronger influence. As I will now go on to exemplify, national values, history and domestic aid constituencies may influence the politics of aid within the local donor community.

Fighting the Thirty Years War

One of the commitments of the Paris Declaration is for donors to harmonize their analyses of the country situation as a foundation to agreeing on a common strategy of support. However, the assumption that all donors can agree a common interpretation of the local context ignores how perspectives may be shaped by a donor country's historical trajectories, undermining the hoped-for harmony of a local donor community.

In a number of EU countries a key political constituency for foreign aid is the church; aid ministries subsidize many of its development activities. At the time about which I am writing, the long-term source of funds for the Bolivian Catholic Church's involvement in poverty and social justice issues was the German branch of the Catholic NGO Caritas and, through Caritas, technical assistance and funding from the German government technical cooperation agency, GTZ.[8] Thus, taking advantage of support from Germany, the Bolivian Bishops' Conference formed in March 1998 a Jubilee 2000 group to campaign for debt relief. During the subsequent government-run National Dialogue on Poverty Reduction Strategy, which was a donor requirement for securing the debt relief, the Church campaigned energetically and successfully to include in the Dialogue's conclusions what it described as a social control mechanism for monitoring the implementation of the Strategy.

Meanwhile, it occurred to a number of donor representatives, including me, that logically harmonization should also mean coordinating our support to civil society as well as to government. If we established a common basket fund to which all eligible civil society organizations could apply on the basis of clear rules of competition, this would do away with the invidious clientelistic nature of donor-NGO relations that we perceived as mirroring the patrimonial character of Bolivian society. It would also demonstrate our commitment to the value of working together. We convinced a number of influential Bolivians of our case and the Office of the Presidency set up a small working group to develop the proposal.

At evening receptions and coffee breaks at donor meetings, I began to hear warnings of the problems we were likely to run into. Mr A became anxious. Was this initiative worthwhile if it would involve us in a major disagreement? It appeared that donors did not wish to surrender their particular, one-to-one relations with specific parts of civil society. There was a clear antipathy to switching to financing Bolivian civil society directly rather than through northern NGOs, an important 'back home' political constituency for the aid programmes of donor governments. Thus, while temporary and limited basket funds for support to Bolivian civil society were deemed acceptable in relation to monitoring the Poverty Reduction Strategy, anything more ambitious was considered 'very difficult'.

It also became apparent that the Church had been actively lobbying to squash the idea, seeing the basket fund as a threat to its own proposed social control mechanism, through which it was aiming to play a leading role. That the basket fund proposal had been designed by a working group that was composed of well-known Bolivian anticlericals only confirmed the suspicions of the Church.[9]

Despite the bilateral aid community having established strong links of trust and collaboration in the Poverty Reduction Strategy process, faultlines developed in relation to this proposal, particularly over our different understandings of the role of the Catholic Church in society. The political constituencies for international aid in different European 'back homes' were the principal driver of this dispute, one that some of the principal protagonists personalized by reflecting on their respective countries' histories and the European religious wars of the sixteenth and seventeenth centuries. Passions ran high. In a heated moment the donor representative from Germany remarked of a colleague from a neighbouring country that he was 'fighting the Thirty Years War all over again in Bolivia'. The influence of back home – its current politics and its past history – was more important in this case than the collective commitment to harmonization. It is also noteworthy that it was another global – in this case religious – institution that exposed the faultlines in the global aid community.

A Global Community

For donors, 'community' bears one of three qualifiers: the international community, the development community and the donor community. There are fuzzy and shifting boundaries between the three. The first variously means the G8 group of states, the OECD countries or everyone with a seat at the UN, UN agencies and international finance institutions, as well as those who have ECOSOC observer status as an international NGO. It is a value-laden concept and thus precious to those who use it, that is, principally people who define themselves and who are defined by others in that community as members.

Although the boundaries of the international community are contentious, for example, when transnational corporations become delegates at UN conferences, within those boundaries is a subcommunity that describes itself firmly and undisputedly as the donor community. My impression is that this public and uncontested recognition of a donor community is fairly new. I do not recollect its use in the 1970s when I first entered Aidland. What may have occurred is a growing formalization of a locus of relations, practice and values that has accelerated with the trend towards harmonization of the aid effort. The donor community can be distinguished from the wider development community, the latter including not only the bilateral and multilateral aid agencies that are the subject of this chapter but also development consultants, those working for international NGOs and development studies institutes. The boundaries are porous. Individuals move from this wider 'community' into official aid, as do the senior officials from aid-recipient countries, recruited into the UN or the World Bank to then negotiate loans and grants with recipients in other countries from the other side of the desk.

Considered another way, donor professionals are a subclass of a global elite of cosmopolitan citizens, a class of professionals whose commitment is to their profession rather than to any particular locus (Isin and Wood 1999). Some home-type cosmopolitan citizens travel frequently but stay most of the time in their home country. However, many donor professionals do not only live symbolically in a global frame of reference but, like employees of transnational corporations, are full-time and long-term nomads. They move every few years to another locality while also being involved on a longer-term basis in a set of relationships, meanings and values defined by a transnational network rather than by territory (Hannerz 1990). Yet, as Rajak and Stirrat (Chapter 8 this volume) point out, this internationalism is 'parochial' in the sense that it is based on a particular set of ideas as to what development is and how it should be attained. Because they stay on the edge, rather than fully engage with diverse cultural experiences, development professionals are not 'cosmopolitan' as understood by Hannerz; rather, they are internationally 'monocultural'. Wherever they go, they find others who will interact with them in terms of specialized but collectively held understandings.

That the global community exerts pressures to conform is illustrated by my second example of a rupture in social relations in the local donor community in La Paz. In this dispute, I was one of the principal protagonists, pushing for a project that the donors' key contacts within the government did not want. Within the local donor community, I was the acknowledged intellectual leader on one of the themes of the Bolivian Poverty Reduction Strategy, 'social exclusion'. Messrs A and B were happy to go along with me. In formal meetings with the Bolivian government they supported my statements on how the government should be more energetic in tackling the causes of exclusion. When a Bolivian researcher brought to my attention the exclusionary consequences for the many Bolivians without identity cards, I persuaded three other bilateral donor agencies, including Mr A's agency, to join with DFID in financing a civil society consortium to tackle the problem by facilitating people to get identity cards and by campaigning for the government to pay greater attention to the matter. Then the other donors got cold feet. Key contacts in government used picnics and parties to tell them to back off. I received an angry letter from the Vice-Minister for Development Co-operation informing me that this was a 'donor-led' initiative, contravening the spirit of 'country ownership'. Mr A decided to pull out, immediately followed by one of the other donors. I was undermining the commitment donors had made to harmonize their support to a government-led strategy (Eyben with León 2005).

That I was able to start this initiative could be attributable to my already having decided to leave my job in DFID and join the Institute of Development Studies (IDS). If my situation had been otherwise, I might not have been prepared to stick my neck out in this way. The decision of the other donor staff to pull out when the government expressed its displeasure was, I suggest, influenced by their intention to remain part of the wider global community and by their wish to take with them the values and ways of working developed in the Bolivian harmonization 'pilot' when they moved to other aid-dependent countries.

The rift I caused in the local donor community led to my no longer being invited to the Sunday picnics. Although everyone came to the British Ambassador's formal farewell reception on my departure, my erstwhile colleagues did not organize for me the informal goodbye party that was the custom for departing heads of country offices before they moved to other posts.

Whereas in the first rupture – 'fighting the Thirty Years War' – the politics and values of 'back home' caused a rift in the local donor community, in the second case the rift was caused by one of the community members (me) deliberately rejecting the donor values that were a reflection of the wider global community to which the donor staff in La Paz saw themselves as belonging. In both cases our social life, constructed and sustained to create shared values and trust, was affected by these disturbances. In the second instance the main offender was 'punished' by being denied an important ritual of transition from one locality to another within the global space. However, because back home offered an opportunity to leave Aidland, this sanction had little impact. However, individuals who sought to remain in that world would have been running the risk of damaging their reputation in the global community. Email gossip, encounters with back home visitors or chats at international conferences all help to ensure that one is already known about before ever arriving in one's new posting. The frequency of meetings between staff from different head offices means that people remain part of this global community even when they are assigned a desk in the ministry back home.

Thus, the normative imperative of harmonization in any particular aid-recipient country is reinforced by ascribed membership in a global donor community, characterized by being relatively exclusive, of relatively long duration and with members united by sentiment with shared knowledge, values, norms and practices. This explains why people do not want to undertake reality checks and risk learning what may be uncomfortable truths. In the next section I will discuss how donor sociality is an essential element in constructing what is acceptable policy knowledge.

Policy Knowledge and the Irrelevance of the Local

The harmonization of aid expenditure in support of government policy requires a single shared diagnosis of the problems of poverty in any aid-recipient country. Undertaking such a diagnosis is a social process. In most cases the donor staff's knowledge and representation of the local is largely derived from their mutual interaction. Old hands tell newcomers what they need to know.

However, some knowledge is gained from interaction with a third set of actors – key individuals from the recipient country, particularly those hired as local staff members or regular consultants, senior officials in government ministries and middle-class leaders of NGOs that subsist on foreign funding. In Bolivia, Mr A, Mr B and their colleagues worked hard to incorporate such individuals into our social as well as professional lives. Unless I made a real effort to go and find my own friends and organize my own social life, it was these individuals that mediated the local for us.

After I left Bolivia, thinking back on the episode of the 'Thirty Years War', I began to explore the literature and interrogate Bolivian friends passing through the IDS concerning the political role of the Church in Bolivia. I found that my friends were happy enough to talk about the issue once I raised it with them, but realized that, as a donor staff member in Bolivia, it was not a subject often discussed in the analyses that Bolivian academics prepared for a donor audience. There were probably many other subjects of which donors were unaware. Although donors funded a considerable number of studies and analyses of Bolivian economy, society and politics, it may be that these studies tended to tell the story of Bolivia in a certain way, sufficient and appropriate for donors in drawing up evidence-based country strategy plans, but staying silent on much of the historical and paradoxical complexity of the local political community. Significantly, the success of Evo Morales in the 2005 Presidential elections came as a surprise to the donor community. They were unprepared.

The Bolivian officials and consultants who came to our receptions, dinners and picnics had a shared understanding with the donors of the way the world worked. This understanding had become so deeply ingrained that we were no longer capable of imagining other kinds of approaches, even when the views of local people broke rudely into our deliberations. On one occasion, crowds were rioting in the main street of La Paz outside the Ministry of Finance. Those of us inside in a meeting with the Director General and his staff were wiping our eyes from the tear gas that had seeped in through the cracks in the windows as we continued to ignore the riot and discuss the contents of the Poverty Reduction Strategy.

International aid practice is currently concerned with coordinating its activities in support of global targets agreed in the global donor community. In that respect the local is messy because it reveals complexities and particularities that obscure the simplicity of the targets. The global donor community serves to shield staff from this messiness and supports the managerial approach to aid that allows donors to protect the purity of their mission and their clear harmonized objectives (Mosse 2005b). This is why any attempt to experience the local, for example through reality checks beyond the confines of the donor community, is likely to be perceived as unnecessary and a waste of time.

Following one reality check visit in Bolivia, I wrote a note to my regional director at head office entitled 'Listening to the Unpalatable'. I had met people whose stories, problems and achievements illuminated and challenged various aspects of our aid policies:

> In Tupiza, farmers spoke of how they felt the Government had abandoned them when opening up Bolivian markets to foreign competition. In the hinterland of Santa Cruz, I met a family making straw brooms in a shed. They buy their straw (a kind of sorghum) from farmers in the Chaco who grow it especially for them. Business was declining because of the importation of plastic brooms from Chile. *Question*: We are supporting Bolivian policies to make its producers more competitive, but the current 'losers' believe no one cares anymore and, in any case, how can straw brooms seriously become more 'competitive'? Obviously urban consumers are benefiting from buying longer lasting plastic brooms but extreme poverty is in rural Bolivia and these are the apparent losers. I am not sure how we can help the broom-makers with our support to free trade principles. A protection for artisan industries used to work well in India for poor rural people but I believe this was abolished when India adopted free trade principles.

I bought a scruffy broom from my interlocutors. It was not sufficiently aesthetically pleasing to display as a symbol of my cosmopolitan lifestyle. I left it behind on a seat at Santa Cruz Airport. My director never responded to my note and soon afterwards I left the country and DFID.

As there was no response to this or similar notes from other visits, I can only speculate on the reactions of the recipients of the notes. From numerous subsequent conversations with staff in DFID and other bilateral aid agencies, it is likely that they did not want to know about the complexity of the local that contradicted pre-established global policy objectives.

The Global Scope of Aid

To understand why the local may be irrelevant to donor staff even when living and working in an aid-recipient country, it is helpful to distinguish between place and space. One way of looking at this is to think of physical localities – or places – where each one of us lives, breathes and runs our daily lives as distinct from what has been described as spaces of engagement where the relationships of the local place are inserted into broader sets of communication and encounters that interact with the local (Marston 2000) .

The Internet revolution has enabled the local place and the space of engagement connected with it to become increasingly irrelevant for those with global agendas. Communication is no longer dependent on geographical proximity but on other kinds of proximities – linguistic, political, cultural, ideological, etc. However, some sense of local place and community is still necessary to support a life in a global space. Most people cannot live in an entirely virtual world and this is why sociality is so important in the everyday life of donors. Hence, the intense social round of meetings, lunches, receptions and picnics were a continuous effort to re-create and sustain the global policy space and to prevent the local political space from disrupting it – as it occasionally did when the tear gas came through the window in our meeting in the Ministry of Finance.

The Internet is a creator of networks with nodes in many different localities that are in constant communication with each other to deliver the same 'product' in much the same way for optimal impact and efficiency (Urry 2005). Thus, the new aid modalities of budget support and harmonization are products of a network of international donors seeking to secure the same effect in many different localities. The Internet has enabled the international aid system to be more effective than ever before in retailing concepts and approaches to poverty reduction that are produced wholesale in global spaces. It has meant that contextually specific projects are being replaced by harmonized expenditure of money that risks being disconnected from having any immediately discernible impact on identifiable beneficiaries.

The Internet is a technology that has facilitated the global harmonization of aid, but donor sociality in particular places employs for this new purpose the long-standing tradition of face-to-face encounters through dinners, tennis parties, receptions and picnics. Sociality serves to exclude knowledge that might undermine what donors need to believe.

Conclusion

The outward form of sociality should not mislead us into imagining that the meaning stays unchanged. For example, throwing parties for head office visitors has been a long-standing element of donor sociality, one with which I have been familiar since first moving to Aidland more than thirty years ago. While the host's purpose of demonstrating his or her status – both to the visitor and the local guests – through his or her convocation power stays constant, there is a new meaning in this event for those aid agencies fully subscribed to the normative imperative of working together. The head office visitor's role is to engage in the local social round to demonstrate approval of and to validate the local harmonination effort in support of a globally established agenda. External threats provoke a collective effort to ward off the uncomfortable reality by constructing a common policy knowledge that for a time at least can ignore its presence (Cadell and Yanacopulos 2006). Sociality enables denial.

The reality of local politics also manifests itself as an internal threat to sociality when a member of the donor community can no longer personally tolerate the divergence between what the recipient government and its donors state they are doing and the reality of the lives of the people in the country being helped. In the case of the lack of identity cards briefly described above, in the first instance I sought to enrol other members of the community to support a project that would change our common perception of the country's reality. In so doing, I challenged the veracity of the relationship between us and the government officials who participated in our social round. The rupture was repaired by my (self-) expulsion.

The other rift described in this chapter concerned the contradictions in the back home agenda and the discursive disjuncture between harmonization and sustaining a domestic constituency for aid. On the same visit, head office visitors may publicly represent themselves as part of the global donor community, hotfooted from an international conference on aid harmonization, but, in private, give warnings to their local representative about politics back home and the need to be cautious about signing up to a particular agenda of the donor community.

Tensions and conflict within the donor community may be more often an outcome of disagreements originating in their various back homes than of any difference in interpretation of reality in the place where staff are temporarily resident. Personal passions and loyalties may come into play regarding how one handles these tensions, and friendships may founder. Nevertheless, the greater threat (and therefore, I suggest, the one less likely to occur because of the stronger sanctions) is when a member of the donor community rejects the knowledge that donor sociality needs to jointly construct with those in the recipient country with whom they share an interest to keep disbursing the money. This is why it is wiser, if one wants to stay in the community, not to make rural reality checks but rather go on picnics to the countryside with one's donor agency friends.

Postscript: La Paz in 2008

Shortly after completing the final version of this chapter, I visited La Paz in early 2008 and interviewed former contacts about the changes that had taken place following the election of a social revolutionary government.

On reading the present chapter, two expatriate staff members from different European aid agencies commented that donor staff were even more isolated in 2008 from local realities than when I had been there. During the political turmoil of 2003–5, the already rare field visits stopped completely and whatever habit there had been of making such visits entirely disappeared. Donor staff were still giving parties, but only for each other. Government officials did not attend, and donors found it much harder to know what was going on. Most of the NGO leaders whom donors used to know, become friends with and invite to their homes had lost political influence, were largely excluded from political decision-making inside government and were replaced by social movement leaders. It appeared that much of the donor socializing was now just a way of spending one's leisure time. Donor parties were no longer a key venue for doing business either with each other or with government and NGO leaders. The social pages were absent from *La Razon* in the week I was in La Paz and I was told that big parties in restaurants and hotels were less common than before.

I found that nearly all those Bolivians with whom donors had had the closest relationship, for example those in the Ministry of Finance, had left government employment. Some had been hired by donor agencies. This was repeating a pattern observed when I was in Bolivia at the beginning of the decade, when those temporarily out of favour drew an income from donors while remaining part of the broader web of social and political relations that made up the ruling elite irrespective of the composition of any particular government. As past and future officials, these 'national professionals' had been useful intermediaries between government and donors and an important part of the social round that I have described in this chapter. It took expatriate staff in donor agencies some time to realize that circumstances had changed. Their Bolivian staff had lost their intermediary role. Those now in government had their own web of social and political relations, one that barely overlapped the one with which donors were familiar and were to some extent part of. Indeed, donors were irritating the new revolutionary government by hiring bureaucrats from the old regime, strengthening the government's suspicion of the long-established donors, turning instead to Venezuela and Cuba.

In its first year, the new government declared no interest in receiving support from Bolivia's traditional donors because of their close ties with the old regime and their alleged role as architects of neoliberalism. Donors' disbursement dropped significantly. Consultants – donors' knowledge brokers who designed and monitored aid projects and programmes – found themselves without employment. Meanwhile, in response to their head offices' requirement that country offices be seen to be implementing the Paris Declaration, donor representatives in Bolivia formed a coordination group to which all were invited other than those from Cuba and Venezuela, whose presence would have constrained donors' scope for political gossip about the new regime. As new staff arrived without the prior experience of how things used to be in the good old days, they realized that the new government was concerned with just one pillar of the Declaration – 'country ownership'; aid relations would be conducted in the way it, not the donors, preferred.

By the second anniversary of the new regime donors were managing to spend a bit more money, but nothing comparable to the large basket funds of yore. Although the donor group spoke of the need for mutually coordinated aid, agencies began to realize that in the interests of their back-home disbursement pressures they would have to negotiate separately with whichever line ministry they could find that might be interested in their aid.

Most interestingly, the new regime has clearly showed its intention to break the knowledge/power collusion between traditional donors and Bolivian officials. A decree prevents any official from being given a contract by an aid agency, as an employee, consultant or NGO coordinator, for up to two years after leaving government employment. As they say in Spanish, *una otra realidad* ('another reality') is informing the government's vision.

Notes

1. From a back to office report of a visit to the Amazon region of Bolivia, 30 January 2002.
2. These activities are certainly very time-consuming. A DFID staff member working in an African country, himself keen to undertake a reality check, recently emailed me:
   'You will ... be delighted to hear (and the classic example of the capital trap) that ... I was confronted by a three-day log-framing workshop (in the Intercontinental Hotel) for the next phase of our budget support which I had to attend. Still trying to struggle with the logic (*sic*) of fitting an input (Direct Budget Support) into a logframe as if it were a project. Assumptions column as a result will be massive, outputs will be conditionalities, as far as I can tell, and activities involve signing a cheque ... Of course it will be made to look much better, but it will remain a curious example of inappropriate linear thinking in a hugely complex context.'
3. http://www.gsdrc.org/go/topic-guides/drivers-of-change; Sida 2006.
4. This section uses the history of British aid as an example. I am not aware of any comparative study of the history and culture of government aid agencies, but from conversations with staff I believe that the overall trend described here was replicated in other agencies.
5. I am grateful to Robert Chambers for reminding me of this and also overall for his helpful comments on an earlier version of this chapter. The chapter also benefited from comments received from the IDS participation team's monthly 'writers' circle', as well as from excellent feedback from this present volume's editor.
6. See my article on 'harmonization' (Eyben 2007). The persistence of the 'one size fits all' approach can be fruitfully explained through various theoretical lenses, including political economy concepts of interest and Gramscian analyses of hegemonic practices (Utting 2006) as well as more Foucauldian understandings of governmentality as a discipline (Mosse 2005b). Another explanation, proffered to me by a very senior international aid official, is that it is a cartelization response by the traditional aid agencies to the growing threat to their authority over aid-recipient countries from the new former Third World donors, particularly China.
7. The Utstein Four was initially an informal group of four women ministers for international development (the U.K., Germany, the Netherlands and Norway) who got together to push forward the new aid agenda.
8. The close relationship between the Bolivian Bishops' Conference and the German government was illustrated by a news item in the Bolivian press (*La Razon*) concerning the visit by the bishops to the Vatican in the week of 8–13 April 2002, followed by a visit to Germany where they had a meeting with the Minister for Development Co-operation.
9. A fuller account of this episode is provided in Eyben 2003.

References

Caddell, M and Yanacopulos, H. 2006. 'Knowing But Not Knowing: Conflict, Development and Denial', *Conflict, Security & Development* 6(4): 557–79.

Cohen, A. 1968. 'Development in Africa: The Problems of Today', *African Affairs* 266: 44–54.

Crewe, E. and P. Fernando. 2006. 'The Elephant in the Room: Racism in Representations, Relationships and Rituals', *Progress in Development Studies* 6(1): 40–54.

Eyben, R. 2003. 'Donors as Political Actors: Fighting the Thirty Years War in Bolivia', *IDS Working Paper No. 183*. Brighton: Institute of Development Studies.

———. 2007. 'Harmonisation', *Development in Practice* 17(4/5): 640–46.

Eyben, R. and R. León. 2005. 'Whose Aid? The Case of the Bolivian Elections Project', in D. Mosse and D. Lewis (eds), *The Aid Effect: Giving and Governing in International Development*. London: Pluto Press.

Hannerz, U. 1990. 'Cosmopolitans and Locals in World Culture', in U. Hannerz (ed.), *Global Culture*. Newbury Park, C.A.: Sage.

Irvine, R., R. Chambers and R. Eyben. 2006. 'Learning from People Living in Poverty: Learning from Immersions', in R. Eyben (ed.), *Relationships for Aid*. London: Earthscan, 63–79.

Isin, Engin F. and Patricia K. Wood. 1999. *Citizenship and Identity*. London: Sage.

Kothari, U. 2005. *A Radical History of Development Studies*. London: Zed Books.

Marston, S. 2000. 'The Social Construction of Scale', *Progress in Human Geography* 24(2): 219–42.

Mosse, D. 2005a. *Cultivating Development: An Ethnography of Aid Policy and Practice* London: Pluto Press.

———. 2005b. 'Global Governance and the Ethnography of International Aid', in D. Mosse and D. Lewis (eds), *The Aid Effect: Giving and Governing in International Development*. London: Pluto Press, 1–36.

OECD. 2005. The Paris Declaration on Aid Effectiveness. Development Assistance Committee. Paris: OECD, www.oecd.org.

Pritchett, Lant and Michael Woolcock. 2004. 'Solutions When the Solution is the Problem: Arraying the Disarray in Development', *World Development* 32(2): 191–212.

Sida. 2006. 'Power Analysis – Experiences and Challenges', Concept Note. Department for Democracy and Social Development. Stockholm: Sida.

Soper, T. 1966. 'External Aid,' *African Affairs* 65(259): 148–59.

Urry, J. 2005. 'The Complexities of the Global', *Theory, Culture and Society* 22(5): 235–54.

Van Gastel, J. and M. Nuijten. 2005. 'The Genealogy of the "Good Governance" and "Ownership" Agenda at the Dutch Ministry of Development Co-operation', in D. Mosse and D. Lewis (eds), *The Aid Effect: Giving and Governing in International Development*. London: Pluto Press.

Chapter 8

PAROCHIAL COSMOPOLITANISM AND THE POWER OF NOSTALGIA

—— ∞ ——

Dinah Rajak and Jock Stirrat

Introduction

The international development industry turns over millions of dollars a year, employing thousands of people. It brings together aid personnel from all over the world, many of them working outside their home countries. For some, these foreign sojourns consist of short, fleeting visits: a week or two here, a month or so there. For others, much longer periods – in some cases their whole lives – are spent away from their 'home' countries. And as part of this world of movement, people working in the aid industry move from one agency to another. Relatively few make their careers in one organization and increasingly careers consist of a series of time-bound contracts varying from a few days to a few years.

On the face of it, those who work in development would seem to approximate to what at least on a popular level one might classify as 'cosmopolitans'.[1] Their peripatetic existence, their continual exposure to varying and ever-changing cultural and political milieux, their commitment to an international rather than a local set of objectives and organizations: all would seem to indicate a highly cosmopolitan world. And of course there is a sense in which this is true. People who work in development tend to see themselves as 'cosmopolitans', able to take a wider view of the world than their colleagues who are tied to particular places, particular cultures and particular polities. Yet at the same time, as we shall show in this chapter, their cosmopolitanism is of a particular kind, nuanced in specific directions, and in many ways can be described as a very parochial form of cosmopolitanism.

In this chapter our aim is to explore some aspects of the world of the development worker. On the one hand, we examine the way in which the development industry and the people who work in it can be understood as 'cosmopolitan' in the sense that they attempt to deny the local and the parochial. But on the other hand, what is equally apparent is that the world of development people is frequently extremely parochial in the sense that it is based on a particular set of ideas as to what development is and how it should be attained, and in the sense that the people involved are often trying to recreate forms of life which, far from stressing the inclusivity of 'true' cosmopolitanism, are based on the exclusivity of parochialism. This in turn, it seems to us, is linked to a sense of nostalgia for an imagined home, a recreation of that home in a foreign land. Yet this is not the only nostalgia to be found in the world of development. If one form of nostalgia looks back to an imagined homeland, another looks back to an imagined world of 'pre-development' similar to Rosaldo's 'imperial nostalgia' where, 'people mourn the passing of what they themselves have transformed' (Rosaldo 1989). So if, as we shall argue later, cosmopolitanism is in many ways a denial of parochial pasts, the cosmopolitanism of the development world coexists – indeed, perhaps depends upon – the nostalgic creations of imagined past parochialisms.

This chapter is based on our experience of working in the development industry over a number of years, either as consultants or social impact advisers on various research and technology transfer projects in the field of aquaculture, fisheries and forestry. Therefore, it does not make the same kind of claims as a conventional piece of ethnography, based on a clearly defined period of participant observation. As former colleagues become the subject of our anthropological interest and enquiry, this dual role of 'participant-insider' is, as David Mosse (2005) warns us, problematic, blurring the lines between 'social investigation and lived experience' (Mosse 2005: ix). But that is, we hope, also its strength. After all, some of the best ethnographic insights come from a level of engagement that can be achieved only by working truly 'inside' the 'field' – whether a development institution or a multinational corporation – even if it makes our position uncomfortable, conflicted and potentially controversial.

The World of Development

Generalizing about the development world is not easy, for it is characterized by its complex and often contradictory nature. Thus, at one extreme it consists of vast, complex bureaucracies such as the multilateral development banks operating at a global or regional level and the various multilateral agencies working under the UN banner, whilst at the other extreme there is a horde of small and often ephemeral non-governmental organizations (NGOs) and civil society organizations (CSOs) concentrating on small and local issues. In between these two extremes there are the official bilateral agencies, often vehicles for the political ambitions of donor countries, the 'international NGOs' working in a range of countries and a few major private foundations. Finally, there are the various commercial companies which in one way or another are active in the world of development.

What links these various organizations is a complicated flow of resources, people and ideas. Resources flow from donors through multilateral and bilateral agencies not only directly to recipient governments but also to the NGOs at international, national and local levels. Similarly, resources activated by international NGOs both from the bilateral agencies and from their own fundraising activities feed through into 'partner organizations' in the developing world. Commercial companies and many NGOs at the national and local level depend on these resources for their operations. The result is a highly interdependent system where in the end most organizations working in development depend on a relatively small number of major donor agencies. This, of course, implies a certain pressure towards conformity. This is not to say that there are not disagreements and argument within the world of development, and many NGOs attempt to present themselves as radical critics of the way in which the development industry works. But these criticisms are managed and muted in various ways, which in the end the critics accept as, after all, they are dependent on the largesse of the donors. In addition, as we will argue later, this dependency creates a centripetal tendency towards conformity within the world of development, a conformity which could be seen as cosmopolitan or parochial.

Just as resources move through the development industry and ultimately produce a form of unity, so too do people. Here it has to be admitted that the picture is even more complex and it is impossible to generalize for all who work in the development industry.

First, the boundaries are unclear and porous. People move in and out, some only working for a year or so, some only for a few weeks, in the development industry. This is particularly the case for those working for commercial companies with specialist technical skills, for instance, engineers or specialist accountants. Others make their whole careers in the industry either within one organization or by spiralling through various organizations, holding contracts of varying durations. Some stay within one sector, for instance, always working for NGOs or specialist relief agencies, whilst others move from one sector to another (see Lewis, Chapter 9 this volume). One of the most common career paths is that which takes a person from working as a volunteer in an NGO, through a paid job within an NGO, up through NGO management into the world of bilateral and multilateral agencies.[2] Some remain 'technical specialists' throughout their lives in development; others move from agriculture or fisheries into more administrative or generalist roles. Recently, due to shifting policy frameworks, an increasing number of development practitioners are moving from the 'technical' to the 'social' or are becoming jacks-of-all-trades. Thus, a technical fisheries development worker commented that 'there's no money in science anymore, but if you can do livelihoods you can get a grand a day from DFID'. For some, the world of development is their only source of income. For others it is combined with other professions, most notably (or notoriously?) academia.

However, what is striking overall is how many people tend to stay within the industry. Admittedly there are people who after five or ten years of working in development move out, yet these are relatively few.

Here some distinctions have to be made, although these distinctions are by no means hard and fast. First, there are the relatively few people in the development industry who have permanent contracts, mainly those working for the large official bilateral and multilateral agencies and the large international NGOs. For them there is frequently a cycling of 'overseas postings', two years abroad being followed by a similar period in the home country. Secondly, there are the short-term consultants, frequently based in their 'home countries' and employed on a series of contracts measured in days and weeks, occasionally months. Finally, there are the longer term contract workers employed for periods measured in years, who move from one contract to another, as far as possible in a seamless fashion. These in many ways form the social 'core' of the industry in the sense of providing a thread of continuity in the development capitals of the world.

Admittedly, there is what might be called 'wastage' in the industry. People do leave and move into other careers not associated with development,[3] but this is relatively rare and most remain associated with development. In part it is a matter of skills: it could be argued that working in development 'deskills' people from following other career options, but it is also something more: it becomes an addiction to a particular sort of lifestyle. And this is a way of life which involves movement, at least of a geographic sort. Very few people working in development spend all their lives in one country, although many attempt this and a few succeed. Much more common is more or less continuous movement. Short-term consultants in particular can rack up an extremely impressive list of countries in which they have worked, thirty or forty not being unusual. And even longer term consultants can show an impressive range of countries in which they have worked over their careers.

Now of course geographical mobility in itself does not necessarily produce a cosmopolitan sensibility and, as we shall argue later, may produce the opposite. Yet the very fact of frequent movement, the continual shifting from one cultural context to another, whether from Europe to Africa or Tanzania to Nepal, does, at least at the simplistic level, create the semblance of cosmopolitanism. Here are people who, to a greater or lesser extent, have lives which are not focused on any one place but rather are focused on a particular process or set of ideas. Indeed, this is how they tend to see themselves and present the lives they lead. The sorts of contrasts that are made are between the changing and exotic worlds they live in and the boring, stultifying and conformist lives they have left behind in their home countries. They present themselves as rootless in the sense that wherever they are is home; that home is not territorially defined in any simplistic sense. Home – at least in the immediate sense – is where one happens to be living.

However, there is more to their claim to 'cosmopolitanism' than simply being rootless wanderers across the face of the earth. They also claim to be the bearers of cosmopolitan values and virtues, and the enemies of parochialism.

Cosmopolitan Values?

Earlier we mentioned that although the architecture of the development industry is complex – one might say confused – in a sense it is highly organized because it depends ultimately on a relatively small group of donors who, to a greater or lesser extent, share a set of common ideas as to what development is and how it should be achieved. These ideas change over time but, even so, at any given time there is general broad agreement as to what should be done and how. So, for instance, policies based on the 'Washington Consensus' were not simply the property of the World Bank or the IMF but were more generally subscribed to throughout the development industry. Similarly, the stress on participatory methods, although it might have been first adopted by the NGO sector, is now general currency throughout the industry.

What is interesting in the present context is not whether one approach is 'better' than another, but that they are presented as having a global significance, as generally true and not in any sense as a cultural production. Thus, the claims that lie behind structural adjustment were based on the premise that there were universal truths about how national governments should and could manage their economies. Similarly, the promotion of participatory approaches to development is premised on the view that participation is not only more effective than other forms of development, but is also based on a universally true and morally correct set of assumptions about the nature of human beings.[4]

What is being claimed here is a transnational, transcultural set of truths: pure rationality unencumbered by social or cultural or indeed political baggage. This is not to say that local particularities and peculiarities are totally ignored, but that they are secondary, a matter of practice and contingency.[5] Furthermore, it is not to say that there are no arguments within and between organizations as to what is 'the truth', but rather to stress that the claims which emerge from these debates are claims to universality.

So, for instance, market relations are seen as embodying a truth about human and social nature. Other ways of organizing exchange are the result of 'cultural' factors, culture somehow preventing the evolution and expression of the 'truth' and the universal and timeless validity of the market principle. As a senior executive in a transnational company put it to one of us, 'the market is like gravity'. Similarly, the appeal for 'participatory' approaches to development is premised on another (not all that different) set of universal values where people are helped to throw off the shackles of culture and domination. And, of course, the overall objectives of the development industry are underpinned by a series of supposedly universal methodologies: cost-benefit analysis, stakeholder analysis, participatory rural appraisal, logframe analysis, etc. Universal tools exercised by a cosmopolitan profession are supposedly as valid in one country as they are in another (Green 2003).

This, then, is at an ideological level a world of cosmopolitan virtues, where universal rationality rather than particularistic cultural assumptions are deemed to be all-important. In this sense the particular geographic situation of development people is irrelevant and, as it were, accidental. Whether it is rural Niger, urban Mumbai or suburban Rio is irrelevant, as these are only the local settings for more general (and more rational) truths to be worked out. Development people are the bearers of this cosmopolitan rationality, sharing a common set of universally relevant tools and sharing a common set of universal goals.[6]

Yet, even if this is the implicit – and at times explicit – claim of the development industry, can it really bear the claim of being cosmopolitan? Whilst the ideas, objectives and methods are increasingly universal, does this necessarily imply that they are 'cosmopolitan' or simply 'transnational'? Certainly, such ideas and methods are common throughout the development world, but this commonality perhaps primarily derives from the dominance of the development industry itself. And if one looks at the principles which underlie them, these have a genealogy which firmly links them into a very specific historical context: that of post-Enlightenment Europe (Henkel and Stirrat 2001). This is most clearly seen in the context of the drive towards market relations which links back to very specific cultural contexts, but is also the case in various other approaches to development which today dominate the development industry.

Thus, rather than the development industry being seen as embodying a set of cosmopolitan ideas and methods, it can be seen as strangely parochial. Whilst there are individuals who display an interest in attempts at developing a Buddhist framework for development or who try to develop an Islamic economics, these are few and far between. Furthermore, the flow of funding ensures a certain orthodoxy in the development world, and stepping too far outside the boundaries is to put this funding at risk. The ideas and practices of the development industry can be viewed as parochial in the extreme, involving a rejection of alternatives and an attempt to 'naturalize' and 'universalize' one particular strand of looking at the world.[7]

The result, not surprisingly, is that all underdeveloped countries look remarkably the same in the eyes of the development industry. The goals towards which development policies and activities are orientated are similar; the problems which have to be faced are also similar.[8] In this sense the development industry is involved in a parochialization of development and the denial of difference.

The Expatriate Lifestyle

For most people, working in the development business involves living in the developing world, often for extended periods. And here again, many development professionals see themselves as 'cosmopolitans'. After all, they bridge different cultures, interact between different worlds and live in but are not part of the country to which they are posted. They pride themselves on their ability to adjust to new contexts, new ways of doing things and new places to explore. The move from one country to another is part of a continuing process whereby development people continually sit on the edge, never quite part of the host country in which they are for the moment placed. Their lives are lives of detachment, premised on the knowledge that their present residence is only temporary and that in a year or two they will move to a new country, a new society, perhaps thousands of miles away. Not surprisingly, this 'edginess' is also apparent in their attitudes towards 'home'. Here there is a certain ambivalence. They present their lives as something diametrically opposed to the narrow and parochial existence of people 'back home'. 'Here I am someone; back in England I am no one' is how one development expatriate put it to one of us. 'I couldn't live in England again: it's so boring, so insular' was another comment.[9] And, of course, there are other comments referring to the standard of living or the availability of servants which the expatriate lifestyle affords.

Yet, although there is a cosmopolitan streak in their overseas existence, it still lacks much of what Hannerz for instance would see as cosmopolitanism. He sees two aspects as being crucial: first, 'an intellectual and aesthetic stance of openness towards divergent cultural experiences' and, second, 'a personal ability to make one's way into other cultures' (Hannerz 1992: 252–53).[10] This is because whilst development people live in exotic places in distant parts of the world, it is extremely questionable whether or not they live up to Hannerz's ideal, whether or not they make their way into the 'cultures' of the countries in which they live or continue to sit, always somewhat detached, on the edge.

The professional world of development professionals is remarkably circumscribed. They tend to work in expatriate teams and are answerable in practice (if not in theory) to overseas donors. They meet other representatives of different development organizations through various consortiums and forums which ostensibly exist to coordinate activities. The result is a shared view of a particular country, a reinforcement of 'normal knowledge' about a country, a view from the outside, free from 'any stance of openness' to different cultural milieux.

Even in their interactions with the 'host community', development professionals tend to be restricted or restrict themselves to certain categories of 'locals'. First, there are those they work with, for instance, government personnel or personnel employed by NGOs. Second, there are the servants, either directly employed or employed through agents. Third, there are the various intermediaries who supply services of various kinds. In other words, their contacts with and views of the local context are heavily determined by these various groups of intermediaries. Dependency on these intermediaries is only exacerbated by linguistic problems.[11] The result is that most contact with 'the locals' is heavily skewed and depends on a form of 'compradore' class, intermediaries between the host population and the foreign development workers who control communication and usually produce what is expected of them. In general there is relatively little social contact between development professionals and the host population at the level of friendship.[12]

Development personnel come into an existing expatriate world and learn from those already in residence. In some places this is institutionalized and codified, as for instance in the *American Ladies Guide to Colombo*. This publication, now in it tenth revised edition, aims to provide handy advice to the newcomer on a wide variety of subjects ranging from Sri Lankan religious traditions to how much to tip servants at New Year and what sorts of towels are best in a tropical climate.[13] However, more generally, newcomers enter into a situation in which they learn from those who have come before and, through these people, they enter into a shared world of understanding the local context. Newcomers learn a shared version of local politics; where there is ethnic difference, they develop a knowledge of the 'character differences' which fit with different ethnic identities. Views of the 'locals' are generated not through some openness to local cultural complexities, but rather from ready-made templates there to be used by newcomers. There is now a growing industry of 'welcome professionals', commonly ex-pats themselves, whose job it is to ease the arrival and adjustment of new ex-pat families, assisting with everything from finding a house, an international school and 'reliable' domestic staff to providing introductions to a ready-made social network of other 'development families'.

These social networks further reinforce the separateness of the expatriate development professional. Thus, in one colonial style bar in Ho Chi Minh City, a group of expatriates known as 'the French' (although by no means all are French) meet three times a week for salsa dancing lessons, given by a French doctor undertaking research on infectious diseases at one of Ho Chi Minh City's main hospitals. Every Saturday the Touch Rugby Club meets for sport, socializing and a few beers sponsored by the local branch of Fosters. The teams are made up of men and women from Australia, New Zealand, North America and Europe who live in Ho Chi Minh City for anything from one month to six years. The one hour bus journey to the sports fields (pristinely groomed pitches outside the city) reveals, on the one hand, the diversity of ex-pats who participate in this social regime and, on the other hand, the insularity and homogeneity of ex-pat social life in the city. Embassy staff from the Australian and British consulates play alongside Scottish fisheries development experts, structural engineers in towns to build a series of bridges as part of multimillion-dollar AUSAID projects, English teachers and NGO workers.

Unlike the St Andrew's Society or the American Ladies of Ho Chi Minh City, this club claims no particular national identity, yet the dominant theme of friendly banter is a gentle competition between nations, played out more formally, when individual teams are created for the annual rugby and touch-rugby tournaments. The most common topic of conversation is the last or next big day in the constant calendar of national holidays marked with grand celebrations hosted by the appropriate society. Australia Day precedes New Zealand Day, which rolls into St Patrick's Day, which is followed by St George's Day and St Andrew's Day. And the scale and intensity with which these national celebrations are imbued would surprise those 'back home'. So, for instance, the St Patrick's Day celebration in Ho Chi Minh City is an exclusive event – tickets for the celebrations, which are held in the suites of one of Ho Chi Minh City's most salubrious hotels, cost thirty dollars. The suites, decked out like a 'Dublin street scene', are filled with ex-pats, all dressed in green, some of the women in tailor-made emerald silk dresses, their husbands in matching cummerbunds, hand-stitched by one of Ho Chi Minh City's numerous cheap tailors. The event of course is sponsored by Guinness. Stalls serve Irish stew and a band, imported from the Philippines, plays a mixture of old and new: from Irish jigs, to cover versions of U2, the Corrs and Westlife.

Similar ethnic issues are apparent elsewhere. At a social event attended by one of the authors of this chapter in Bangkok, six long-term development professionals were present with their Thai wives and children. The table divided neatly into two, Thai wives and children at one end and expatriate husbands (and other expatriates, including expatriate women) at the other. The major topic of conversation amongst the expatriates was the issue of who was to be the next 'chief' of the Bangkok St Andrews Society, the problem being that the obvious candidate had a Thai wife and the rules of the Society specified that the chief and his wife should be Scottish! One of the men at the table joked that his wife might be Thai but she was taking Ceilidh dancing lessons and added, in a rare moment of self-awareness: 'I've been here 10 years and still can't speak Thai properly, but my wife can dance like a true Scot.'[14] In this case the development professionals had in some sense rejected the mobile, detached and insulated social world of the development industry, establishing, through marriage, a kind of rootedness and connectedness to their host country. At the same time, communal life remained structured by the same parochial concerns and exclusive social regimes.

The overall result of these processes is a somewhat ghettoized existence. Development workers tend to exist in a social cocoon, socializing with each other and reproducing not only differences between the expatriates and the host community but also national differences amongst the expatriates.[15]

Interaction between development professionals and the local population tend to take place on terms set by the expatriates. In some places this separation is far stronger than in others. In Dhaka, for instance, where alcohol is not widely available, the constraints (both legal and social) of the society of the host country means that the social world of development practitioners is largely insulated within a series of ex-pat clubs. Here there are separate clubs catering for the Scandinavians, the Americans, the Australians, the Germans and the British. Each of these serves as a place where 'the locals' are only present as servants, as guests or as 'honorary foreigners'.[16] Here information is generated and a common view of 'the local' is developed, safely insulated from the local context. The extreme case involves humanitarian aid workers working in unstable areas of the world who tend to live physically as well as socially ghettoized lives within the walls or high fences of UN compounds.

Now of course there are individuals who escape the ghetto-like existence of the majority of development personnel working in developing countries. There are some who learn the language and there are some who refuse to be imprisoned within the development circle. Some even 'go native', never to reappear. But these are a very small number. In general, far from being 'cosmopolitans' engaged in an open relationship to other cultural traditions, development personnel are imprisoned within a narrow world, looking out at their host culture through lenses which distort and reinforce existing stereotypes of that culture.

It has to be said that in many ways this state of isolation is forced upon development people and is neither their choice nor the reason they entered the industry. The world they work in demands of them certain ways of behaving and certain ways of doing. There is a sense in which neither the host community nor the expatriate community allows space for a 'true' cosmopolitanism. Being a development professional involves hard work and long hours. It is simply much easier for all concerned if people slip into the ghetto-like world of the expatriate community. Given the limited nature of most contracts, it does not pay to be seen as an eccentric; rather, being a 'good chap', fully participating in the expatriate social world, is a means of maintaining a reputation and developing connections. For many, romantic ideals of free, unmediated contact and the experience of divergent cultures ('true' cosmopolitanism) were instrumental in their choice to enter the world of development, but the demands of the industry are such that there is little room for such dilettantism.[17]

Nostalgias: Home and Away

Thus, at the heart of the development profession there is a small tragedy. To live and work within it requires abandoning youthful dreams and aspirations. The transnational and peripatetic lifestyle it involves does not create any cosmopolitan sensibilities, but instead a rootlessness. There is no turning back, no 'going home'. Not surprisingly in such a situation, national identities reassert themselves through the rituals of the expatriate year and, like nationalisms everywhere, these tend to indulge in forms of nostalgia, not for the 'home country' left behind, but for an idealized version of that home.

Returning for the moment to the St Patrick's Day celebrations in Ho Chi Minh City, the street was of course meant to be a nineteenth-century street, and the Vietnamese waitresses serving the Guinness were dressed in the costumes of nineteenth-century Ireland. The Ireland which is being celebrated is a nostalgic invention of the past, shorn of poverty or its colonial status.[18] Other national celebrations are similarly archaic inventions, nostalgic imaginings of what the past should have been. The food served in the Bhagga club in Dhaka appears to be modelled on public school fare of the 1920s, if not earlier. More generally, there tends to be a nostalgia, at least amongst the British, for a 'warm beer and cricket' sort of nationalism, a world where things were clearer and demarcations were more exact. So, when talking about their futures, development professionals will remark on how Britain has changed so much, how its 'culture' has been transformed, how it would be impossible to fit into today's Britain, and the contrast is made with a distant past. Indeed, there is a sense in which what is most problematic about 'the home country' is the degree to which it has become a 'cosmopolitan' country. It is easier to be 'British' from a distance.

Nostalgia for an imagined past of one's 'homeland' is perhaps not all that surprising or exceptional. Indeed, it seems to characterize many groups of expatriates, not just those working in development. What is more surprising is that development professionals also frequently indulge in romantic nostalgic invocations of the pasts of the countries in which they are working, which are as much inventions as the pasts of their own countries.

Frequently, development professionals will contrast the present of the country they are working in with the past: 'You should have been here ten (or fifteen, or twenty) years ago. Then it was so different, so unspoilt.' Old hands in Cambodia, Laos or Indonesia, for instance, will romance about a 'different world' which has now been spoilt. 'Development', the very objective of the development industry, is seen to have eroded a previous pristine state. The complaints are that the 'character' of, for instance, Bangkok has been destroyed by massive and rapid urbanization. And it is not just the physical nature of these countries, but also the nature of the people: 'Then, people were more honest; they didn't try to cheat you', 'There was an innocence then. Not much of that now' or 'We were appreciated for what we were doing in those days. But now we aren't respected in the same way'.

On a different level, the nostalgia for a lost past comes out in the tendency amongst many development professionals to 'collect' the past.

At times this becomes somewhat pathological. Thus, when Cambodia was opened up to the major agencies in the late 1980s, there was a rapid and exhaustive accumulation of 'traditional' works of art. Whilst some of this aggressive collecting was certainly for commercial gain, it was also motivated by a desire to 'own' the Cambodian past. In Sri Lanka, one prominent figure in the aid business during the 1990s was notorious for his fine collection of Sri Lankan antiques. Again, there may have been a commercial angle to his activities, but much more important was his fascination with the past of Sri Lanka.[19]

This nostalgia for the past, this time a colonial past, similarly comes out in choice of hotels. Where visiting consultants should stay is often a complex issue which involves considerations of status, facilities and cost, but also considerations of style. Frequently, old colonial style hotels are favoured over their modern counterparts. Indeed, snide comments are often made over which people from which agencies choose which hotels. 'Old colonial' is somehow morally superior to 'new capitalist'. However, it has to be said that anthropologists are just as guilty of this form of imperialist nostalgia as their development counterparts.

Much of this revolves around issues of 'authenticity'.[20] Caught in a transnational world, many development professionals, like many expatriates, seek to identify what is 'truly authentic' about their surroundings. And this is largely concerned with 'othering' both the places and the people of the host community. The expatriates experience the world they live in as a world of confusion (or of complex hybridity) where there are no clear lines of demarcation between us and them or, more importantly perhaps, between modernity and tradition.[21] Given that to a great extent the development industry is premised on a distinction between the 'developed' and the 'underdeveloped', anything that threatens this distinction threatens the position of the development professional. Thus, rather like tourists (or certain brands of anthropologists), there is a perpetual search for and invention of the 'authentic'.[22] Moreover, this 'authenticity' may be as much a colonial as a precolonial past, for at least in the colonial world the lines of distinction were clear.

One aspect of this is the ambivalence often felt towards 'compradores' – those people from the host community on whom the expatriates depend and who in turn make a living from the expatriates. Of course, there are often extremely good and close relations between development professionals and their counterparts, but there is at times a certain distrust and distancing, as if the counterparts are potential competitors for jobs in the development industry. More significant are the traders, merchants, rental brokers, etc., the people who make life possible in a strange land, and here there is much more distrust and at times active antipathy. But what is most distressing to the seeker for authenticity is precisely the amphibian qualities which enable them to act as go-betweens. The obvious parallel is the way in which the British distrusted and despised the 'Babu' class in nineteenth-century India, who were considered as neither 'modern' nor 'traditional' in British terms.

The nostalgic search for the 'authentic' comes out most clearly in perhaps the most important ritual of the development industry, the 'field trip'.[23] Most development professionals spend the majority of their time in offices in cities surrounded by the panoply of 'modern' life. Yet this was not what they entered the industry for, and it leaves them isolated from the 'real people': the poor, the marginal and, most importantly of all, the rural whom the industry is attempting to benefit. The 'field trip' is the means by which development professionals can attempt to escape from their daily lives and make contact with 'authenticity'. Here they can meet 'real' farmers in 'real' places and see things as they 'really' are.

However, it has to be stressed that this is a ritual. Field trips are carefully orchestrated by counterparts at various levels, and the development professional is shepherded in specific ways to meet particular people reading in effect from prearranged scripts. Only very rarely does the field visit throw up new knowledge or new issues. Development professionals are of course aware of this on one level. After all, they are not fools and they know only too well the ways in which field trips are managed and manipulated. Indeed, they are often involved in precisely this manipulation and management when faced with visitors. Yet, even so, there is a ritual to be gone through, often involving vast expense.[24] Both development professionals and their counterparts expect such events to take place. What they do is to provide a ritual arena within which 'the authentic' can be put on show and the development professional can make a link with an imagined past. In this sense the field trip is an exercise in applied nostalgia.

Put slightly differently, as various authors have made clear, nostalgia is always about the present and holds a critical mirror up to the present (Bissell 2005: 239; Stewart 1993: 23; Ylijoki 2005). So too with the exotic (Eaton 2006). Yet with 'development' destroying any semblance of the exotic, what one is left with are alternative and complementary nostalgias which both embody a deep-seated recognition of the rootlessness of the contemporary world and a yearning for the primal order of a colonial past. The 'field trip' of today is a pale shadow of the circuits of the past.

Conclusion

What we have tried to do in this chapter is to explore some aspects of the world of development professionals. We have tried to argue that although they would see themselves as 'cosmopolitans', in fact they are caught up in particular forms of 'parochialism'. On the one hand, this is a function of the intellectual underpinnings of development thought and practice which leaves little room for alternative ways of thinking and doing. On the other hand, they are caught up in circumscribed expatriate lifestyles where, far from escaping the social and cultural forms of 'home', they are actively engaged in creating a specific and self-enclosed social world which, to use the term in a non-derogatory sense, is a parody of 'home'. They fail to be cosmopolitans both in Hannerz's terms of being able to move between cultures or in terms of those writers such as Bhabha (1996) and Gilroy (2000) who would see cosmopolitanism in terms of a blurring of boundaries, hybridization and even 'mongrelization'. Furthermore, these self-conscious bearers of 'development' and 'modernity' are on one level aware of the rootless nature of their existence and thus develop various forms of nostalgia which look back to imagined worlds where things were 'simpler', either a nostalgia for an imagined past of home or an 'imperial nostalgia' for a world which notionally preceded the discontinuities, disjunctions and displacement of the world of development.

Acknowledgements

The authors would like to thank both the U.K. Department for International Development (DFID), which at various times has given them access to the world of development, and the U.K. Economic and Social Research Council, which has supported their separate research activities.

Notes

1. At this point we do not wish to hazard a definition of 'cosmopolitanism'. For the moment we would prefer to follow Pollock et al.'s comment that we cannot define it, 'because specifying cosmopolitanism positively and definitely is an uncosmopolitan thing to do' (Pollock et al. 2000: 577)!
2. See Stirrat 2006 for more details.
3. This is particularly true of volunteers who, having tried development, decide it is not for them.
4. '[N]eoliberal cosmopolitan thought is founded on a conformist notion of what it means to be a "person" as an abstract unit of exchange': Pollock et al. 2000: 581).
5. So, for instance, there may well have been a move away from 'market fundamentalism' signalled by the rise of the so-called 'post-Washington consensus', and organizations such as the World Bank may recognize the importance of the institutional and perhaps ideological 'embeddedness' of markets (Jenkins 2003), but at the base there is still an adherence to a set of essentialist notions of 'truth' about the market and the individual.
6. Thus, Robert Fine (2003: 454) remarks on how one can see the 'rationality of cosmopolitanism as the fulfilment of the enlightenment project' in the context of 'cosmopolitan', as distinct from 'international' law.
7. One is tempted to draw a parallel between the supposed universality of certain ways of thinking about the economy and debates about the universality of human rights. As Turner (amongst many others) has pointed out, human rights can be seen as 'irredeemably associated with western values' (Turner 2002: 46).
8. To take one example which one of the authors was recently involved in, 90% of the conclusions of two studies of the same sector in Ghana and Cambodia were identical. This is what Maia Green (2003) refers to the 'standardization of development'. See also Ferguson 1990.

9. In some ways their comments are reminiscent of those Nava reports for British expatriates in 1930s Europe: '"Home" in this imaginary landscape tended to be prosaic, class bound, emotionally and sexually frustrating' (Nava 2002: 90).

10. For similar approaches to cosmopolitanism which stress 'openness', see Beck 2002 and Nava 2002.

11. The degree to which development personnel are competent in the languages of the places they work in varies enormously: young tend to be better than old and long-term residents more competent than short-term visitors. In some countries (e.g., Indonesia) there is a relatively high degree of competence. In others (e.g., Sri Lanka) very few speak indigenous languages. Whether anthropologists are any more competent is a moot point.

12. In Colombo this was remarked upon by both expatriates and Sri Lankans. Each party saw the other as aloof and standoffish.

13. This guide is most easily available in the shops catering for expatriate taste in upmarket Sri Lankan memorabilia.

14. We hasten to add that by no means all marriages between development professionals and partners from host countries are like this, and that there are many cases where the relationships involved are much more balanced. However, there are more extreme situations. In one Asian city, which should perhaps remain nameless, a system of 'temporary marriages' developed in the 1990s. Out of a project team of six men, four had taken 'wives' for the duration of their contracts. However, the increasing feminization of the industry will presumably transform these relationships in unpredictable ways.

15. It could of course be argued that these expatriate groupings form 'self enclosed cosmopolitan enclaves or bubbles' (Lasch 1995: 47, quoted in Nava 2003). Yet this would be to adopt a somewhat parochial definition of cosmopolitanism.

16. An extreme case of what goes on in these clubs is provided by White, who describes 'the expatriate club serving aid and embassy staff, which held a "pyjama party" one week, and the next a "Bengali party", in which the "fancy dress" consisted of the clothes that Bangladeshis wear. The disparagement of Bangladesh and all things Bangladeshi was the common currency of talk in the bar at expatriate clubs' (White 2002: 409).

17. Thus, in a limited sense development professionals can be seen as 'victims' of the development industry. However, we hasten to add that this is somewhat different from the 'abject cosmopolitanism' described by Nyers (2003).

18. On the selectivity of nostalgia as a form of remembering, see Stoler and Strassler 2000.

19. The significance of collecting is unfortunately not a theme we can develop in the present context. Hiwever, there are parallels to be drawn between present-day 'collectors' in the development business and their colonial predecessors. See for instance the fascinating recent monograph by Maya Jasanoff (2005) and Natasha Eaton's work on the eighteenth-century trade in Indian art (Eaton 2006).

20. The relationship between 'nostalgia' and 'authenticity' is well discussed by Fairweather, who argues that whilst 'nostalgia' refers to 'a process of remembering the past', 'authenticity' refers to an 'image of the past (Fairweather 2003: 282).

21. This of course raises the issue of how far nostalgia is an inherent and inevitable aspect of modernity, or at least that vision of modernity which is central to the development industry. See for instance Robertson 1990.

22. It is worth noting that this is nothing new. Bissell quotes Fortes as writing that 'nostalgia for the "unspoiled savage" is usually found amongst those who get their living from breaking up primitive societies and "corrupting" the savage – government officials, traders and missionaries' (Fortes 1945: 223). However, Bissell also goes on to point out that well into the 1970s (and one might say much later), 'nostalgia continued to serve as the secret sharer of anthropological thought' (Bissell 2005: 224). See also Pham 2004.

23. See Harriet Stanley's thesis for an excellent discussion of the 'field visit' in the Nepali context (Stanley 2001).

24. The largest scale field visit either of us has taken part in involved six Land Rovers, each holding eight people.

References

Beck, U. 2002. 'The Cosmopolitan Society and its Enemies', *Theory, Culture and Society* 19: 17–44.

Bhabha, H.K. 1996. 'Unsatisfied: Notes on Vernacular Cosmopolitanism', in L. Garcia-Moreno and P. Pfeiffer (eds), *Text and Nation*. Columbia S.C.: Camden House, pp. 191–201.

Bissell, W.C. 2005. 'Engaging Colonial Nostalgia', *Cultural Anthropology* 20: 215–48.

Eaton, N. 2006. 'Nostalgia for the Exotic: Creating an Imperial Art in London', *Eighteenth Century Studies* 39: 227–50.

Fairweather, I. 2003. '"Showing Off": Nostalgia and Heritage in North-Central Namibia', *Journal of Southern African Studies* 29: 279–96.

Ferguson, J. 1990. *The Anti-Politics Machine. "Development", Depoliticization and Bureaucratic Power in Lesotho*. Cambridge: Cambridge University Press.

Fine, R. 2003. 'Taking the "Ism" Out of Cosmopolitanism. An Essay in Reconstruction', *European Journal of Social Theory* 6: 451–70.

Fortes, M. 1945. 'An Anthropological Point of View', in R. Hinden (ed.), *Fabian Colonial Essays*. London: Allen and Unwin.

Gilroy, P. 2000. *Between Camps*. London: Allen Lane.

Green, M. 2003. 'Globalizing Development in Tanzania. Policy Franchising through Participatory Project Management', *Critique of Anthropology* 23: 123–43.

Hannerz, U. 1992. *Cultural Complexity: Studies in the Social Organization of Meaning*. New York: Columbia University Press.

Henkel, H.M. and R.L. Stirrat. 2001. 'Participation as Spiritual Duty: Empowerment as Secular Subjection', in B. Cooke and Uma Kothari (eds), *Participation – The New Tyranny?* London: Zed Books, 168–84.

Jasanoff, M. 2005. *Edge of Empire. Conquest and Collecting on the Eastern Frontiers of the British Empire*. London: Fourth Estate.

Jenkins, R. 2003. 'International Development Institutions and National Economic Contexts: Neo-liberalism Encounters India's Indigenous Political Traditions', *Economy and Society* 32: 584–610.

Lasch, C. 1995. *The Revolt of the Elites and the Betrayal of Democracy*. New York: Norton.

Mosse, D. 2005. *Cultivating Development. An Ethnography of Aid Policy and Practice*. London: Pluto Press.

Nava, M. 2002. 'Cosmopolitan Modernity. Everyday Imaginaries and the Register of Difference', *Theory, Culture and Society* 19: 81–99.

Nyers, P. 2003. 'Abject Cosmopolitanism: The Politics of Protection in the Anti-deportation Movement', *Third World Quarterly* 24: 1069–93.

Pham, J. 2004. 'Ghost Hunting in Colonial Burma. Nostalgia, Paternalism and the Thoughts of J.S. Furnivall', *South East Asia Research* 12: 237–68.

Pollock, S., H. K. Bhabha, C.A. Breckenridge and D. Chakrabarty. 2000. 'Cosmopolitanisms', *Public Culture* 12: 577–91.

Robertson, R. 1990. 'After Nostalgia?', in B.S. Turner (ed.), *Theories of Modernity and Postmodernity*. London: Sage, 45–61.

Rosaldo, R. 1989. 'Imperialist Nostalgia', *Representations* 26: 107–22.

Stanley, H. 2001. 'Distant Friends and Intimate Strangers: Desire and the Development Encounter', unpublished DPhil thesis, University of Sussex.

Stewart, S. 1993. *On Longing: Narratives of the Miniature, the Gigantic, the Souvenir, the Collection*. Durham, N.C.: Duke University Press.

Stirrat, R. 2006. 'Mercenaries, missionaries and misfits: Representations of Development Personnel', *Critique of Anthropology* 28: 406-425.

Stoler, A.L. and K. Strassler. 2000. 'Castings for the Colonial: Memory Work in "New Order" Java', *Comparative Studies in Society and History* 42: 4–48.

Turner, B.S. 2002. 'Cosmopolitan Virtue, Globalization and Patriotism', *Theory, Culture and Society* 19: 45–63.

White, S. 2002. 'Thinking Race, Thinking Development', *Third World Quarterly* 23: 407–19.

Ylijoki, O-H. 2005. 'Academic Nostalgia: A Narrative Approach to Academic Work', *Human Relations* 58: 555–76.

Chapter 9

TIDY CONCEPTS, MESSY LIVES
Defining Tensions in the Domestic and Overseas Careers of U.K. Non-Governmental Professionals

David Lewis

Introduction

The identities of development professionals and activists can usefully be analysed in the context of the dominant policy ideas and models within which their expertise is constructed and given value and meaning. Recent ethnographic research has used the life-history method to understand the longer term trajectories of people who cross between governmental and non-governmental careers and, more generally, to learn more about the motivations, working experiences and worldviews of activists and professionals (Lewis 2008a; Lewis 2008b).[1] In this chapter I consider the experiences of a particular subset of individuals in the U.K. who have built careers within two distinctive domains within the broader non-governmental sector. One group has worked primarily in the U.K. domestic setting, where they have sought to tackle issues of poverty 'at home', while another has built international careers doing overseas work within so-called 'developing' country settings. Expertise and professionalism among these two groups of people has been differently constructed in relation to two main models or institutional 'maps', both of which are explored in this chapter. The first is the model of the three 'sectors' of institutional life (government, business and 'third' sector), which has become central to current global concerns with good governance. The second is the still-prevailing postcolonial separation of professional third sector work spaces in the U.K. into categories of 'domestic' and 'international development'.

The life history narratives collected take us further into what Apthorpe (Chapter 10 this volume) has termed 'the virtual reality of Aidland', enabling a more detailed exploration of these two key issues in the world of ideas relating to professional non-governmental activities in the U.K. There is a ubiquity to the 'three sector' model of state, market and civil society as a central framing device and organizing principle of contemporary policy landscapes, yet this simple but persuasive institutional idea tends to sit uneasily with 'real' worlds of history and practice (Lewis 2006; 2008a and b). An important element of the identity and role of the development professional is the need to continuously mediate and 'broker' the relationship between disparate everyday work practices on the one hand, and organizing ideas of policy on the other hand, in the pursuit of stability, coherent meaning and order (Mosse 2005; Mosse and Lewis 2006). Yet this process of brokerage can simultaneously subvert and destabilize the three-sector model, because the process depends upon – and makes apparent – many relationships and activities that operate across sector 'boundaries', including the boundary separating government and non-government, and in so doing blurs and complicates policy assumptions about these boundaries.

The second issue analysed in this chapter is the stark and highly artificial division in the U.K. non-governmental sector between the 'domestic' and the 'international' as domains that constitute 'parallel worlds' of professional life (cf. Lewis 1999). While this distinction is becoming increasingly untenable within the globalized world of development practice, where for example microfinance approaches to tackling poverty developed in the 'Third World' are now increasingly applied to settings in Europe and North America, the distinction persists within the realm of professional practice. Both issues help to illustrate the ways in which policy models tend to operate through a reliance on heroic levels of ahistorical oversimplification.

Before turning to the life histories of these professionals, I will first discuss the background to the three-sector model and the idea of a 'third sector' as one of its components. I will then briefly consider the rise of the ideology of 'non-governmentalism', before introducing what I have termed the two 'parallel worlds' of domestic and international work in the UK third sector.

The Three-Sector Model

The concept of the third sector – which is often conflated and used interchangeably with familiar terms such as the 'voluntary sector', the 'not-for-profit sector', 'non-governmental sector' and 'civil society'[2] – has in the past two decades become a dominant organizing idea within the frameworks that policy makers and activists now use to think about society, economy and policy. This third sector idea is important at two levels: first, as recognition of the importance of organizational forms that are seen as distinctive from state or business, represented by a wide range of third-sector, non-profit, non-governmental or charitable actors; and, second, at the level of a three-sector model – linking the state, the market and the third sector – which increasingly informs the framing of policy in both Western and developing country contexts in support of good governance, and organizational pluralism in the delivery of social services, as prevailing policy discourses.

Ideas about the third sector are politically important in the U.K. As Kendall (2003: 1) writes

> In 2003, the voluntary, third or non-profit sector occupies centre-stage in public policy discussions in the UK. Not since the late nineteenth century, when voluntary action was integral to contemporary concepts of citizenship, and the associated institutional infrastructure of charities and mutuals were the cause of considerable national pride, have organisations occupying the space between the market and the state commanded so much attention.

In March 2006, the U.K. government appointed a Minister for the Third Sector, Ed Miliband, who quickly set about extolling the virtues of the sector both as a key agent of social service delivery within what is now termed 'the mixed economy of welfare' and as a critical campaigning force within a democratic society.[3] (In 2010, the new Conservative/Liberal Democrat coalition government renamed the Office for the Third Sector as the Office for Civil Society, a term that was perhaps seen as more in keeping with the government's efforts to promote its idea of the 'big society'.) The economic importance of the sector is also now considerable. Kendall's data shows that in 1995 almost 1.5 million full-time equivalent workers were employed in what he terms 'the broad non-profit sector', accounting for more than six percent of the economy as a whole, more than the 1.1 million employed in the National Health Service, the largest single employer in the UK. Turning his attention to the phenomenon of volunteering, Kendall (2003) shows that a total of 16 million people volunteer in the U.K., committing hours equivalent to a further 1.7 million full-time employees.

These trends in the U.K. are part of a broader international phenomenon, with diverse roots in recent political and economic change. On the one hand, for example, organizations such as CIVICUS were born out of the rediscovery of the ideas of 'civil society' among anti-authoritarian activists in areas of Eastern Europe and Latin America during the 1980s, often influenced by Gramscian ideas about civil society and resistance. On the other hand, it was liberal thinking on civil society that informed the growth of the 'good governance' agenda of the World Bank and other international development agencies during the 1990s, and which envisaged new roles for non-governmental organizations (NGOs) alongside states and markets (Lewis 2002). The 'good governance' policy agenda rested on a key mobilizing idea – that it was possible to create 'better' citizens through building of associations – and this required a policy model that assumed an interdependent and supportive relationship between the market economy, the state and civil society. Within this model a 'virtuous circle' was asserted between all three institutional sectors such that a productive economy and a well-run government would sustain a vigorous civil society, a well-run government and a vigorous civil society would serve to sustain growth and a well-managed economy and a strong civil society would help to produce efficient government (Archer 1994).

It is first useful to unpack the proliferation of terms that characterize discussions of this 'third sector'. Each term can be seen to have a distinctive historical and contextual origin. For example, the term 'non-profit' organization comes from the U.S., where organizations of this kind have long been contrasted with the dominant organizing principle of the market and the profit-making business organization, while the term NGO was first used in the context of the UN in 1945, when it was agreed in the UN Charter that selected non-state actors would be given observer status in UN assemblies and meetings. 'Voluntary organization', the term most frequently used in the U.K., refers back to Christian notions of charity and volunteering, while the more recently fashionable 'civil society' emerged as a term rediscovered from political theory by activists. As a result, it makes more sense to take these terms as a group or 'set' rather than to debate the merits and characteristics of each, since all may be seen as manifestations of the broader phenomenon of 'non-governmentalism' (Lewis 2007). In this chapter I will use the term 'third sector' as a shorthand for this cluster of broadly similar ideas.

Najam (1999: 143) has noted the relatively small amount of scholarly research on the third sector, despite the recent surge of policy interest. He argues that 'our conceptual understanding of this terrain is even more scant than the terrain is expansive' and characterizes what literature that does exist as predominantly 'descriptive' and 'parochial'. In a similar vein, Tvedt (1998: 3) suggests that research in the field lacks conceptual clarity and that 'definitions have tended to be normative and ideological or so broad as to make discussion and comparison difficult'. Nor have anthropologists paid much attention to the phenomenon of the 'third sector', either in terms of analysing its role as an increasingly ubiquitous organizing idea within landscapes of 'neoliberal institutionalism' (cf. Mosse, this volume, Chapter 1) or in considering its other main sense as a loose description of a diverse collection of organizations that exist in an institutional space between the state, the market and the household (Lewis 2006).

Indeed, the precise origins of the third sector term remain somewhat obscure. The U.S. sociologist Amitai Etzioni (1973) is believed to have invented the term, but around the same time, apparently independently, the management specialist Theodore Levitt (1975) wrote *The Third Sector: New Tactics for a Responsive Society* in relation to social activism. Daniel Bell (1973) also refers to the third sector in his book *The Coming of Post-Industrial Society*. Etzioni (1961) constructed a conceptual framework with three basic organizational forms, centred on his concept of organizational 'compliance'. The type of power relations required to achieve it could take one of three forms: coercive, which is the application or threat of physical sanctions (such as pain or restrictions on the freedom of movement); remunerative, based on control over material resources and rewards such as wages or benefits; and normative, based on the manipulation of symbolic rewards and deprivations, the use of the power of persuasion, and on appeals to shared values and idealism. Third-sector organizations were extremely diverse, but Etzioni suggested that they chiefly used degrees of normative power to achieve compliance. They built commitment of workers, volunteers and members, and compensated them primarily through symbolic reward. This line of thinking led to the idea of a third sector as a loose category of organizations that are not government or for-profit businesses but which were held together by the 'glue' of value-driven action and commitment.

Ideas about the third sector did not remain confined to organizational and sociological theory, but were also taken up within various types of policy thinking during the 1980s. The 'discovery' of the third sector fed into several different areas of the changing policy landscape: as another potential delivery system for services, as an area of 'private' activity into which the government could shift more of its responsibilities; and as a public arena or space within which individual citizens could be encouraged to organize social action. In the next section I consider the broader political and institutional context in which policy ideas about the third sector have become prominent.

The Rise of 'Non-governmentalism'

From the late 1980s, a set of ideas that I suggest can loosely be characterized as 'non-governmentalism' emerged as a dominant and influential ideology in the fields of public policy, including international development. This was manifest in a policy discourse that 'talked up' the roles of the third sector, NGOs and civil society. It was associated with the ascendancy of ideologies of neoliberalism that brought with them the discourse of privatization and a disillusionment with states and state-led development, as well as a set of new more activist agendas of 'alternative development' (Lewis 2005).[4] Neoliberalism was a return to the preoccupations of an earlier economic liberalism in the nineteenth century that privileged the market as 'the proper guiding instrument by which people should organise their economic lives' (MacEwan 1999: 4).

This market-oriented policy agenda brought market competition and theories of comparative advantage centrestage and it shifted ideas about government away from national planning and state provision of services towards markets and third-sector actors. It envisaged a new 'enabling' role in which the role of government was to secure the conditions in which markets could operate more fully across a range of areas of social and economic life. For example, within international development, an influential World Bank volume edited by Paul and Israel (1991) set out the reasons for the Bank's decision to begin 'an institution-wide effort to expand its work with NGOs' (Beckmann 1991: 134). This decision was based on the recognition that states and markets had limited capacity to reduce poverty, while NGOs had distinctive competences such as closeness to the poor, committed leadership and capacity to build access to services for the poor. This was the beginning of an explicit recognition of the role of NGOs within the unfolding neoliberal development agenda, which had gained ascendancy rapidly following the end of the Cold War.

Interest in the third sector was also an outcome of the bundle of different ideas and approaches implied within new public management (NPM) perspectives (Ferlie et al. 1996) that formed part of the efforts to reshape public administration from the 1980s onwards, based on ideas about linking efficiency and accountability. To varying degrees, this thinking has been the dominant model of government reforms throughout the industrialized and developing worlds. NPM has led to structural reforms and changes in practice which generally include the restructuring of the public sector through privatization, the introduction of internal markets and the contracting out of public services to both market and non-market agencies (such as third-sector organizations), a reduction in the overall scale of the civil service and the use of a raft of new managerial techniques for improving efficiency, such as the use of performance indicators and incentives (Minogue 1998).

This was the context for an increasing the role of the third sector within social policy. Ideas such as the purchaser/provider split in public service provision, the use of agency contracting in order to link performance and incentives, and efforts to improve accounting transparency based on quantifiable output indicators all contributed to a policy climate in which new roles have now been opened up for third-sector organizations in service provision as government roles had been redefined and reduced (Turner and Hulme 1997). The attraction for governments and donors of working with third-sector organizations within this general paradigm was primarily one of improved efficiency. Third-sector organizations are seen as more cost-effective vehicles for service provision than other forms, able to reach certain sections of the population with specialized services, and with potential gains from the 'synergy' which could be created between government and NGOs working in 'partnerships'. This type of thinking carries a strongly functionalist logic in which third-sector organizations are represented as having a set of comparative advantages in relation to public sector agencies (Cernea 1988).

In Britain, the gradual shift in the 1980s and 1990s towards using private social service delivery with a reduced government role was termed 'the mixed economy of welfare', bringing uneven results in terms of the quality of provision, despite making more government resources available to the sector (Kendall 2003). In the developing world, the adoption of structural adjustment policies by African governments, for example, led to cuts in social services, with the result that third-sector organizations were left attempting to fill the gap. In Zimbabwe, church missions provide sixty-eight percent of all hospital beds in rural areas, while in Zambia the third sector – which is mostly church-based – provides forty percent of health services in rural areas. In Uganda, many rural schools are being managed and funded by parent-teacher associations, despite being still nominally under the control of the state (Robinson and White 1998).

In this way, the third sector can be seen as a prominent idea that has helped to frame policy primarily within neoliberal governance processes. What all these variants of the third sector idea have in common is that they form part of an increasingly ubiquitous way of defining institutional landscapes and policy parameters with versions of a 'three-sector model' – whether in terms of development donors' 'good governance' agenda or within the U.K. government's current vision of the reform of public services. However, an ethnographic perspective suggests a disjuncture between the model's easy clarity in the way that it offers up a tripartite separation between three distinct areas of institutional life and the messy realities of professional life revealed in the life histories.

This disjuncture is revealed through an examination of the movement of particular individuals across these sector boundaries. There are both those who build careers within the third sector and then 'cross over' into a new job within a government agency, as well as those who maintain interests and relationships in both sectors at the same time (Lewis 2008a). In the U.K., the Department for International Development (DFID) has recruited many staff from the NGO sector, since they may have relevant experience, sometimes creating new informal sets of relations between them. Such persons may simultaneously serve to uphold the idea of difference between government and non-governmental sectors, while subverting it through a transfer of ideas and knowledge, often in informal and less visible ways (Lewis 2008b). For example, Oxfam, a large and long-established U.K. NGO, now has numerous former employees in senior positions across a range of U.K. government agencies. Use is made of these individuals, referred to by some as 'ex-fams', by Oxfam to gather information about policy processes and to build alliances as the NGO goes about its work. At the same time, the U.K. government agencies make more and more use of secondments and placements, bringing key policy thinkers from non-governmental settings into government, broadening 'big tent' politics but also arguably reducing dissent and criticism of government policy (Lewis 2008a). The boundary between the third sector and the government is therefore far more complex and porous than the three-sector model suggests. In the next section, we turn to another aspect of the conceptualization of the U.K. third sector which seeks to simplify a complex and messy set of historical and political relationships, namely the parallel worlds of work lives in domestic and international settings.

The Parallel Worlds of the U.K. Third Sector

The British 'third' sector has long been divided into two quite distinct subsectors which in a sense form two separate 'parallel worlds'. One is apparently outward-facing and contains the various NGOs that have worked overseas in 'developing' country contexts; the other is the world of more inward-facing 'voluntary organizations' that are concerned with domestic, U.K.-focused work 'at home'.[5] Despite the organizational diversity found within both subsectors, these two broad clusters of organizations are of an essentially similar type. Although they work in different geographical areas, many undertake broadly comparable types of activities (grassroots community work, service delivery, lobbying and advocacy). Yet there are few links and little communication between these two subsectors and, as a result, two different and separate communities of third-sector professionals coexist uneasily in the U.K. (Lewis 1999). The persistence of these two professional worlds reflects a dominant and problematic binary worldview that continues to separate problems of poverty and social justice in the U.K. from those in the rest of the world (Jones 2000). The binary worldview seeks to conceal – and indeed largely obscures – a range of continuities and connections in relation to migration, displacement, trade, conflict, transnational institutions and many other interrelated elements among broader landscapes of colonial history and globalization (Kothari 2005; Jones 2000).

Life-work history interviews[6] were conducted with individuals from within both contexts, making it possible to learn more about people's reasons for choosing to work in one or other of the two domestic or international 'subsectors'. The narratives revealed an unexpectedly sharp division between these worlds of domestic and international work, and of particular interest were the stories of people who had tried to challenge or subvert this prevailing dualistic order. These efforts to rupture the expert consensus that has emerged around the two 'parallel worlds' of the U.K. non-governmental sector suggests ways that ethnographic research, with its capacity to reveal and explain the less visible aspects of policy processes, has the potential to contribute to understanding the ways in which expertise is socially situated.

Ideas about the third sector have therefore become important as a site for the construction of knowledge about global and local poverty, and of strategies for addressing poverty reduction. Professional identities among third-sector personnel in the U.K. have as a consequence been shaped historically by the creation and maintenance of a conceptual boundary that helps to determine choice, first about whether to work in a non-governmental or governmental setting and, second, whether to work 'at home' on domestic poverty and social welfare issues or whether to focus instead on international development issues and the 'Third World'. But this is not a simple one-way causality because, as we will see, the maintenance of professional identities and interests also generates boundaries of protection in which both sides uphold the division. In the U.K. third sector, part of the way that this bounded knowledge community operates is by restricting the movement of individuals between these two professional worlds and, as will be demonstrated from some of the accounts below, it ultimately serves to limit the exchange of ideas and information across them.

Working in the Parallel Worlds

Raymond Apthorpe (Chapter 10 this volume) draws attention to what he terms the 'virtual reality of Aidland' as a useful tool for framing new thinking in the anthropology of development:

> Of course the world of aid is real enough to those who have to plan, manage and deliver it. Those subject to it know it well too. But looked at in another way – allegorically – it is different: an inauthentic world of only virtual reality. Indeed sometimes those who live and work in Aidland, not just travel through it with a donkey or a consultancy, will say so. So this must be true! ... What is 'virtual' about Aidland is its trick *trompe l'oeil* quality of being both there and not there. Not a nowhere exactly but inexactly a somewhere, with the characteristics of a nowhere. An idea of a somewhere but about which more is desired – or feared or neglected – than known.[7]

Reading Apthorpe's chapter led me back to reflect on my own earlier identification of these two 'parallel worlds' of the U.K. third sector (Lewis 1999), which seemed a striking, albeit little-explored, area of the 'virtual reality' of policy land. The dichotomy was clearly derived from elements of an 'othering' relationship between West and non-West, with continuities back to colonial relationships. Such a dichotomy has long been central to the construction of ideas about 'development' itself (Gardner and Lewis 1996; Cooper and Packard 1997; Kothari 2005).[8] This binary distinction at the level of worlds of policy can clearly be understood in relation to work on the ways in which the power of 'experts' is exercised through the act of 'simplifying' the world and 'resolving it into simple forces and oppositions' (Mitchell 2002: 34), and in new approaches to the anthropology of development which argues that policy can be analysed as a set of practices that are enacted through the construction and constant maintenance of coherent representations of meaning and action (Mosse 2005). What came through strongly in the life history narratives, and which seemed to require further explanation, was the strength and persistence of this category boundary among a community of people within the broad U.K. third sector whose moral and political outlook, and day-to-day working environment, might be expected to encourage a relatively high level of reflection and exchange in relation to global social and political issues. It seemed parochial rather than cosmopolitan if cosmopolitans are defined as those 'who identify more broadly with their continent or with the world as a whole' (Norris 2003: 289), and it seemed significant that the operation of these two subsectors appeared to be holding out against, and to some extent refusing, the logic of a more globalized order.

While the extent and extremes of poverty in areas of Asia, Africa and Latin America cannot be compared to disadvantage and inequality in the industrialized societies of 'the North', it makes little sense to obscure or deny the global relationships and continuities which connect social and economic change within such different contexts. Poverty is not nor has ever been confined to a 'third world', but is also a condition also experienced by many individuals and social groups in better-off societies. Organizational responses within the third sector to poverty and marginalization may increasingly be comparable and interconnected within the broad logic of neoliberal policy frameworks, and intervention strategies such as microfinance or participatory planning are increasingly exported between settings in different parts of the world. The restructuring of welfare systems (involving the use of third-sector organizations as service contracting agents), as well as the organized resistance to the growing marketization of service provision imposed by international financial institutions, are common phenomena within institutional and policy landscapes in many areas of the world. For example, Lind (1996) has analysed women organizing in the third sector to construct communal soup kitchens in Peru, seeking to influence policy in Bolivia and fighting violence against women in New York, all within a single global conceptual framework that links gender rights and organizational responses to poverty.

However, informants working in the U.K. third sector speak of having to make clear either/or choices between a professional identity based on either working 'at home' or focusing on 'Third World' contexts. For the individuals involved, this leads their subsequent career trajectories into quite separate worlds of practice, within either voluntary organizations or NGOs, despite the common challenges of poverty, exclusion, participation and accountability found within the policy contexts of both spheres, and the comparable tools and techniques deployed to try to tackle them.[9] Sometimes the parallel worlds can exist even inside the same organization.[10]

The Ethnography of 'Home or Away'

We now turn to explore some of the ways in which the subjects of my research spoke about their decisions to embark upon work in local or international contexts, and the ways in which such decisions have helped to construct professional identities. Research reveals a complex bundle of motivations and circumstances that operate to determine a person's choice of work context. The non-governmental professional is motivated by various factors: political solidarity, humanist compassion, an exploratory worldview, an interest in trying to escape one's own culture and family, or a sense of religious or humanitarian mission, among others.

In the U.K., a decision to work overseas may be expressed in quite romantic terms, drawing on an interest in travel, adventure and extending one's general experience. For example, one informant, working in an NGO, talked about a strong predisposition towards travel and international service from a relatively early age:

> I think I was interested in a wider world, not necessarily the 'doing good' end of it but, you know, the wider geography. I was always interested in … travel and finding out more, and seeing more. So there was a sort of … a cultural thing as well, and then there was this class thing, and probably community service 'cause that's … my parents were very strong in … you know, if you're a member of the community and you ought to support it, and I'm sure that got embedded in very early on actually. So there was all that … I can see all the bits of it, but I don't know what sparked it. But … by the time I left university I wanted to save the world anyway, that was quite clear …

The desire to construct a more cosmopolitan identity as a young white British person, by exploring the possibilities of combining international work with elements of self-realization, comes across in the following account:

> [My first job] … was actually a gap year between school and university and I went to India ostensibly to change the world and make a difference and so on, which I very quickly had beaten out of me or drummed out of me by realising that a white, middle-class, eighteen year old who'd travelled but not lived, had very little to offer to people in a rural village community in central India, except perhaps a little bit around English, the use of the English language and so on. But that … that whole experience, that whole year I worked for an organisation … it did give me a taste for different realities, I'd say, and different experiences and different ways in which people live their lives and so on. And I went from there to study development studies at university … My work direction has always been overseas-focused and always been … kind of development-orientated … [I]t was probably the single most concentrated period of learning in my life, I'd say that one year overseas just in terms of knowing who I was and my own resources, how I cope with adversity …

Both of these accounts resonate with those of other observers of the world of U.K. development agencies. In her work on aid agency personnel,

Kaufman (1997) explores the idea raised by one of her informants that many U.K. NGO staff can be described as in some way culturally 'disassociated' people, for example, people who had grown up overseas with a sense of being away from home. Her data suggested a more general idea that such persons tended to have 'had their horizons extended at an earlier age' (1997: 126) more than most others of their peer group, and that this sometimes led them into overseas work.

The motivation of a person from a more cultural and geographically diverse background within a minority community in the UK is likely to reflect a less binary – or more cosmopolitan – justification for working internationally. For example, a British Asian man who had grown up in East Africa worked, after completing university studies, in the U.K. voluntary sector. He saw this job as far less 'separate' from international work than the other informants:

> [T]here weren't many Asian models [of] people working on development issues in Africa at the time. And there was quite a lot of tension when I was growing up between the whole 'Africanisation' agenda in these countries and so on. And one of the things I grew up with was a very strong feeling that actually ... I'd really like at some stage to see more Asian people working in the development field in Africa. So immediately after finishing university ... this was 1981, I began to think about ... how do I ... go overseas and work, because that's where I saw the real challenge of what I wanted to do. I made some initial inquiries with a number of voluntary organisations, the UN system, NGOs and so on, and everywhere where I went, people said, 'Well, actually ... you don't really have any real experience'. So it was quite a difficult path. I eventually took my first job working in a night shelter for young homeless people in London ... after having done that for a year, I decided ... my dream was still to work overseas, and I made some enquiries with UN Volunteers. And I was selected for a post to work as a community worker [in an African country] ...

Many informants offered political or ideological analyses of why they decided to work in the U.K. as opposed to overseas. This was particularly true for those informants who had begun their working lives in the 1970s amid discussions of the politics of social work and community organizing. These arguments can be read partly as the desire to avoid what Midgley called 'professional imperialism' in the social work field, which imposed 'alien theory and techniques on developing countries, which were unsuited to their cultures and development needs' (1981: xiii).

Such decision-making makes explicit a political analysis that expresses discomfort with working in distant postcolonial contexts, as this informant explained:

I was involved in community development programmes and … the choices you made about where you were going to go and live and work could be in the U.K., or they could be in … some sort of international 'third world'-type context. There was a pretty strong feeling that it was really important to do things in the rest of the world, but actually it was really important to do work 'at home' too. It was almost like the rediscovery of poverty type stuff, at the end of the nineteenth, early twentieth century … not quite, not as dramatic as that … but a sense that 'hang on a minute, we've got a lot of awful problems here' and it's fine … and important … to go and do work internationally … but if you're not doing anything here, then it's a bit of a cop-out …

Accepting that there is a vague sense of unease rather than a firm position on this issue, another informant spoke of her concerns about the politics of work with distant others:

… there is a something in there … a worry about disaster tourism, or about disaster employment … that sort of thing … I know that that's not what it is about. But there's still a little bit of me that feels very reserved about it. I was in … oh … an Islington women's group [laughs] that I'm in. One of the women in it is an advisor on women and medicine for the developing world, works with [an aid agency] on that. I mean she was presenting her work on that, you know it was fascinating, you know, really interesting stuff, and I kept thinking … not 'Why are you doing that', but rather 'You're talking about a world that connects to mine politically, and in terms of morality and ethics, but it still feels like a different world. And somehow you are telling me a story from a strange land …' Whereas another woman telling me about what she is doing something about … prostitution in King's Cross doesn't feel like that …

Lifecycle pressures and the fear of weakening social and family networks are also an important set of factors which influence a person's decision to continue working internationally. While dislocation may help to trigger the desire for international work, its lack of resolution may also feed the tension between 'home and away', perhaps related to sense of place, of ageing and of family. This dislocatory tension may ultimately inform an attempt to try to 'cross back' between the two worlds, as another informant explained:

And then I came home, back to the U.K. I'd been away for a quite a few years and my parents had got older, my nieces and nephews … I was really aware that I was kind of losing touch with my family. People would come out and visit me, and as much as I loved [an

Asian country] – and I probably will go back there … or anywhere else I've worked, because I like that – but I really thought 'Now I really have to go back home and start investing back in personal relationships, back here', because you know, I'd been away a bit …

The (Dis)organization of Professional Knowledge

These short extracts from the life histories provide glimpses into narratives of decision making that suggest that the 'parallel worlds' distinction remains a feature of the U.K. third sector, serving not only to construct non-governmental professional career identities but also to segregate certain areas of expert knowledge. Professional lives in the third sector are influenced and constrained by policy assumptions at two main levels. First, they take shape within the broader three-sector model, which creates a separation between three institutional spheres which obscures the messy boundaries and connections that exist between them in practice. Second, the further construction of the two 'parallel worlds' within this third sector serves to create artificial and ahistorical boundaries between the domestic and international work. This latter distinction is expressed by one informant, who speaks of the fact that it is usually difficult for both people and ideas to move across the boundary:

> I do see the international development sector as really almost a 'sub-sector' or a 'co-sector' really, alongside … you know … the voluntary, the U.K. voluntary sector. And I think there's … little movement probably between international development and U.K. voluntary sector.

The boundary exists as a barrier to the travel of ideas, even where there may be useful potential for exchange and learning across contexts. The importance of possible 'policy and theoretical convergence across boundaries' is recognized by Jones (2000: 240) in his analysis of why it is 'alright to do development "over there" but not "here"'. For example, he finds increasing areas of common need around issues such as participation and citizenship in both 'First World' and 'Third World' contexts.

A key problem that can be identified in relation to these parallel worlds is a general lack of exchange and communication that seems to exist between the respective subsectors (Lewis 1999). This state of affairs appears to be continuing and is supported by many of these new narratives. For example, this NGO staff member speaks of her experience of a general lack of openness to cross-learning between domestic and international settings:

> [T]he saddest thing is that I find in [the NGO] is [that] I don't think we're open enough to ideas coming in from all sorts of places.

Because I think so many people have come up [through] straight routes and they don't know that there is a life out there. And that's what I worry about all the time, that people aren't seeing the potential from these other places. Like the Humanitarian Department, we've done this [new plan] and we've put a lot of ... stuff into getting our humanitarian [approach] really slick ... [F]rankly, it's been really hard work to persuade them to go and look at emergency services in other places, including the NHS. And you just think 'Oh for heaven's sake' ... and they finally did go to say, the County Council for example, to look at their emergency procedures ...

This lack of openness to other sources of ideas is attributed to the fact that people tend to come into the international NGO sector and stay there during their careers, moving between a relatively small number of organizations. Unable to imagine that useful knowledge or relevant lessons might be available from within the U.K., NGO colleagues restrict their consultations to other similar NGOs, sometimes drawing on their own previous jobs in these broadly similar organizations. Part of this is an unwillingness, according to this informant, to connect 'developed' and 'developing' country contexts.[11]

The same informant continued her account in which her previous work in the U.K. health service tended to be undervalued by her 'development' colleagues, even where she felt there were potentially relevant comparisons about accessing more directly the views of service users/beneficiaries:[12]

And there is that thing about not seeing that there are relationships, because I think I know quite a lot about development actually, not in the sense of Africa and all that ... but when you get round to it, the skills and the things you do, they are so similar really... I mean, I didn't know much about delivering humanitarian stuff, and then I got into debates about actual beneficiaries and their ability to comment on services and things. And I was thinking, wait a minute, I've been here before with patients, you know, and all the same things are just there ...

In order to get around the problem that her knowledge from the domestic subsector was not valued by her international colleagues, she explained that she sometimes found it necessary to pretend to know less than she actually did in some meetings. This, she said, was a response to the negative power of people's preconceived expectations about the value of 'her' knowledge as against 'their' highly specialized knowledge field of development:

I [had previously done] all this work on quality at [a U.K. organization], and ... a new accreditation programme and all that ... And eventually [at the NGO] I sort of started writing some stuff down … about the different ways … you have accreditation of individuals, you have accreditation of organisations … all those sorts of things that you think about looking at, in terms of quality. And at first it looked like I was completely out of my mind … there were one or two words about 'She's never worked in the humanitarian sector before, you know' … And you just think, honestly, this is terrible, really. [W]e ended up doing peer reviews which again, I think I have spent quite a lot of my time slightly pretending I don't know as much as I do about some things, so that people can discover them for themselves. And that's what happened … I feel I've had to learn how to be very … gentle … [T]here's a very heavy culture and I don't just mean in [this NGO], I mean in that whole sector, you know, … you can get change to happen, but if you look like you're bringing something hard from … you know … *outside*, I think you've got trouble.

Another informant explained certain other ways in which knowledge was segregated. She had come to know of work in the NGO world in relation to the evaluation of community-level interventions because her sister worked in an NGO, but did not find it easy to interest her colleagues in exploring possible opportunities to exchange ideas between the subsectors. She was unusual in that she was about to start a new job in an international NGO, having spent most of her professional career in the domestic sector. She characterized her colleagues as introverted and unwilling to consider the international context as a valid source of knowledge:

I think there's very little cross-fertilisation. I think one of the things that I really find interesting is … a whole of debate about impact and evaluation … in the voluntary sector generally. I know … there are sort of parallel debates going on in international development … You don't get the cross-fertilisation, you don't get, you know, the learning from the international development sector coming into the U.K. It's like … they're just talking amongst themselves. They don't talk to the broader voluntary sector. I mean, that's my take on it, and I'm quite interested to see, when I move into [an NGO] if it's true.

The compartmentalization of the two subsectors – and the professional identities that this tends to shape – makes movement by professionals between them comparatively rare. Where people do develop an interest in moving across, there are barriers that result from the different knowledge communities each subsector represents. From a perspective within the U.K. voluntary sector, some informants view the world of international development as exotic and exciting. For the following informant, the view of the international part of the U.K. third sector is a somewhat idealized one and is expressed as part of a desire to 'escape' from the everyday into something more exciting. She suggests that people who do make it across do so as a kind of 'one-way traffic' from which there is an unlikely chance of return:

> I think it's quite difficult to get into the international sector you know, if your experience is mainly U.K. And once you're in the international sector people don't tend to want to come back to the U.K. sector. And I can see the reasons for that. There's some sort of excitement, perhaps, about working overseas, but also the need. You can't really compare the needs of kids in Africa to the needs of, you know, even the most deprived kids in the U.K.

All this can pose difficulties for people who wish to blur the boundary between these two professional worlds, since they find that their knowledge may be differently valued. One senior NGO staff member interviewed recalled being asked about her earlier career in the U.K. public sector during her NGO job interview. Under increasingly hostile questioning from the panel about the status and validity of her U.K.-based knowledge and experience, she reflected during her narrative:

> ... you know, I was starting to think, but I *do* know about development ... I mean someone said to me, 'But you never had ... "dirt under your fingernails"'. And I said, 'Well, I've had grime under my fingernails in inner London, you know, is that not the same thing?'

The organizing principle of the parallel worlds, while operating at the level of general policy discussion in the U.K., also informs individual agency, whether as an idea helping to structure decisions over choices of work location or in conditioning managerial responses to challenges of everyday work practices.

Conclusion

This chapter has drawn on life-work history data in order to explore the complexities of professional identities among those who work in the U.K. 'third sector', both in the domestic sphere and in the parallel world of international aid and development work. The personal narratives highlight the significance to these professionals' career histories of values, political and religious commitments and family histories, as well as relationships to wider historical and political events. The stories reveal ideas about, and tensions within, the separation of the state from the third sector, and about the distinguishing of work at home from that abroad. The life histories work to construct and reproduce, as well as to subvert, these sector divisions and dominant policy models.

The life histories combine two important elements within current dominant rationalities of aid and governance. The first is the tripartite model which provides a framework for neoliberals to conceptualize a 'good governance' agenda that first disaggregates and then finds synergies between the state, the market and a 'third sector', thereby helping to create a persuasive rationale for policy simplifications such as ideas about organizational 'comparative advantage'. The second is a colonially rooted discourse that distinguishes poverty in the U.K. from poverty in the 'Third World', thereby denying both the interconnectedness of global social inequalities and links with the poverty-related domestic issues of immigration and racism. The obscuring of such continuities is reinforced by the ahistorical character of the three-sector model, the boundaries of which map uneasily and often unconvincingly on to local and global institutional landscapes, yet they achieve a power that continues to organize policies of aid and governance.

The professional life histories presented here begin to reveal ways in which these dominant policy models are constructed and how they operate. In relation to the first issue of the boundary between the public and the third sector, boundaries are in practice more complex, subtle and unstable than the three-sector model tends to allows for. For example, 'non-governmental' actors are linked in potentially important ways to government through movements of people, resource flows and transactions, even though such links may be far from visible. They may include kinship relations within elite families, age-sets or alumni groups which connect NGO staff with colleagues in other spheres, the embeddedness of employees within wider communities, and funding streams which generate ambiguous roles, allegiances and identities among individuals (Lewis 2008a and b). In relation to the second issue of the separation between home and away, a set of 'defining tensions' helps to construct the identities of these non-governmental professionals in the U.K. within a highly simplified frame. At the level of policy, a key function of the dichotomy is to deny the connections around international development and domestic policy. At the level of practice, the distinction functions to create and maintain spheres of professional expertise through the construction of 'relevant' and 'non-relevant' areas of competency and knowledge.

Such policy maps may become increasingly anachronistic as the links between the three sectors are rendered more apparent, and the international relationships and networks which transcend such simple binary thinking about domestic and international subsectors become more visible and less avoidable. For the present they remain relatively fixed and form part of this 'virtual reality'. However, this reality appears to contain a 'mirror image': while the boundaries of the three-sector model are increasingly complicated in practice under current neoliberal governance arrangements in the U.K. and elsewhere – as the life histories of 'cross-overs' indicate – the model itself remains in place, sustained within the good governance policy discourse; but in the case of the domestic and international distinction, the model is increasingly unsustainable as themes and techniques such as microfinance converge, yet at the level of professional practice the division has been reproduced and appears to be stronger than ever.

Notes

1. Research was funded by the U.K. Economic and Social Research Council (ESRC), Grant Reference RES-155-25-0064, as part of its Non-Governmental Public Action (NGPA) Programme. The study was based on the collection of professional life histories in three countries: the U.K., Bangladesh and the Philippines. A complementary study was also undertaken in a fourth country, Mexico, by Alejandro Natal Martínez, at El Colegio Mexiquense. An overview can be found in Lewis (2008b). This chapter takes as its focus some of the life histories from the U.K. I wish to thank Nazneen Kanji and Hakan Seckinelgin for their useful comments on earlier drafts, and David Mosse for his perceptive editorial input.
2. These overlapping terms each have distinctive histories and are embedded in different geographical and cultural contexts, which are briefly discussed below.
3. *Third Sector*, 10 December 2006. The weekly U.K. newspaper *Third Sector* for 'charities, voluntary organisations, social enterprise' boasts a circulation of more than 17,000.
4. In the development sector, for example, NGOs became seen as a *tabula rasa* onto which were projected ideas such as empowerment and participation, and new forms of management and organizing (Lewis 2005).
5. Despite the lack of any clear analytical or terminological logic to the distinction, here I am following the convention among those working in the U.K. third sector in which the term 'NGO' is used for organizations working in international development and the term 'voluntary organization' is used for those working in the U.K.
6. A detailed description of the strengths and weaknesses of the life history method, and the experience of using life-work histories within the wider ESRC research project, can be found in Lewis 2008a.
7. This quote is taken from an earlier conference draft of Apthorpe's chapter, which has unfortunately disappeared from the later published version!
8. When Oxfam launched a small U.K. programme in 1996 after six decades of working internationally, arguing that expertise acquired through its years in developing countries was transferable to Britain, the *Daily Mail*'s headline was 'Stick to the Third World!' (NCVO News 1996).
9. Pearson (2000) for example writes of the ways in which certain types of microcredit schemes have been adapted from Asia for use in interventions in poor communities in the U.K.
10. Organizations such as the Save the Children Fund (SCF) which operate both domestic and overseas programmes have tended to reproduce this division within their organizations and, until comparatively recently, the two halves of the SCF organization remained very separate, with little communication or exchange of ideas between them. On the other hand, Christian Aid must be careful not to involve itself directly in the rights of refugees in the U.K., since this is seen as the preserve of another non-governmental agency also linked to the Church of England.
11. However, evidence suggests that when structured opportunities for learning and exchange between contexts are presented, they are eagerly taken up. For example, an issue of the international practitioner journal *Participatory Learning and Action (PLA) Notes* on this topic has been particularly well received in recent years (PLA Notes 38: Participatory Processes in the North, International Institute for Environment and

Development (IIED), June 2000, Guest Editors: Charlotte Flower, Paul Mincher and Susan Rimku, available from www.iied.org).

12. There is also sometimes a parallel language dividing the discussion in the U.K. and 'development' settings such that, for example, people labelled 'users' of voluntary sector services in the domestic U.K. setting are frequently termed 'beneficiaries' among NGOs working in developing countries.

References

Archer, R. 1994. 'Markets and Good Government', in A. Clayton (ed.), *Governance, Democracy and Conditionality: What Role for NGOs*? Oxford: INTRAC.

Beckmann, D. 1991. 'Recent Experience and Emerging Trends', in S. Paul and A. Israel (eds), *Nongovernmental Organizations and the World Bank: Cooperation for Development*. Washington D.C.: The World Bank.

Bell, D. 1973. *The Coming of Post-Industrial Society: A Venture in Social Forecasting*. New York: Basic Books.

Cernea, M. 1988.'Non-governmental Organizations and Local Development', *World Bank Discussion Papers*, Washington, D.C.: World Bank.

Chambers, R. 1996. *Challenging the Professions*. London: Intermediate Technology.

Cooper, F. and R. Packard. (eds). 1997. *International Development and the Social Sciences*. Berkeley, C.A.: University of California Press.

Etzioni, A. 1961. *A Comparative Analysis of Complex Organizations: On Power, Involvement and their Correlates*, New York: The Free Press of Glencoe.

_____ 1973. 'The third sector and domestic missions', *Public Administration Review* (July/August): 314–27.

Ferlie, E., L. Ashburner, L. Fitzgerald and A. Pettigrew. 1996. *The New Public Sector Management in Action*. Oxford: Oxford University Press.

Gardner, K. and D. Lewis.1996. *Anthropology, Development and the Post-modern challenge*. London: Pluto Press.

Jones, P.S. 2000. 'Why is it Alright to Do Development "Over There" But Not "Here"?: Changing Vocabularies and Common Strategies of Inclusion across the "First" and "Third" Worlds', *Area* 32(2): 237–41.

Kaufman, G. 1997. 'Watching the Developers: A Partial Ethnography', in R.D. Grillo and R.L. Stirrat (eds), *Discourses of Development: Anthropological Perspectives*. Oxford: Berg.

Kendall, J. 2003. *The Voluntary Sector*. London: Routledge.

Kothari, U. 2005. 'From Colonialism to Development: Oral Histories, Life Geographies and Travelling Cultures', *Antipode* 37(3): 49–60.

Levitt, T. 1975. *The Third Sector: New Tactics for a Responsive Society*. New York: AMACOM, American Management Association.

Lewis, D. 1999. 'Introduction: The Parallel Worlds of Third Sector Research and the Changing Context of Voluntary Action', in D. Lewis (ed.), *International Perspectives on Voluntary Action: Rethinking the Third Sector*. London: Earthscan.

_____ 2002. 'Civil Society in African Contexts: Reflections on the "Usefulness" of a Concept', *Development and Change* 33(4): 569–86.

_____ 2004. 'On the Difficulty of Studying "Civil Society": NGOs, State and Democracy in Bangladesh', *Contributions to Indian Sociology* 38(3): 299–322.

_____ 2005. 'Individuals, Organisations and Public Action: Trajectories of the "Non-governmental" in Development Studies', in U. Kothari (ed.), *A Radical History of Development Studies*. London: Zed Books.

_____ 2006. 'Elusive Spaces and Organisational Forms: A Partial Recovery of the History of the "Third Sector Idea"', Paper for the *Manchester ESRC seminar series on 'Rethinking Economies'*, University of Manchester, 15 December.

_____ 2007. *The Management of Non-Governmental Development Organizations*, 2nd ed. London: Routledge.

_____ 2008a. 'Using Life Histories in Social Policy Research: The Case of Third Sector/Public Sector Boundary Crossing', *Journal of Social Policy* 37(4): 559-578.

_____ 2008b. 'Crossing the Boundaries between "Third Sector" and State: Life-work Histories from Philippines, Bangladesh and the UK', *Third World Quarterly* 29(1):125-141

Lind, A. 1996. 'Gender, Development and Urban Social Change: Women's Community Action in Global Cities', *World Development* 25 (8): 1205–23.

MacEwan, A. 1999. *Neo-liberalism or Democracy: Economic Strategy, Markets, and Alternatives for the 21st Century*. London: Zed Books.

Midgley, J. 1981. *Professional Imperialism: Social Work in the Third World*. London: Heinemann.

Minogue, M. 1998. 'Changing the State: Concepts and Practice in the Reform of the Public Sector', in M. Minogue, C. Polidano and D. Hulme (eds), *Beyond the New Public Management: Changing Ideas and Practices in Governance*. Cheltenham: Edward Elgar.

Mitchell, T. 2002. *Rule of Experts: Egypt, Techno-Politics, Modernity*. Berkeley, C.A.: University of California Press.

Mosse, D. 2005. *Cultivating Development: An Ethnography of Aid Policy and Practice*. London: Pluto Press.

Mosse, D. and D. Lewis. 2006. 'Theoretical Approaches to Brokerage and Translation in Development', in D. Lewis and D. Mosse (eds), *Development Brokers and Translators: An Ethnography of Aid and Agencies*. Bloomington, C.T.: Kumarian Books.

Najam, A. 1999. 'Citizen Organisations as Policy Entrepreneurs', in D. Lewis (ed.), *International Perspectives on Voluntary Action: Rethinking the Third Sector*. London: Earthscan.

NCVO News. 1996. *Tackling Injustice in our own Back yard*. London: National Council for Voluntary Organisations.

Neilsen, W. 1979. *The Endangered Sector*. New York: Colombia University Press.

Norris, P. 2003. 'Global Governance and Cosmopolitan Citizens', in D. Held and A. McGraw (eds), *The Global Transformations Reader*, 2nd ed. Cambridge: Polity Press.

Paul, S. and A. Israel 1991. *Nongovernmental Organizations and the World Bank: Cooperation for Development*. Washington, D.C.: The World Bank.

Pearson, R. 2000. 'Think Globally, Act Locally: Translating International Microcredit Experience into the United Kingdom Context', in D. Lewis and T. Wallace (eds), *New Roles and Relevance: Developed NGOs and the Challenges of Change*. Bloomfield, C.T.: Kumarian.

Robinson, M. and G. White 1998. 'Civil Society and Social Provision: The Role of Civic Organisations', in M. Minogue, C. Polidano and D. Hulme (eds), *Beyond the New Public Management: Changing Ideas and Practices in Governance*. Cheltenham: Edward Elgar.

Tvedt, T. 1998. *Angels of Mercy or Development Diplomats? NGOs and Foreign Aid*. Oxford: James Currey.

Chapter 10

CODA

With Alice in Aidland: A Seriously Satirical Allegory[1]

Raymond Apthorpe

Introduction

The recent emergence in anthropology-and-development of 'the ethnography of aid' ('aidnography')[2] has much to offer in depicting and interpreting the institutional culture of 'Aidland' at large and the 'expert knowledges' that inculcate and sustain it. Several aspects of these prove to be in some ways more virtual than real – hence the degree of virtual reality of Aidland. Social anthropologically-informed aidnography probes and ponders the *representations collectives* and *classifications sociales* by which Aidmen and Aidwomen say they order and understand their world and work, whether these are virtual or real.

The Aidland in this account is thus a macro construct, whose micro applications are interesting. Aidland has its own mental topographies, languages of discourse, lore and custom, and approaches to organizational knowledge and learning. Driven from without, thus only semiautonomously,[3] it generates and sustains to an extent its own politics and economics, geographics, demographics and other -ics such as 'cultur-ics', though as yet the latter field is without standard texts. It even has its own handed-down secular-inspirational sort of 'ten commandments', the 'thou shalt' UN Millennium Development Goals.[4]

The following few candid, sketchy, 'with love from Aidland' postcards seriously, allegorically and satirically portray some of the surreal virtuality of the story of the 'why' of international development, humanitarian and peacebuilding aid, where it comes from and then goes, how it gets there and what happens then. They tell part of our story, Alice's and mine, about our decades of travels 'abroad', which are now over. The great and the good of Aidland might find it difficult to see the point,[5] but our motive is one not of hurrying the 'end of aid' (whatever that might mean, given international relations and the humanistic eternalities of altruistic 'help').

Rather it is to situate aid practices in a sort of *sociologie totale,* so that broader, indeed the broadest contexts are given their due.

Some epistemic space opening up in anthropological theory has made such conceptualization and empirical research as aidnography possible. For example, in some schools a discourse and culture focus succeeded anthropology's received concerns with language and culture; an engagement with agency to an extent shifted structure from its former pride of place; intersubjective pluralities conquered some of the old ethnographic-objective singularities. Multisite research comes into its own where earlier it was derided.

'We' planners, administrators, human rights campaigners, development and humanitarian studies professors, researchers, aid-workers and others are perhaps even more astonishing candidates for political, economic and social – including social class and social mobilization – observation and analysis (which is fair game for Alice, back from Wonderland and now off on new adventures), than are 'they', the peasantries and tribes of a number of varieties of unreconstructed social science, the displaced and the dispossessed who are 'our' normal subjects/objects of study.

Development-speak as if you will a Barthian 'sociolect', has many markers, mostly of its own making. For example, what cutely and cozily it likes to call 'the human factor' (in other declensions 'the social', or 'the cultural' seen as an 'aspect' or 'factor') owes more to the ways of the intervening agencies and *their* sociology than those of its ostensible subjects. Shades of Anais Nin, things 'over there' seen not as they are, but as we are. Alice is agog. Aidnography explores Aidland through its own speaks, that to a degree fancifully, fitfully and again only in a semi-*sui generis* way are constituted by the *trompe l'oeil* it paints for itself on the looking glass. What starts as virtual, in the name of real, becomes in the process also somehow real, both for its protagonists and sometimes everyone (think for example of the national election in Afghanistan that has just taken – and not taken – place).

Here then are some séances, some slices; Aidland seen as a parallel universe with its own truths that, outside the fold, are more bizarre *invraisemblances* than verisimilitudes. Some 'true social science fiction' as one might say.

Views of Aidland

I

A virtual world of inauthentic reality. 'Modernization' in Tunisia, as was remarked half a century ago, in some ways brought not the promised new dawn but an artifice *'sans intégration effective du milieu humaine ou géographique ... El Habibia avec ses canaux, ses routes and ses maisons blanches*

... un petit morceau de planète étrangère, un jeu de l'esprit mais non le premier stade d'une évolution progressive de la paysannerie locale' (Poncet 1964: 326). Another planet that this planet has created. More recently, Achille Mbembe (1992) writes at large on the 'post-colony' as a form of *'virtual reality ...* mayors, attachés, official hostesses ... often miscast [yet playing] their roles with great vigour [and] infinite potentiality – the capacity for individuals to virtually transform themselves into anybody they want to be'. Think too of Friedrich Kratochwil (2007) on 'the surreal quality' of, for example, the introduction of the International Criminal Court for Rwanda and similar reforms which 'proceed on the basis of organizational answers whose remedial capacities have no [realistic, let alone idealistic] relationship to the local circumstances'.[6]

Truths in one universe that are astonishing falsities in another are of course nothing new, and may anyway be benign, harmless, possibly comforting. They become perhaps even murderous only when, whether by conceit or deceit, beggaring belief, cunning conspiracy or just ignorant incompetence, one universe is mistaken for another, and such substitution matters. If utopian propensities, whether for diagnosis or prognosis, have now more or less died (before rising again) everywhere else, they continue to be robust in the world of aid. But given the high expectations held of it, the evidence on aid ineffectiveness is massive. In case after case, both in 'just helping' as in international humanitarian assistance (as Zoe Marriage brilliantly reveals on the evidence of her own extensive travels)[7] and in 'forced entry' such as armed *HumanitarianIntervention* (or strongly conditional 'enforced' international development assistance), there are outcomes concealed as far as possible from public scrutiny, so that the myth may be preserved.

While real enough to those who have to plan, manage and deliver it – those subject to it also know it well – Aidland's trick *trompe l'oeil* quality is one of something being both there and not there. Not a nowhere exactly but inexactly a somewhere with the characteristics of a nowhere. An idea of a somewhere but one about which more is desired – or feared, neglected, denied or evaded – than known or learned.

The travel writer Jan Morris in her memoir *Trieste and the Meaning of Nowhere* relished her expatriate's idea of a Trieste long ago where she could 'feel suspended [as if] "nowhere at all" [in a] highly subjective place [that inspires] fancies ... an allegory of limbo in the secular sense of an indefinable hiatus' (Morris: 2001: 4–5). Adventuring through the looking glass into the land of the trails and travails of Aidland, Alice is astonished to find so much there of 'nowhere at all', *terra nullius*, unhistory, ungeography, uneconomics. Fancy-free falling *up* (one intervention success will surely generate another), as well as down (as in 'domino' effects).[8] In gravity-free Aidland, provided only that it is 'implemented', anything is possible.

The wonderful world of aid is a Marc Augean sort of place-that-is-not-a-place. As worded by its Aidmen and Aidwomen, it is both immaterial and material, infinite and immediate, in its figurative potentiality. An uttered, surreal, Baudrillard-like semiotic universe (1991) which appears to be settled more in the sky above than on the ground beneath. In surreal *DevelopmentEconomics* (and sometimes other university disciplines) weightless stylistic facts are given a gravitas that is far from the gravity they defy.

Morris' idea of 'secular … hiatus' is pertinent for our allegory also. Ask any First Secretary in any country's embassy abroad why he or she is there. 'Why of course [stupid] for our national interests' will be the reply. Not for world citizenship, particularly not, thought Alice, for migrants and refugees. Consider also what Australia demanded, but failed to get, a few years ago for its police on an aid assignment in Papua New Guinea (PNG): immunity from the ordinary laws of that country beyond the normal diplomatic immunity. The mundane facts of that case were that the PNG government objected to the demand, and Australia's foreign minister refused to back down. However, PNG's judiciary then successfully established that what the donor country demanded would be in breach of PNG's national constitution. Australia was forced to withdraw its police. An interesting course of events indeed, muses Alice, for what donors commonly call a 'failed' or 'failing' state.

II

Lewis Carroll's darling girl Alice. It was her penchant for 'in yer face' asperity and accuracy about what she thinks is bleeding obvious[9] that attracted me to Alice; her way of picking on what is 'beyond belief' – as in 'you're kidding surely, yet you seem not to realize that' – about what she thinks is unmistakably as plain as a pikestaff and delights in saying so.

An aid recipient country's foreign minister complains that the foreign *NonGovernmentalOrganizations* 'are running a parallel government' to the government in his country, rather than aiding that country and its own governance institutions. Consider also the view taken by all three of Norway's most prominent and best informed peace studies directors, that Norway's military *PeaceBuilding* role in Afghanistan is 'largely defined by security interests related to maintaining its own [that is, Norway's not Afghanistan's] good standing both in NATO and its bilateral relations with the US' (Surkhe, Stand and Harpviken 2002). Alice is amazed. How and why could that be the true rationale for aid? Whatever has happened to the *GoodGovernance* that *AidDonors* prescribe for others when, again as in Afghanistan, '[d]ifferent donor governments and different policy instruments tend to undermine one another and with even the UN Security Council, UNSMA, and UNOCHA are pursuing three mutually conflicting policies there' (Atmar and Goodhand 2002: 13)?

Alice has every reason to be often astonished by what the Aidpeople she meets say to her, and the surprising facts of the *AidWorkers'* universe. Remarkably, not one but two heads of the World Bank were among the chief architects of America's murderous wars (in Vietnam and Iraq). Admittedly at times she can be exuberantly over-rationalist in her reactions. *Uber* cool, she can be far less quick to remark on the part that the under-rational plays in world-making then in keeping it going. Her not entirely rhetorical question, 'Are UN experts people who are experts on getting employment with the UN?', is not the best conversation opener when at dinner at their tables (neither is the supplementary: 'Don't you think that perhaps *less* pay and perks and politics might result in more serious appointments?').

Some of the real – not allegorical – people[10] she and I meet are far from being uncool themselves in the heat. Many wear their masks and say the 'right things'; others say they are 'just cogs in a machine, really', with the day's job to be sorted and done and 'a good cooperation to try to achieve in whatever way we can' (perhaps more in ignorance of the codes and protocols to which their head offices have signed up so as to be 'good donors' than aware of, and following them). But others are as sharp as she. As for what Aidpeople may think of Alice's minder, another academic on the loose (and a non-economist at that), a poor misguided native-loving sort who just doesn't get it; guess we are a pair.

III

Some cracks in the glass. The internal corporate frontiers of Aidland that were never crossed a couple or so decades ago now frequently are. Someone you met last year in a UN special agency is now with an *InternationalNon GovernmentOrganization (INGO)*. Or there has been a reverse shift. She moved across because the job, the pay and other career aspects were right. Or because nothing else was going. Certainly it syncs perfectly with such crossings over, both that there is less *AlternativeDevelopment* around than there used to be and that what there is can pop up virtually anywhere.

Set against what has changed is what definitely has not: Aidland's major, governmental/intergovernmental/non-governmental power divide. The NGOs who genuinely want to get their own act together ethically nevertheless continue to be driven greatly by fear of anything that might tip the balance of power in their world even more in favour of the *Donor Governments* on whom they heavily depend for assignments and resources. Is that why in 2006 Oxfam U.K. thought it best to 'stand together' on one platform with that country's New Labour government (and a wealthy pop star) so as to appear to jointly command *The WarOnPoverty*? Or was it rather some ditzy, dizzy 'governance without government' moment that politicians as well as aid agencies like to spin?

As for the aidfever occurring under the rubric of 'making poverty history': a Chancellor of the U.K.'s Exchequer is on a Mad Hatter few away days' of rolled-up business shirt sleeves in 'the Third World' promising to 'double aid and halve poverty'; and a U.K. Prime Minister no less spinning like March Hare his 'goodbye to ideology', 'hello to values' farewell and hail (Taylor 2005). 'Halving' presumably as in 'cheating by halves', 'doubling' as in 'double-crossing', thinks Alice – aware that given the very minor proportion that international aid accounts for in the total of world financial flows, even in fairyland economics and mathematics, two times a figure that typically is much less than one percent adds up to not much.

Internally, Aidland is made up of several Aidlands. Not all INGOs are the same in their politics. Unlike Oxfam, Médecins Sans Frontières (MSF) U.K. certainly would not have appeared in public in such governmental company. Note too that policy positions taken by the various national MSFs (or other agencies) around the world differ. The international is also the national, there being only discursive space 'in between'.

As well as variable horizontal frontiers, Aid has vertical layers, horizontal differentiations, variable adiabatic cooling rates and such. Discontinuities and disjunctures that differently inflect their different categories of staff – head office and field, short-termers and regulars, foreign and national, relief and rescue and development people. Thus, to be more precise, the Aidland in this account is a composite of somewhat different Aidlands that, at times, can differ considerably from one another, sometimes according to the sector and type of aid they ply, sometimes because of their different resources and histories, sometimes according to whether confessionally they are religious faith-based or not.

IV

A little of what you fancy does you good, an endless supply does you even better. Fancies in Aidland are prolific and live a merry life, until they drop. Notoriously, fads and fashions in Aidland come and go, and come round again. Once in Manila at the ILO (*International Labour Organization*) office Alice and I were told a good one about the 'informal sector'. An earnest young staffer enthused about discussions on an ILO summit to be held in Rome 'to formalize the informal sector, a wonderful idea don't you think, so full of possibility'. He was apparently unaware of the social and economic history of the informal sector as, among other things, a realistic, protesting, search against the formal for better alternatives to it.

For another example, think of Australia where for a couple of centuries (continuing until relatively recently) *terra nullius* served as a very fine fancy indeed. A master metaphor perhaps for everything these postcards are about. An idea of a nowhere somewhere, that allows an actual land, which clearly *is* owned and inhabited, to be treated for the purposes of foreign incursion and dominion as if it were not. As if, to borrow an American urban planning concept (for the forcible renovation of cities), it were an 'eminent domain' to be tamed through a sort of adverse possession – which is dispossession – and resettlement. It was only a few years ago that the High Court of Australia (in the *Mabo* case) rejected that, as a matter of law,

Australis belonged to no one before the colonials came and grabbed it, certainly not to its indigenes. The visible is said to be invisible. Now what sort of sense is that?

Terra nullius was a convenient legal fiction that was most likely unknown to Australia's white settlers when they landed on New Holland's shores. Rather, it arrived much later (and not as one might have thought from England, but from Algeria, where it was used to justify an occupation of land in Mauretania over which there was said to be no sovereignty, let alone ownership). No matter. Wherever it came from, and whatever particular type of 'policy transfer' (Larmour 2005) it may represent, as a metaphor it sums up perfectly the sort of supposed *tabula rasa* that Aidlanders make theirs to fret and fancy over, to dream and scheme on, to inscribe at will. Including when claiming in the name of 'local ownership' not to be 'in the driving seat' while in actual practice never giving that up.[11]

Missionaries go about their business of denying and partially dispossessing in the name of 'salvation' ('good religion' to chase out 'bad'). Imperial adventures and colonial regimes do their denying and dispossessing in the governance-correct name of *pax*, 'peace' (through war for 'civilization'). *InternationalAid* dispossesses while aiding but also through aiding as for example when, acting as its own client, an *AidAgency* 'capacity-builds' for the compliant version of whatever at the time suits its agendas best. Yes of course a proselytizing religion, empire building and international aiding are different sorts of international undertaking. That is not at issue here. What is at issue is that an enveloping shroud can wrap in any number of ways, including through innocence and the best of intentions, not through pre-emptive strikes and dominion only, even while some of the actual 'help' promised may also be delivered as a result of some fantasm being part-realized.

Busy buzzwords. Alice learns that little watchwords like *Local Ownership*, as well as big ones like *HumanitarianIntervention*, are words to watch, to see what in their name is done or undone. It can turn out to be quite surprising, often alarming. She decides that such keywords ought also to be called lockwords, because they can be disengaging while engaging, and concealing/blocking while revealing and framing. What keywords (which also work as 'lockwords') mean is seen on the plane of what they do as critical discourse analysis unwraps.

Of course, all human worlds are constituted partly but significantly through the metalanguages and foundational discourses built round the keywords they choose to prefer and put forward the most aggressively. But to its unspeakers, Aidspeak can appear as world-making through world-talking gone mad: 'Fiji' is (or was) 'set to become East Asia in the Pacific'; 'Sri Lanka must change into a Singapore'; a humanitarian 'haven' (as in Bosnia) is 'safe'; against 'terror' there must be a 'war'; Papua New Guinea, whose government as already noted won a constitutional legal case against Australia, is a 'failed', or at least a 'failing', state.

V

Who benefits? An adventure in Aidland worth telling is about a mission in Malawi, commissioned for an *Aid Effectiveness Evaluation* of the United Nations Development Programme (UNDP)'s *Sustainable Participatory Livelihoods Development Project (SPLDP)*. Under a UNDP contract, joined by two Malawians – Pierson Ntata, a lecturer in sociology at the University of Zomba, and Blessings Chisenga, at that time at the same university researching 'the politics of poverty' in his country (so this assignment was far from being the usual sort of a foreigners' big game poverty spotting safari) – I (plus Alice incognito) was charged with reviewing what progress that *Participation* project had made 'on the ground', how and why, to what effect, and what should happen next.

The project's bosses who worked around the world out of their HQ in New York were of the view that, until their *Participation* project came along, in *AfricanTraditionalCulture*, for example, in Mchinji village (or probably any African village), 'coming together to analyse a problem and devise a solution was simply not part of the local culture' (Heatherside 1998). Our view (informed by lived experience)[12] was the very opposite. Getting together to work things out, along of course with all its antimonies, paradoxes, permutations and other types of social relations (such as 'hierarchy', 'competition' and 'conflict'), must in fact have been around in Mchinji's case since the beginning of human history. To pitch one hyperbole against another, pretty much the whole of what is now Malawi is not far from where quite possibly humankind actually originated millennia ago and where, after one vicissitude and another, a chunk of it is still; thanks to having no idea about cooperative problem-solving? Alice was perplexed.

Besides the SPLDP's extraordinarily arrogant premise and crooked design being in our view fatally intellectually flawed, 'on the ground' it was anyway perfectly open to observation in our case village that the substantive SPLDP project outcome was absolutely nil. The modest, ongoing livelihood developments that were perfectly open to view there owed nothing whatsoever to that project. Indeed, to a point they ran contrary to it and thus belied it.

Eventually, after visiting some other project sites, we returned to Lilongwe, Malawi's capital, to present our overall findings. Pretty well one hundred percent negative; for Malawian villagers that is. What the SPLDP had done for the UN in New York, is, of course, another story that we did not have access to learn, the 'indoors' and HQ 'upstairs' of aid being typically excluded from consultants' enquiry.

Thus daring to challenge the SPLDP's false premise head-on, as well having peeked at the nakedness of the emperor, naturally gave great hurt and offence to the earnest honchos who by then had flown in from New York. They accused us (as well as 'traditional Mchinji') of the most heinous sin in their book, anti-participation, adding for good measure (a nice try) that we had anyway confused single cases of 'wrong implementation' with 'the good idea' and sincere resolve 'behind' them (eventually, having no counter-evidence to put on the table to contradict ours, suddenly they became agnostic about demonstrable outcomes, whether of 'success' or 'failure').

Back to Lilongwe. Late one evening, a few days after the presentation-confrontation convened in the Office of the Resident Coordinator of the UN, over a beer or two in the bar, some of the *SLPDP*'s *LocalCounterparts*, who up to then had not publicly taken sides, came clean (to us). They said their silence in the Office had not been because they disagreed with our findings (with which they now said they agreed completely). Rather, it was because if they had spoken out, their employment with that *AidProject* would have been jeopardized through 'disloyalty' and there was no other work around.

Alice again is truly astonished. A sustainability village development project's staff are its principal beneficiaries, not the villagers? Humpty Dumpty she was sure would have hrumphed: 'Hear me, "sustainability" is what I, not you, say that it means.'[13]

VI

Discourse geography. Virtualities come in various shapes and sizes. Often in Aidland, instead of earthly geography (aside from moans about the heat and flies or exceptionally the cold) and topographical topography (other than groans about the roads), there is something else: 'discourse geography' (Beljic et al. 2002: 6). The landscape that the looking-glass reflects is one not of physical, but moral peaks and troughs. Aidland's atlas is no help at all to anyone actually trying to get around (no matter how repaired the road). Painted-on frescoes owe everything to the appetites and talents, and fears and frauds, of those who come up with them; little or nothing to the place as it is known and lived in by those whose place it is.

The social anthropologist James Ferguson (1990) in a landmark study showed the World Bank in the name of geography and economics proceeding on another mission altogether: to define, so as to rule, its own version of Lesotho, not that of the Lesothans who live there. The economist Richard Brown (1992) showed IMF doing something very similar: inventing a country through traducing Sudan's actual economy for another that, while 'not there', fitted its own mandate and agenda and which it could then recognize and propose to reform.

The social anthropologist Theodore Trefon's (2004a) edited monograph on the Congo critiques the 'heart of darkness' Conrad/Kaplanesque portrayal of nothing but chaos and disorder. Yes, in Kinshasha there is no 'Weberian political order with its functioning bureaucracy, democratically elected representatives, tax collectors, law enforcement agents and impartial judicial system ... [as] advocated by Western development theorists [though] the state remains omnipresent on the social, economic and political landscape'. But no, that does not mean that there is only breakdown. Rather, 'despite the outrageous problems [some] new and remarkable patterns of stability, organization and quest for well-being have emerged ... the transition from authoritarian rule and the multiple implications of conflict has been a period of intense social stress [but rather than] fall[ing] apart in this context ... [there is] diversifying and even strengthening' (2004a: 2–4).

Totally ungeographical (and as we will see unhistorical) contrasts and comparisons are common currency in Aidspeak, where 'periphery', 'north', 'south', etc., live ageographic lives of their own.[14] Think too of former White House spin about 'US troops at the end of the World War 2 in Japan and now in Iraq as being in the same general kind of situation' ('tell that one to the marines!' says Alice!). As for that 'road map' to 'peace in the Middle East', if such road-mappery can be so devoid of actual roads, roadblocks and walls, let alone the chaps – and refugees and displaced persons and others – that you would normally expect to find on maps, wouldn't that be better described as unmappery?

Out-of-body geography, cartography imagined at will, indicators serving more as vindicators than descriptors, a sociography of moral compacting not social contracting. An *AidAgency* ranks a country's *Human Development* in an index according to whatever indices and ways of scoring and indicators are best for *its* devotions and potions, not of anyone else's (except where by chance they coincide). Neither earthly economic geography nor historical political economy are allowed to count for anything in such fancy-free (fancy-saturated) league tables that are insensitive to natural resources, good ports, strategic entrepot position, last year's development and humanitarian achievements as endogenously understood, and other things that count on earth but are ignored in Development's marks and scores.[15]

What *HumanDevelopmentReport* tables or indices really show (beyond the face of their texts) are pointers to present, and perhaps also future, candidate areas for engagement – or disengagement – as suit the *Aid Agency* that comes up with them. Another *AidAgency*, another indicator, another league table. Another *HumanitarianIntervention* and another 'eminent domain' are found to justify going in either alone or with a *Like MindedCoalitionOfThe Willing*. Not international law.

VII

Sociology nullius. The rise of 'gender and development' – later 'governance and development', later still 'democracy and freedom' – allows the bases for recruitment of *DevelopmentExperts* to broaden a bit in terms of university disciplines and civil society programmes. Leonard Frank wrote in his *Granta* gem 'The Development Game' about a consultancy team's leader getting lucky when a 'soft and warm' (usually female) sociologist joins the team's harder (usually male) economics people 'to keep us happy', and 'get the social right' (Frank 1986: 234) . Hmm. Anyway, serious sociologists for the most part don't go to Aidland. They are not welcome there, and anyway say they have better things to do. Is there even one seriously sociological study say of social class and wealth and poverty and socioeconomic mobility, all conceived together in one frame for a highly aid-recipient country, with a focus on the *PovertyEradication* aid it receives and what can be attributed to that?

Getting sociology into Aidland is as hard as getting a ship out of the bottle: very difficult without breaking the ship or the bottle! 'Sociology even in my country', said one of its most famous political thinkers addressing some 'post conflict' aid to national constitution building at large, tends to be 'treated as a criminal activity'. In the relative absence of sociology, the 'social groups' or categories that an *AidProjectManagement* recognizes are those that 'exist(s) only in the project personnel's imagination and report' (Nyamwaya 1997: 189); service-delivering agencies 'target' according to only their own ideas of vulnerable groups (see Harrigan and Chol 1998).

Tony Barnett's (1977) sociological work on the Gezira cotton scheme in the Sudan and its broader context is an exception. He found that it was the educated bureaucrats in their offices and on tour who were the 'slow adopters' of agricultural 'innovation', not peasants and others in the woodwork of so-called premodern society. In a smart cocktail party at an overseas development studies institute in London at around that time, shocked by one of Barnett's Gezira books, someone could be heard saying at the top of her voice that besides being 'a dangerous lefty, Marxist, crank', its author must be 'completely sick' (she did not like facial hair either), adding that she wanted it to be perfectly clear that she was speaking for her (presumably closely shaven) *DevelopmentEconomist* husband even more than for herself. What was disgracefully wrong with 'that sort of book', she said, spitting the word out, was that it was 'ideological'.

Consider another exception. Eventually the faux sociological empirics, with the help of which 'the informal sector' concept in the ILO's *Development And Employment Studies* was launched, could be replaced by some sound empirical social research specifically on the deemed social attributes of that 'sector' by social anthropologists working out of Bergen (Sklar 1985), but that made not one iota of difference by way of correction to what either the ILO in particular, or Aidland at large, continued to say about 'the informal sector'.

The ebbs and flows of dogmas and their tides in Aidland that do occur have more to do with 'new initiatives' taken by the top management of a donor or an INGO or NGO, and the politics of organizational policy (as that authority sees them), than with any reality checks on the *Development Projects* and their performance 'on the ground'. Whether an *AidProject Evaluation* is or is not properly, independently, transparently, professionally done 'over there' matters less than what is seen and deemed to be the case right here. Indeed, the 'reality checks' to which assiduous attention is paid concern the far from virtual domestic reality at home whence a donor country's aid and foreign policy comes and goes. A crisis 'at home' is far more determining than a crisis 'over there'.

VIII

History nullius. Aidland is also peculiarly innocent of history (other than the sequences of its own periods or stages it likes to paste dates on) or subject to self-serving pseudohistory ('now the war is over').[16] What has been said of American 'democracy assistance' by one of its most indefatigable and accurate critics seems generally true for all *International Aid*: it 'tends to live in an eternal present. Democracy promoters talk at times vaingloriously of participating in "history in the making," yet they rarely have much sense of history with regard to the countries in which they are working, or to the enterprise of using aid [and its limits] to promote a democracy' (Carothers 1999).[17]

That such a 'lack of institutional memory' is one of the features of Aidland that is as much remarked on by Aidpeople themselves as by their visitors and guests should also be noted. 'What happened last time?' is not a question that it is good to ask in Aidland if for no other reason than that even Aidmen and Aidwomen themselves have little at their disposal with which to answer it. Future history (Apthorpe 1997a) is never rehearsed either, such as what (else) might (or might not) happen if *International Aid* were somehow – to whatever small extent – actually to 'eradicate' 'poverty'. Beginnings and ends are illusory and 'new' in Aidspeak as; for example in 'a new partnership approach', almost never means 'novel'.

So, when an *AidAgency*'s official discourse runs to charts, indicators, periodizations, cut-off points and the like, this is primarily to reveal a little of what it suits to tell about itself. What most strongly influences rises and falls in, say, the amount and kind of *PovertyEradicationAid* tends to have little or sometimes nothing whatsoever to do with the rise or fall in an actual *DevelopingCountry*'s 'poverty level'. Again the 'crises' and 'needs' that a governmental or non-governmental agency chooses first to utter and then to manage are determined superordinately, if not entirely, by its own interests, values, mandates, discretions, resources and opportunities, no one else's, certainly not those of the poor or the victims.

Yes, wouldn't it be marvellous if the world were as GATT writes (and trade wars and bilateral treaties were recognized and researched for what they are), if durable solutions (and 'best practice') reigned; if the neoclassical gaze did not have so much equilibrium in mind (on the brain) that it simply has no real chance of understanding disequilibrium. If 'space' made 'in the UN' for 'civil society' to 'come in' really did open things up for nonstatal parties to make some serious difference in today's post-Westphalian 'international society' of states then the academic,

International Relations, 'English school' conception of the international social relations of states could have a field day.

Being a world largely of its own making, Aidland is captive to characteristic modes of time-reckoning (some of which are strangely atemporal, as we have seen). A week may be a long time in politics, but where there is the stranglehold of annual funding for an aid programme a year may be all there is. Is that good for aid effectiveness in international roles, for example, in peacemaking, let alone state building? Alice is sure that it is not.

IX

Uneconomics. Palgrave Macmillan's *The Real World Economic Outlook* confronts the IMF's *World Economic Outlook*, claiming to be well aware of some of the inauthenticity involved in the standard forms of economic reporting about *Developing Countries*. True, some versions of 'institutional economics' that went before *Development Economics* and *Development Sociology,* and the 'the new institutional economics' that followed, are not completely one-eyed, yet are generally far too astigmatic to qualify seriously as interdisciplinary. (Will 'the new behavioural economics' be any different? Alice suspects not, but waits to see.)

Conventional economics texts that take their task seriously model 'poverty' and 'wealth' together in this worldly, two sides of the same coin terms – not alternative different currencies. Aid texts on poverty economics in contrast do not; even those that qualify as being somewhat radical are averse to such an integrated frame. Famed public intellectuals such as Gunnar Myrdal, who in their day were masters of both aid and non-aid studies, had pretty much two personas (coming nearer the present, consider Amartya Sen on conventional welfare economics, then 'the same' writer on *Development*, even *Economic Development*, also *Freedom*). One persona, when a scholar, is uppermost, but Jekyll is also Hyde, quite another when performing as a preacher, prophet or policy adviser. The carefully problematizing Myrdal on social and cultural values in economics theory is astoundingly also the recklessly idolizing and demonizing *Asian Drama*'s main author (the methodological appendices of that monument to modernization are the work of others) on 'Indian social and cultural values', 'hard' and 'soft' states, etc. (in contrast, for example, W. Arthur Lewis's scholarly and public profiles were remarkably integral).

Exactly as the former World Bank Chief Economist Joseph E. Stiglitz put it, 'third rank students [of economics] from first rank universities' (2000: 56) are indeed part of the story of 'the typical' economist in *International Aid*. But not of its stars, whose story is more complex, nothing straightforwardly 'typical', but something closer to the errant ways of 'celebrity'.

X

Metaphysical mathematics. At their most inflated, the discrete charms (*Poverty Eradication, Participation*, etc.) of the aid bureau-bourgeoisie and their 'policies' and similar 'sexing-up' (which is not unknown in national security intelligence) bubble babble moments like Orwell's NewSpeak can 'give solidity to pure wind' like no others. In the mist of aid, as in the fog of war, the trick is partly to conjure not with numbers as statisticians in other worlds and ordinary mathematicians know them, but to juggle instead with 'numberoids' – shades of Dan Smith's menus, fears and desires glossed with 'numerical characteristics' – as political and other appetites require; neither real quantities nor true; not percentages but percentoids; not statistical figures but figures of speech.

A *DonorGovernment* proudly and compassionately announces some huge amount of 'new' post-tsunami money 'for Indonesia'[18] but, for one thing, typically such 'new' largesse comprises a lot of 'old', so precisely what is now 'pledged' is unclear. Second, normally it is in any case totally unpredictable quite how much of either the old or new promised will ever materialize. Third, there is what no aid minister worth his or her cabinet seat will fail to say or imply to parliament when arguing for a bigger *Aid Budget* (while equally robustly taking an opposite view for another constituency): 'hear me, never fear, however big the figure "we all" gain because by far the greater part of *OverseasAid* is spent "at home". So, folks, "for the poor", fork out (to me and my department) generously!'

Other such fancied figurations (or configurations) of appetite and desire, Alice thinks, are idiotic diddledeedums, not sums. For example, any 'need-assessment' counts of the hungry, sick, dead, maimed or displaced as governmental and non-governmental agencies may respectively call for and adopt are seldom self-standing. The 'higher' counts can justify demands by *DevelopingCountryGovernments* for more aid; while by claiming 'lower', the *AidAgencies* doing the actual emergency services distribution and delivery can put themselves in a better light after the event because then they can say that, despite limited resources, truly they 'reached all' (however, they too prefer 'higher' when appealing for more funding). This is policy driving 'numbers', not 'numbers' policy.[19] If somehow a 'number' gets attached to one of the UN's *Millenium Development Goals,* or any other such grand *DevelopmentTarget*, another mystery is whether such 'targets' can be measured reliably, if in some cases at all, let alone be achieved, as claimed (Saith 2006: 1171).

XI

Unpeace. Our last postcard for now is about the 'peace' of Aidspeak's *Post Conflict*. One thing is that especially 'after' long, recurring or endemic conflict – as in Israel-Palestine as well as Iraq and Afghanistan – typically different wars are being fought simultaneously, with each (and different sides in each) having its own aims, programmes, resources, backers, etc. Thus, even if one war may be ending, another, perhaps all the others, may not be. Another thing is that when for example OECD's Development Aid Committee (and the governments that report to it) speak of 'conflict' as in *Conflict Prevention And Peacebuilding* with (as they much prefer of course) 'peace' in mind, they refer only to armed, military action and its violent agendas, not to civil class conflict in whatever shape or form, let alone ideological war, even though there is plenty of evidence that internal wars around the world are far from being just mindless resorts to arms.

Is Aidland's last taboo one about 'conflict,' as in its 'development and conflict' writing, in which the former is always cast as the casualty of the latter, never possibly its product – only as 'the answer', never as the 'question'? Alice or rather her minder remembers for example that what the UN originally meant by its 'failed state' expression was not a state that was at war in some sense, but one lacking in pro-poor public policy, also that the *Peace Dividend* heart-wringing (in long-gone pre-'human security' days) about what, if spending were not on the military, the extra could do for 'development and peace'.

Facing up to 'conflict' cannot altogether be avoided, although *Conflict SensitiveAid* is perhaps as far as Aidspeak can get. While Iraq and Afghanistan and other such theatres of war may be seen as provinces of Aidland, being wonderlands of contrived fancies (about 'freedom' and 'democracy' and such), they are of course also murderous infernos of fatalities where even Dante's guide Virgil[20] might not dare to go (Alice is fearless).

'Postconflict' serves as a site where a yet higher (possibly the highest) degree of foreign and/or international forcible intervention gets legitimized in what normally should be internal affairs of the state concerned. In the name of *InterventionAndStateBuilding*, all aid and foreign policy divides are down. Normally it tends to be aid, not foreign policy, that says it should be governed by 'big ideas' (such as *Basic Needs, Human Rights, Structural Adjustment*, etc.). In unpeace situations the boot is typically on the other foot.

Understandably, where a conflict has involved much loss of life, limb and livelihood, there are strong pressures to put other considerations aside so as to waste no time in responding to the new and urgent needs of the moment. But if, as so often in Aidland, that entails just blaming the conflict for the conflict, whether or not ethnicity or some other single dimension is seized upon exclusively or predominantly, another casualty of war is: namely ascertaining what, besides the violence, it was about in the first place and that continues to be important, as well as learning what has survived and perhaps even strengthened since.

No more cards or views of views now, but an addendum.

Why the Bubble Does Not Burst

The *trompe l'oeil* that is Aidland is about a virtual nowhere, but it is not from a nowhere that it comes (or goes). Aidland's blend of an underlying real and an overwriting virtual is distinctive but not unique. All worlds like communities are both imagined and real. What is most special about Aidland is its provenance, which over the decades becomes somewhat more, not less, open and unashamed. A good part of what is perceived to be 'other' or 'exotic' about *DevelopingCountries* is the Orientalist, or Balkanist, or other Other-ing imprint they are obliged to bear of the fancies and fears, and the best and other intentions, of their foreign aiders.

Aidland can usefully be imaged as a bubble, a balloon, or, as worded, a babble, that in a special mix is pumped and powered up but is at the same time strongly resistant even to pricking, let alone bursting, from without or within; a balloon that while aloft, as well as while in the hangar, is firmly tethered by the strings of conditionalities. Untied aid only gets rarer in the world – it may soon disappear for good.

In the Aidland bubble there is little new knowledge making, no broadening of the mind. A Swedish international civil servant in his memoir on his life in the UN, where it seems he was mostly based in New York, wrote that his colleagues there who 'lost contact with their home countries were handicapped in some way: they saw the problem only from the international point of view and had little feeling how one would react in the national capitals' (Carlson 1964: 5–6). What, wonders Alice, does that say about 'cosmopolitanism' and 'the international community'('like-minded' donors' coalitions and the 'third world' UN voting bloc in the UN General Assembly aside)?

The (counterfactual) role of firewalls against accountability to intelligence, let alone society and culture, that is built into *InternationalAid's* very foundations and some of its other preserves is lethal to responsible aid. 'The international aid business is one of the most un-regulated markets in the world, with few internationally agreed standards [yet it] literally deals in life and death issues for missions of people, … spend[ing] thousands of millions of dollars of other people's money', wrote Peter Walker (1995: 23) not long ago (since when notably he and other ethical reformers have done their utmost to right some of its wrongs through some introduction of oath-like codes and protocols). However, there remains little advocacy anywhere for an international court or tribunal – or some other form of institutional provision – for intellectual crimes against humanity.[21]

Seen as a virtual, parallel[22] universe, dedicated perpetuating institutions install Aidland and keep it in shape as a multicentrally planned, market-informed, apolitically ('no politics please we are experts'), ageopolitically ('if you are not with us you are against us'), moralistically imagined while bureaucratically led, ostensively victim-centred arena. For example, humanitarian assistance organizations like to label afflicted populations as 'victims', despite the widely held (but little reported) rule of thumb among the most experienced and free-speaking in the trade that 'only ten percent' (for which read 'only ten percentoid') of survivors of conflicts and disasters 'owe their survival to international aid'. In other words, a huge proportion survive through their own efforts – and 'generally speaking [they] are not at all as paralysed and helpless as donors are inclined to believe, but often act more rationally and efficiently than the foreign assistant worker' (Foreign Ministry of Sweden and Sida 1986). Social strategies of escape and development are at work (among survivors). Rather than being ignored or written out by *AidAgencies*, they should be considered from the very outset when designing and implementing their programmes.

Inside Aidland, among the powerful perpetuating plays at work there is also a perverse effect of what could be termed seeking 'identity beyond function'. For example, the UN World Food Programme successfully performs logistical miracles in sourcing and delivering emergency food to where it is needed, with remarkably small margins of delay and error that evaluations examine and report on, often very positively. Once, however, when in Rome with my evaluation team at a debriefing in Head Office after our weeks-long travels in West Africa,[23] having reported favourably on such functionality as we had seen, we were reprimanded: 'is that *all* that you think that we do and stand for?' Their point was that, over and above achieving functional, logistical excellence, an international organization must seek something else as well: an identity beyond the fact, a rationale and a transcendence, a reform vision and agenda for a new day, not to say era, beyond help now. Also, there is what notably UNICEF appears to excel in doing, namely being highly aggressive, glamorous and successful in the marketing of itself, as itself – along with associated celebrities – for itself. What amount (if any) of the funds raised is spent on a results-oriented appraisal to ascertain the value and meaning of its aid to those for whom it states it is primarily intended? In Aidspeak 'beneficiaries' not customers or clients.

Consider, too, the extent to which typically *International Aid's* hired-in management *Independent Consultants* act as other defences to bubble bursting, in respect now not of internal sociation requirements trumping individual responsibility, but a sort of 'embedding' (similar to an extent to that of the journalists given access to the American military in its war in Iraq). 'Careerwise, I cannot afford to upset the World Bank … I get two thirds of my income from [it]', writes a most unusually frank (and, like 'Leonard Frank' of the *Granta* piece already mentioned, anonymous) *DevelopmentEconomics* consultant 'Peter Griffiths', in his extraordinary *The Economist's Tale: A Consultant Encounters Hunger and the World Bank* (Griffiths 2003: other researchers, less dependent on consultancy income, who find their expertise directed away from identifying the concerns and interests of local peoples or refugees, towards the internal informational needs of aid agencies, withdraw their services; see Apthorpe 2004). No prizes for guessing what even 'five years work [done] in four months' and 'six years or so in eight or ten countries' – and 'every month … learn[ing] the names of a hundred new people and a hundred new places and then forget[ing] them' (Griffiths 2003: 105) can do. Beyond which is, to borrow from Robert Wade's critique of the World Bank's misreading the East Asia 'miracle',[24] 'polishing paradigm management' so as to ensure that things are kept as they are and not reformed.

It is Aidland's very thick skin that enables it to withstand (and sustain) the sheer high density of the very hot air that – again as in Orwell-land – relentless exuberant use of vogue keywords like *Participation, Partnership* and *Local Ownership* builds up to pressures just below bursting point. On her adventures this side of Wonderland, Alice frequently recalls Doris Lessing's *Canopos-in-Argos Archives* about other planets, their occupying representatives busy with *RuralDevelopment* and such, Canopos' *Development Officers* falling so routinely into mental and verbal disorder after their long service and constantly changing postings that for any cure possible into a hospital for rhetorical diseases they have to go. Definitely not to a Staff College.

'Which way? Which way?' asks Alice. If this time round she is asking what practical use 'ethnography of aid' will actually prove to be for 'the aid industry', she will I suspect as a result of her travels be thinking less about aidnography as such and more about what cultural studies can help reveal: something broader, namely that the 'expert knowledges' of which our postcards tell turn out on inspection to be neither greatly expert nor notably knowledgeable. Meanwhile, Aidland's complacent, also complicit, 'we tried, they failed' practice of attributing any project success exclusively to its own good aid practice relegates the role of 'the other' in the situation merely to that of complying with the donor's 'right approach'. Hmm.

Notes

1. This allegory started as 'The Virtual Reality of Foreign-aid Land' for an anthropology conference at Kyoto University in 1999, a first draft of which had been improved thanks to a characteristic 'few points' offered by Peter Larmour. The next version – 'Postcards with Love from Aidland' – was given, at a 2004 Tsukuba University seminar, again at the kind invitation of Yasushi Uchiyamada. The third, prepared for the ASA conference in Keele in 2006, David Mosse kindly presented for me. The fourth I gave in 2006 at a special seminar organized by Rosalind Eyben at the IDS, Sussex. Each year in the period 2005–9 Alice was warmly welcomed in my International Humanitarian Assistance courses in IR at the Australian National University (and recently she joined me at the Peace Research Institute Oslo and Copenhagen Business School). Thus, many friends and associates over a decade urged me to get this paper, in any version, out, outed perhaps, as it was already in evidence.
2. The term 'aidnography' I think makes its first appearance in Gould and Marcusen 2004.
3. American academic IR writing on international organizations (see, e.g., Nielson and Tierney 2003) appears to lack robust (perhaps any) conceptualization of 'semi-autonomous' function and identity, while perceptively raising certain other issues.

4. For an excoriating critique of these goals and the process that led to them, see Saith 2006.
5. To judge for example from one White Knight of Aidland's exasperation who accused it of wanting to end aid.
6. See also Oliver P. Richmond on *'virtually* liberal post conflict states and governments' (2007: 261, emphasis added); and forthcoming work, for example, by John Hethershaw and St Andrew's University IR LPII project.
7. While Marriage takes a games theoretical approach in her work (2006), it is not necessary to share in this fully to appreciate the acuity of her findings and insights.
8. Thus, for example, Draper (1995): 'The falling domino "principle" is ... a mechanistic theory, because it assumes a necessary succession from an initial starting point to a fore-ordained end ... but the loss of Vietnam [to the American project] did not bring about the communist takeover of all South East Asia'.
9. Compare for example Ralph Grillo's writing (e.g., 1997) on 'development anthropology' and 'anthropology and development'.
10. For example, at the University of Sussex and the Institute of Development Studies, Anne-Meiker Fechter, Rosalind Eyben and others are researching real, not allegorical Aidworkers and their lives, beliefs and doings, sometimes with the help of autobiographical accounts.
11. For a country case study of 'local ownership', 'the driving seat' and the like, see Abdulrahman and Apthorpe 2003; for a global synthesis, see Guimaraes, Apthorpe and de Valk 2003.
12. Blessings when young lived in a neighbouring Chewa village, while Pierson has relatives nearby. As for me, in my twenties I had social anthropologically researched at intervals over three years in a Nsenga village (with some Chewa connections) just across the border in Zambia, thereby acquiring a sort of intellectual capital, the returns on which get simply constantly reinvested.
13. Four or five years later, Alice and I were in New York for a visit when a young Aidman there, whom we knew, told us that finally the SPLDP had been terminated ignominiously. Quite how it met its end he did not disclose, but certainly that would not have had much if anything to do with a single consultancy report, warmly complimentary though he was about ours on that day.
14. Decades ago in *Development Studies* such terms did make some serious political economy sense. Then, when they no longer did, they were challenged from within – for example, in DSA meetings in the U.K. in the 1970s – but to no effect whatsoever.
15. On which, for some broader comment, see Apthorpe, 1997b.
16. For a collection of insightful short pieces relating to the U.S. President's 'Mission Accomplished' speech in Iraq, see Tsing et al. 2005.
17. Thanks to Christopher Hobson when at the ANU for this reference.
18. For an analysis of one example of in that case one billion dollars, see Research Note, Parliament of Australia, Department of Parliamentary Services, 2004, 2004–5, ISSN 1449-8456.
19. On 'numbers' and policy, a broader analysis is my 'Reading Development Policy and Policy Analysis: On Framing, Naming, Numbering and Coding' (in Apthorpe and Gasper 1996).
20. Michel Acuto introduced Alice to Dante's Virgil, Matt Davies twice took her out to breakfast, in classes in IR at the ANU, as once another Ph.D. candidate in IR, Daniel Biro did too.
21. Intellectual crimes against humanity might extend for instance to such severe methodological irresponsibility in poverty assessments as identified and reviewed for example by Hanmer, Pyatt and White 1999.
22. Where, as with Aidland , there is some link with what a 'parallel universe' is parallel to, 'intersecting' may be a better adjective than 'parallel'.
23. For an account of a two-month period of travel with a consultancy (and a team and a four-wheel drive) and what happened then, see Apthorpe (2001) in a collection of several such team leaders' experiences elsewhere.

24. Wade (1996) saw the World Bank's misreading the East Asia 'miracle' as partly reflecting the extent to which none of the very many economist staffers concerned actually had the kind of regional, intercultural experience that should have prevented such misunderstanding, as well as ensuring as usual that its own ownership and interests continued to matter more than its borrowers'.

References

Abdulrahman, M. and R. Apthorpe. 2003. *Egypt: A Policy Evaluation of Current KTS Practice in Technical Assistance.* Stockholm: Sida.

Apthorpe, Raymond. 1996. 'Reading Development Policy and Policy Analysis: On Framing, Naming, Numbering and Coding', in Raymond Apthorpe and Des Gasper (eds), *Arguing Development Policy: Frames and Discourses.* London: Frank Cass.

————. 1997a. 'Development Studies and Policy Studies: In the *Short* Run We Are All Dead', *Journal of International Development* 11(4): 535–46.

————. 1997b. 'Human Development Reporting and Social Anthropology', *Social Anthropology* 5(1): 21–34.

————. 2001. 'Mission Possible: Six Years of Emergency WFP Food Aid in West Africa', in Adrian Wood, Raymond J. Apthorpe, and John Borton. (eds), *Evaluating International Humanitarian Action: Reflections from Practitioners.* London: Zed Books.

————. 2004. 'Humanitarian Action and Social Learning: Notes and Surmises on Ten Consultative Tools', *JCAS Symposium Series* 21: 213–43.

Atmar, Haneef and Jonathan Goodhand. 2002. *Aid Conflict and Peacebuilding in Afghanistian: What Lessons Can Be Learned?* London: International Alert.

Barnett, T. 1977. *The Gezira Scheme: An Illusion of Development.* London: Cass.

Baudrillard, Jean. 1991. *The Gulf War Did Not Take Place.* Bloomington, I.N.: Indiana University Press.

Brown, Richard. 1992. *Public Debt and Private Wealth: Debt, Capital Flight and the IMF in the Sudan.* London: Macmillan.

Beljic, Dusan I. and Obrad Savic (eds). 2002. *Balkan as Metaphor.* Cambridge, M.A.: MIT Press.

Carothers, Thomas. 1999. *Aiding Democracy Abroad: The Learning Curve.* Washington, D.C.: Carnegeie Endowment for World Peace.

Cornwall, Andrea and Karen Brock. 2005. 'What Do Buzzwords Do for Development Policy? A Critical Look at "Participation", "Empowerment", and "Poverty Reduction"', *Third World Quarterly* 26(7): 1043–60.

De Waal, Alex. 1997. *Famine Crimes: Politics and the Disaster Relief Industry in Africa* .London: African Rights, International African Institute, James Currey.

Disaster Relief for Development: A Study Commissioned by the Foreign Ministry of Sweden and Sida. 1986. Stockholm: DSUD.

Draper, Theodore. 1995. 'McNamara's Peace', *New York Review of Books*, May.

Ferguson, James. 1990. *The Anti-politics Machine: 'Development', Depoliticization and Bureaucratic Power in Lesotho.* Cambridge: Cambridge University Press.

Frank, Leonard. 1986. The Development Game. *Granta* 20: 229-43.

Gasper, D. 1987. 'Motivations and Manipulations: Some Practices of Project Appraisal and Evaluation', *Manchester Papers on Development* 3(1): 24–70.

Gould, J. and H.S. Marcussen. 2004. *Ethnographies of Aid – Exploring Development Texts and Encounters.* Roskilde: International Development Studies Occasional Paper, No. 24, Roskilde University.

Griffiths, Peter. 2003. *The Economist's Tale: A Consultant Encounters Hunger and the World Bank.* London: Zed Books.

Grillo, R.D. 1997. 'Discourses of Development: The View from Anthropology', in R.D Grillo and R.L Stirrat (eds), *Discourses of Development: Anthropological Perspectives.* Oxford: Berg.

Guimaraes, J., R. Apthorpe and P. de Valk. 2003. *Contract-financed Technical Cooperation and Local Ownership: Synthesis Report*. Stockholm: Sida.

Hanmer, Lucia C., Graham Pyatt and Howard White. 1999. 'What Do the World Bank's Poverty Assessments Teach Us about Poverty in Sub-Saharan Africa?', *Development and Change* 30: 795–823.

Harrigan, Simon and Chol Changath Chol. 1998. *The Southern Sudan Vulnerability Study*. Nairobi: The Save the Children Fund (UK) South Sudan Programme.

Heatherside, C. 1998. Development Through Participation. *Choices* 8. New York: UNDP.

Kratochwil, Friedrich. 2007. 'Looking Back from Somewhere: Reflections on What Remains "Critical" in Critical Theory', *Review of International Studies* 33: 25–45.

Larmour, Peter. 2005. *Foreign Flowers: Institutional Transfer and Good Governance in the Pacific Islands*. Honolulu, H.I.: University of Hawaii Press.

Marriage, Zoe. 2006. *Not Breaking the Rules, Not Playing the Game: International Assistance to Countries at War*. London: Hurst.

Mbembe, Achille. 1992. 'Provisional Notes on the Post Colony', *Africa* 62 (1): 3–37.

Morris, Jan. 2001. *Trieste and the Meaning of Nowhere*. London: Faber & Faber.

Nielson, Daniel L., and Michael J. Tierney. 2003. 'Delegation to International Organizations: Agency, Theory and World Bank Environmental Reform', *International Organization* 57: 241–76.

Nyamwaya, D. 1997. 'Three Critical Issues in Community Health Development Projects in Kenya', in R. Grillo and R. Stirrat (eds), *Discourses of Development: Anthropological Perspectives*. Oxford: Berg.

Poncet, Jean. 1964. *Paysages et problemes ruraux en tunisie*. Paris: Presses Universitaires de France.

Richmond, Oliver P. 2007. 'Critical Research Agendas for Peace: The Missing Link in the Study of International Relations', *Alternatives* 32: 247–74.

Saith, Ashwani. 2006. 'From Universal Values to Millennium Development Goals: Lost in Translation', *Development and Change* 37(6): 1167–99.

Sklar, H.O. (ed.). *Anthropological Contributions to Planned Change and Development*. Gothenburg: Acta Universitatis Gothoburgensis.

Stiglitz, J. 2003. 'What I Learned at the World Economic Crisis. In William Driscoll, Julie Clark (eds.) *Globalization and the Poor: Exploitation or Equalizer*. New York: The International Debate Education Association.

Surkhe, Astri, K.B.Harpviken, and Arne Strand. 2004. *Conflictual peacebullding: Afghanistan after Bonn*. Bergen: Chr. Michelsen Institute.

Taylor, Ian. 2005. 'Advice is Judged by Results, Not by Intentions', *International Affairs* 81(2): 299-310.

Trefon, Theodore (ed.). 2004a. *Reinventing Order in the Congo: How People Respond to State Failure in Kinshasha*. London: Zed Books.

———. 2004b. 'Introduction: Reinventing Order', in T. Theodore (ed.), *Reinventing Order in the Congo: How People Respond to State Failure in Kinshasha*. London: Zed Books.

Tsing, Anna, Bregje van Eekelen, Jennifer Gonzales and Bettina Stotzer eds). 2005. *Shock and Awe*. Los Angeles, C.A.: Institute of Advanced Feminism, UCLA, New Pacific Press.

Wade, Robert. 1996. 'Japan, the World Bank, and the Art of Paradigm Maintenance: The East Asian Miracle in Political Perspective', *New Left Review* 217: 3–36.

Walker, Peter. 1995. 'Conflicts, Contract Culture and Codes of Conduct', in P.Walker (ed) *Aid under Fire: Relief and Development in an Unstable World*. UNDHA, in collaboration with ODI, ODA and ActionAid, New York: UN.

Notes on Contributors

Raymond Apthorpe, formerly a part-time visiting fellow at Australian National University between 1992 and 2009, is a Professorial Research Associate in Social Anthropology and Development Studies at SOAS, London, and Associate at the Institute of Social Studies, The Hague.

Rosalind Eyben is a Fellow at the Institute of Development Studies (IDS), University of Sussex. She previously worked for many years as a development practitioner. She has published extensively on aid relations, including *Relationships for Aid* (2006) and, with Joy Moncrieffe, *The Power of Labelling. How People are Categorised and Why it Matters* (2007).

Maia Green is Professor of Anthropology at Manchester University. She is professionally engaged in the development sector as a social development specialist and policy analyst, and currently researches into social and institutional transformation in Tanzania around health services, development participation and governance. Her recent publications include the Special issue of *Critique of Anthropology* on Anthropology and Development (2000) and *Priests, Witches, Power: Popular Christianity and after Mission in Tanzania* (2003).

Ian Harper is a senior lecturer in social anthropology at the University of Edinburgh. He studied medicine and worked in public and community health in Nepal and India before 'retraining' in anthropology. He has published widely on issues related to tuberculosis, public health and development in Nepal, as well as ethics related to anthropology and interdisciplinarity. He was the ASA Ethics Officer between 2004 and 2007. He recently finished researching on an ESRC DFID-funded research project, 'Tracing Pharmaceuticals in South Asia', and between August and December 2008 worked with the Nepalese government in developing their TB programme.

David Lewis is Professor of Social Policy and Development at the London School of Economics. He specializes in research on South Asia, development and non-governmental organizations, and is currently working on a book on Bangladesh. He is coauthor – with Katy Gardner – of *Anthropology, Development and the Postmodern Challenge* (1996) and his most recent book is *Non-Governmental Organisations and Development* (2009 with Nazneen Kanji).

Tania Murray Li is Professor and Canada Research Chair in the Department of Anthropology at the University of Toronto. She has written extensively on questions of development, indigeneity and agrarian class formation in Indonesia. Her most recent book is *The Will to Improve: Governmentality, Development, and the Practice of Politics* (2007).

Desmond McNeill is a professor, and former Director, at SUM (Centre for Development and the Environment), University of Oslo. His research interests include the political economy of multilateral organizations and development ethics. His recent books are: *Global Institutions and Development: Framing the World?* (2004, edited with M. Bøås); *Development Issues in Global Governance: Public-Private Partnerships and Market Multilateralism* (2007, with B. Bull); and *Global Poverty, Ethics, and Human Rights: The Role of Multilateral Institutions* (2009, with A. Lera St Clair).

David Mosse is Professor of Social Anthropology at the School of Oriental and African Studies, University of London. He has also worked for Oxfam in south India, as a social development adviser for the DFID and as a consultant for various international development agencies. Recent books include *Cultivating Development: An Ethnography of Aid Policy and Practice* (2005); *The Aid Effect: Giving and Governing in International Development* (2006, edited with D. Lewis); and *Development Translators and Brokers* (2006, edited with D. Lewis).

Asuncion Lera St Clair is Professor of Sociology at the University of Bergen, and Associate Senior Researcher at the Chr. Michelsens Institute (CMI). She is also Lead Author of the IPCC 5th Assessment Report (AR5) Working Group II. She has recently published in the journals of *Global Governance, Global Social Policy, Globalisations and Global Ethics*. Recent books include *Global Poverty, Ethics and Human Rights: The Role of Multilateral Institutions* (2009, with Desmond McNeill); *Climate Change, Ethics and Human Security* (2010, with Karen O'Brien), and *Development Ethics: A Reader* (2010, with Des Gasper).

Dinah Rajak is a lecturer in social anthropology at the University of Sussex. Her research interests cover the anthropology of development and global capitalism. She has worked on the role of transnational corporations and public-private partnerships in development with a focus on the global mining industry and South Africa.

Jock Stirrat is Honorary Senior Research Fellow and formerly Professor of Social Anthropology at the University of Sussex. He specializes in the anthropology of Sri Lanka and has carried out research there at various times since 1969. His research focuses on aid and development and publications include *Discourses of Development: Anthropological Perspective* (edited with R. Grillo) and *Power and Religiosity in a Post-colonial Setting: Sinhala Catholics in Contemporary Sri Lanka* (1992).

INDEX

VOL 6 Berghahn | STUDIES IN PUBLIC AND APPLIED ANTHROPOLOGY

GENERAL EDITOR: **SARAH PINK**, *University of Loughborough*, **and SIMONE ABRAM**, *Town and Regional Planning, University of Sheffield*
The value of anthropology to public policy, business and third sector initiatives is increasingly recognized, not least due to significant innovations in the discipline. The books published in this series offer important insight into these developments by examining the expanding role of anthropologists practicing their discipline outside academia as well as exploring the ethnographic, methodological and theoretical contribution of anthropology, within and outside academia, to issues of public concern.

Adventures in Aidland
The Anthropology of Professionals in International Development
Edited by **David Mosse**

The contributions are framed by a brief, but rich introductory chapter that contextualizes the anthropology of professional expert knowledge. The volume is concluded by a wonderful (in several meanings), entertaining essay by Raymond Apthorpe. **Forum for Development Studies**

By denying developing countries cultural specificity, aid agencies can arrogantly perpetuate their own insularity. This is fascinating and underexplored territory for anthropologists and development theorists alike, making this an important collection. **Times Literary Supplement**

Themes are . . . consistently woven throughout the book, particularly ethnographic approaches considering mechanisms by which expert knowledge is transmitted. . . . This book fills a gap in the consideration of expert knowledge and its application to consultancy that has not been addressed since Morris and Bastin (2004). **Anthropological Forum**

Anthropological interest in new subjects of research and contemporary knowledge practices has turned ethnographic attention to a wide ranging variety of professional fields. Among these the encounter with international development has perhaps been longer and more intimate than any of the others. Anthropologists have drawn critical attention to the inter-faces and social effects of development's discursive regimes but, oddly enough, have paid scant attention to knowledge producers themselves, despite anthropologists being among them. This is the focus of this volume. It concerns the construction and transmission of knowledge about global poverty and its reduction but is equally interested in the social life of development professionals, in the capacity of ideas to mediate relationships, in networks of experts and communities of aid workers, and in the dilemmas of maintaining professional identities. Going well beyond obsolete debates about 'pure' and 'applied' anthropology, the book examines the transformations that occur as social scientific concepts and practices cross and re-cross the boundary between anthropological and policy making knowledge.

David Mosse is Professor of Social Anthropology, School of Oriental and African Studies, University of London. He has also worked for Oxfam in south India, as a social development adviser for DFID, and as a consultant for various international development agencies. Recent books include *Cultivating Development: An ethnography of aid policy and practice* (2005); *The Aid Effect: Giving and Governing in International development* (2005, ed. with David Lewis); and *Development Translators and Brokers* (2006, ed. with David Lewis).

ANTHROPOLOGY

berghahn
NEW YORK · OXFORD
www.berghahnbooks.com

Cover photo: Maia Green

9 781782 380634